PENOLOGICAL ESPERANTO AND SENTENCING PAROCHIALISM

Authors:

Professor **Malcolm Davies** is Director of the Criminal Justice Centre in the Law School at Thames Valley University. He worked in California as a senior research fellow in the Attorney General's Office and is a visiting professor in the Law Faculty at the University of Helsinki. In 1998 and 1990 he was a visiting scholar at the Center for the Study of Law and Society, Berkeley, and in the Law School at UC Davis. He is author of *Punishing Criminals: Developing Community-Based Intermediate Sanctions*, (1993), Greenwood Press: Connecticut, USA; and is joint author with Dr Hazel Croall and Jane Tyrer of *Criminal Justice: An Introduction to the Criminal Justice System in England and Wales*, (1995), Longmans: London.

Jukka-Pekka Takala is a researcher at the National Research Institute of Legal Policy, Helsinki. He is joint editor with H. Klingemann and G. Hunt of *Cure, Care or Control: Alcoholism Treatment in Sixteen Countries* (1992), Albany, New York: SUNY.

Jane Tyrer is a magistrate, barrister, law lecturer and programme leader for the Criminal Justice degree at Thames Valley University. She is joint author with Dr Hazel Croall and Malcolm Davies of *Criminal Justice: An Introduction to the Criminal Justice System in England and Wales*, (1995), Longmans: London.

Penological Esperanto and Sentencing Parochialism

A Comparative Study of the Search for Non-Prison Punishments

MALCOLM DAVIES with
JUKKA-PEKKA TAKALA and
JANE TYRER

Dartmouth

Aldershot • Brookfield USA • Singapore • Sydney

Published by
Dartmouth Publishing Company Limited
Gower House
Croft Road
Aldershot
Hants GU11 3HR
England

Dartmouth Publishing Company
Old Post Road
Brookfield
Vermont 05036
USA

British Library Cataloguing in Publication Data
Davies, Malcolm, 1946-
Penological esperanto and sentencing parochialism : a comparative study of the search for non-prison punishments
1.Alternatives to imprisonment 2.Sentences (Criminal procedure) 3.Community service (Punishment)
I.Title II.Takala, Jukka-Pekka III.Tyrer, Jane
364.6'8

Library of Congress Cataloging-in-Publication Data
Davies, Malcolm, 1946-
Penological esperanto and sentencing parochialism : a comparative study of the search for non-prison punishments / Malcolm Davies with Jukka-Pekka Takala and Jane Tyrer.
p. cm.
Includes bibliographical references and index.
ISBN 1-85521-772-4
1. Alternatives to imprisonment–California. 2. Alternatives to imprisonment–England. 3. Alternatives to imprisonment–Finland. 4. Community-based corrections–California. 5. Community-based corrections–England. 6. Community-based corrections–Finland. 7. Sentences (Criminal procedure)–California. 8. Sentences (Criminal procedure)–England. 9. Sentences (Criminal procedure)–Finland. I. Takala, Jukka-Pekka, 1948-. II. Tyrer, Jane, 1951- . III. Title.
HV9276.5.D38 1996
364.6'8–dc20

95-52506
CIP

ISBN 1 85521 772 4

Printed in Great Britain by Galliard (Printers) Ltd, Great Yarmouth

Contents

List of Tables

Acknowledgement

The research projects reported in this book were funded and supported by many individuals and organisations and we are grateful to them all, especially those criminal justice officials in California, England and Finland who participated in the focus group panels.

In California the research was made possible by the California Attorney General's office, the Law School at the University of California, Davis and by the Guggenheim Foundation, Center for the Study of Law and Society at Berkeley. The project was very dependent on the support and encouragement of Jim Rasmussen, Head of the Bureau of Criminal Statistics; Brian Taugher, Department of Justice; Sheldon Messinger and Malcolm Feeley, Center for the Study of Law and Society, Berkeley; Floyd Feeney, Law School University of California, Davis; Quint Hegner of the California Department of Justice; and John Berecochea and Ben DeGroot of the Department of Corrections. Special thanks to Michele Rose from the California Department of Justice, and Saralee Buck from University of California, Davis for the time, energy and help they put into the administration of the research.

The research in Finland was conducted by the National Research Institute of Legal Policy (NRILP) with the collaboration of the Law School at the University of Helsinki. For their encouragement of the project in Finland we would wish to express our gratitude to Raimo Lahti, Professor of Criminal Law, University of Helsinki; and Kauko Aromaa from the NRILP. We are heavily indebted to Matti Joutsen for his support and for the use of some of his translations and formulations in Chapter 4 (Joutsen 1995). For help and comments we would wish to thank Tapio Lappi-Seppälä from the Ministry of Justice and Patrik Törnudd from NRILP. For help in setting up and recording the sessions we thank Eira Mykkänen, and those who offered their encouragement and advice in the Ministry of Justice and the Probation and Aftercare Association.

In England the research was conducted by the Criminal Justice Centre at Thames Valley University. For help with the empirical work and the organisation of the research in England we would like to thank Angela Legg and Gary Smith.

Some of the research material used in Chapter 2 on California had been previously used in the report from the California Department of Justice, *A Policy Role for Focus Groups: Community Corrections*, 1991 and in *Punishing Criminals: Developing Community-Based Intermediate Sanctions*, published by Greenwood Press, Connecticut in 1993.

The authors would also like to thank Jacqueline Burns from the Criminal Justice Centre at TVU, for the considerable amount of time and energy she put into the preparation and production of the manuscript for this book.

The authors and publisher wish to thank the following for their permission to use copyright material: California Attorney General's Office for extracts from the *Blue Ribbon Commission on Inmate Population Management*, (1990); Greenwood Press for extracts from *Punishing Criminals: Developing Community-Based Intermediate Sanctions*, by Malcolm Davies (1993), an imprint of Greenwood Publishing Croup, Inc., Westport, Connecticut; HMSO Crown Copyright Unit; Kluwer Law and Taxation Publishers, for extracts from Peters, A. G. (1986), 'Main Currents in Criminal Law Theory', in van Dijk, J. *et al* (eds.), *Criminal Law in Action*. Reprinted by permission of Kluwer Academic Publishers; Malcolm Feeley and John Simon for extracts from 'The New Penology: Notes on the Emerging Strategy of Corrections and its Implications', *Criminology*, vol. 30, pp. 449-74; Mike Maguire (1988), for an extract from the Book Review section of the *British Journal of Criminology*, vol. 28, p 557; National Research Institute of Legal Policy, Helsinki, for extracts from Törnudd, P. (1993), *Fifteen Years of Decreasing Prisoner Rates in Finland*; State University Press of Louisiana, for an extract from Sandoz, E. (1990), *A Government of Laws: Political Theory, Religion, and the American Founding*; University of Wales Press, for an extract from Zedner, L. (1995), 'Comparative Research in Criminal Justice', in Maguire, M. and Levy, M. (eds.), *Contemporary Issues in Criminology*: and, the University of Chicago Press for extracts from Zimring, F. and Hawkins, G. (1991), *The Scale of Imprisonment*.

Introduction

This book is about sentencing policy and the search for non-prison forms of punishment. It reports the results of empirical studies undertaken in California, Finland and England on developments in community sentences. The trends in sentencing practice and policy with respect to the use of community sentences with adults are outlined, and the changes in recent years and the response to them provide the basis for theoretical comments about the cultural basis of law and the implications for a comparative analysis of criminal justice.

The book describes the use of imprisonment and community sentences and the shifts in policy in these three jurisdictions that aimed to make greater use of community sanctions. Policy and legislative changes indicated a growing official acceptance of the need to provide community sentences in the light of the cost and consequences of imprisonment. The book looks at the reasons behind these developments, the responses to them, and to the subsequent implications for sentencing policy.

The views of criminal justice officials were sought about the purpose, appropriateness and credibility of community sentences and to discover what forms of non-custodial punishments would be acceptable to meet the policy-directed ambition to make less use of incarceration. The research focused exclusively on the development of community sentences with respect to adult offenders. The logic of using focus groups as a tool for research and consultation is explained and the methodology described.

Contribution to the comparative study of criminal justice

We start from the proposition that the criminal law is a cultural phenomenon and does not have a significance as a body of regulatory norms merely by its enactment, but achieves its significance through the meanings given by the participants involved in operating and interpreting the law. From this perspective, law is not a series of rules that are self evident outside of the cultural context of a given society. To understand the way the criminal law and criminal justice system works we need to understand the perspectives provided by the interpreters, implementers and receivers of law. These perspectives have implications for the nature of comparative studies between different cultures and is the reason why we used focus groups to explore the cultural assumptions and perspectives in respect of the use of community sentences.

How can a researcher interested in comparative policy developments across jurisdictions make sense of the documents and data that exist? It was our view that greater insight into the progress of policy innovations was to be found by moving beyond a reading of the documents and the collation of statistical data and listening to the views of criminal justice officials involved in the policy developments. Focus groups offered us a way of doing this.

Methodological significance of focus groups

Focus groups were used to examine and record the views expressed by the people who implement sentencing decisions in the three jurisdictions. The research explored the views and opinions of criminal justice officials and sentencers about their assumptions regarding the use of community sentences.

Focus groups as a means of consultation have many advantages as they involve real actors in relatively natural settings; they provide an opportunity to explore the tacit and explicit assumptions of participants; and allow for a more accurate reflection of the ambiguities and complexities in the responses given by the participants on topics where there is no simple answer to the questions posed. As such, they more accurately mirror the real life situation of policy makers than do other means of assessing responses to policy developments via opinion polling, or the more overtly political responses from professional interest groups and single-issue pressure groups. Where focus groups involve key decision-makers and criminal justice officials, they can provide important insights into the political and professional support for a reform and the practical problems of implementing a reform

Chapter 1 explains the uses and limitations of focus groups. It sets out the stages of a focus group inquiry and provides advice on how to conduct focus groups, whether for the purpose of research or as a method of consultation in the criminal justice system.

Sentencing theory and policy

There are three chapters in the book providing the empirical core of this project. They give details of the results obtained from the research conducted in California, England and Finland between 1990 and 1995. These three jurisdictions were at about the same time engaged in policy debates about the need to expand community sentences. The response to these developments was the central issue of our research. Central to an understanding of the impact of this policy for sentencing practice is the degree of confidence that criminal justice officials and judges have in the aims of community sentences and their implementation. Thus, the credibility of sentencing policy is explored with specific focus on the acceptability of community sanctions as either intermediate sanctions or alternatives to custody. Intermediate sanctions are defined as sanctions that are more severe than routine probation but less severe than imprisonment. Community sentences that are presented as alternatives to custody are regarded as substitutes for imprisonment, hence they are considered as equivalent to imprisonment.

These three jurisdictions have sentencing principles based on proportionality and uniformity. A key issue for a sentencing process based on the retributivist criteria of proportionality and uniformity is that of where to anchor the sentencing tariff in practice. Comparing the way officials in different jurisdictions responded to the idea of community sentences as punishments would help to give an insight into the nature of the sentencing tariff in the three jurisdictions.

California, England and Finland

These three jurisdictions were chosen because they had a common policy commitment to expanding community sentences in the period 1990 to 1995; the period covered by our research. In 1990 the Finnish Community Service Act was passed allowing for an experimental period of three years initially, later extended until the end of 1996. In 1990 in the UK the government department responsible for the criminal justice system, the Home Office, published a report on sentencing and penal policy, *Crime, Justice and Protecting the Public.* A month earlier the Blue Ribbon Commission presented to the Governor and the legislature of California the results of an official inquiry which had been set up to investigate the problems of managing the overcrowded prison system. The reports in California and the UK came to a similar conclusion about the need to expand the availability of community sentences.

These jurisdictions share common commitments to a democratic system of government, to retributivist sentencing principles, as well as the development of a community sentencing policy. However, despite the similarities there are important differences between these three jurisdictions.

The first point of contrast is that Finland is one of the few countries where the prison population is declining. In 1987 the daily population in prison in Finland was 3,824. This number declined to 3,295 in 1992. The Californian prison population has seen a phenomenal rise since 1977 from 22,000 to 120,000 in 1993. In England and Wales the prison population has made a less dramatic increase up to 50,000 in 1988 since when it declined only to start to rise again in 1994.

Demographically the jurisdictions vary. In 1994, Finland had a population of 5.1 million, California a state population of 32 million, and England and Wales 51 million. The rate of imprisonment, that is the proportion of the population imprisoned, is highest in California and lowest in Finland

Sentencing options in Finland were limited to the fine, imprisonment or conditional imprisonment, which means a suspended sentence of imprisonment in which nothing happens if the person does not re-offend. In 1991 an experiment started with the introduction of community sentences. In 1994 community service was extended throughout the country. 'The vast majority of those sentenced for an offence (some 93 per cent in 1991) are sentenced to a fine. Two thirds of these are for a traffic offence. Annually, some 14,000 are sentenced to a conditional (suspended) sentence of imprisonment, and 10,000 to unconditional imprisonment' (Joutsen, 1995, p. 34).

The size of the penal estate and the distribution of sentences in the three jurisdictions studied varies markedly. In Finland there are only seven central prisons for adults, and eight county prisons which are used for those remanded for trial. 'The daily average prison population in Finland has decreased from a high of almost 5,600 in 1976 to slightly below 3,200 during 1993. In 1986, there were 86 prisoners per 100,000 in the population. By 1993, this had decreased to 67' (Joutsen, 1995, p. 34).

In California there are 25 prisons and a state prison population of 134,000 (California, 1995b). The fine is rarely used except in the case of fixed penalty motoring offences. Of the three jurisdictions, California has restored the death penalty and in 1992 executed its first criminal since the death penalty was restored in 1977. The rare use of the fine is in marked contrast to its use in England and Finland. The high proportion of those who receive a custodial sentence in the form of either a term in county jail or state prison and the lower proportional use of probation represents a very different approach to the use of custody and probation in California compared with English and Finnish criminal courts.

In 1992 the lower and superior courts in California sentenced

200,119 criminals. Sentencing distribution figures for that year show that the fine was used in only 1.4 per cent of all sentencing decisions in the Lower Court and 0.1 per cent of cases sentenced in the Superior Court. In 1992 the Lower Court used jail in 11.2 per cent of those sentenced. More typically, an offender got a combined sentence of probation with jail in 69.8 per cent of all dispositions by the Lower Court, and probation was given in 15.4 per cent of all sentences by the Lower Court. In the Superior Court, of all those sentenced in 1992, 37 per cent were sent to state prison; 54.8 per cent were given probation with jail, 0.8 per cent jail and 5.5 per cent probation (California, 1994b, p. 17). While the use of imprisonment has risen in recent years the use of probation on its own has fallen as a proportion of all sentences given in the Superior Court to 5.5 per cent in 1992 (California, 1994b, p. 17).

In England and Wales in 1995 there are 134 prisons and a prison population of 50,000, which gives a prison rate of 100 per 100,000 population. In 1992, 1,503,900 offenders were sentenced by the Crown Court and the magistrates' courts in England and Wales. The fine is the most frequently used sentence. In 1992 the fine was used for 85 per cent of those sentenced for non-motoring summary offences and in 93 per cent of all summary motoring offences; this data does not include fixed penalty motoring fines. In the Crown Court the fine was the most frequently used sentence for the more serious category of indictable offences, and was used in 34 per cent of all sentences. Community sentences include probation orders, supervision orders with juveniles, community service orders, attendance centre orders. In 1993, 98,458 offenders commenced a court-ordered community sentence (Home Office, 1994, p. 10). In 1992 a community sentence was given to 23 per cent of those sentenced that year for indictable offences in the Crown Court and one per cent of summary motoring and one per cent of summary non-motoring offences in the magistrates' courts (Home Office, 1993, p. 149). 'About 42,900 persons aged 21 and over were sentenced to immediate imprisonment for all types of offences in 1992' (Home Office, 1993, p. 146). For the most serious category of indictable offences, the proportionate use of custody with adults was 16.1 per cent in 1992.

Another marked contrast is in the saliency of sentencing issues and the influence, if at all, of popular opinion on policy making. In Finland the politics of law and order is noticeably absent and policy makers tend to listen to the advice of experts. Since the late 1970s in California, crime policy and sentencing issues have been high on the political agenda and the electorate make their demands very clear through the ballot box and in the

Public Initiatives or referenda that are used to clarify state policy. In England, law and order has become a salient issue in the last twenty years, but still professional elites make their influence felt on matters of sentencing policy, most noticeably the judges, but also the Home Office officials and the magistracy.

The saliency of crime in politics will be in part a reflection of public perceptions of the crime problem in the three jurisdictions, which are influenced by the extent of crime, the fear of crime and, related to the latter, the extent to which the media and politicians provoke an interest in crime issues.

The crime picture varies dramatically between the jurisdictions. A comparison of the number of non-traffic crimes recorded by the police in 1992 shows the total in California was 1,092,832 (California, 1994b, p. 108), Finland was 390,000 (Statistics Finland, 1994, p.8) and England and Wales 5,591,717 (Home Office, 1994, p. 23).

The clear-up rate of crimes recorded by the police varies considerably between the three jurisdictions. In England for 1993 it was 25 per cent (Home Office, 1994, p. 22). However, estimates based on data provided by the British Crime Survey, a victim survey, conclude that only 3 per cent of all crimes committed result in a sentence of a caution for an offender. The crime clear-up rate for the six crime categories recorded on the California Crime Index has remained consistent over the years with a 23.4 per cent clear up rate in 1988 and 22.0 per cent in 1993 (California 1994a, p. 119). 'The clearance rate for offences in Finland is relatively high from an international perspective. Somewhat over one half of all reported property offences and some 90 per cent of all reported violent offences are cleared' (Joutsen, 1995, p. 34).

In England and Finland the crime rates are based on crimes recorded by the police. In California crime trends are measured through the California Crime Index (CCI). This index is based on six offence categories: wilful homicide, forcible rape, robbery, aggravated assault, burglary and motor vehicle theft. The CCI showed a steady increase from 1953 to 1980. It peaked in 1980 and declined over the next four years and then began to rise again from 1985 but has not reached the 1980 rate (California, 1994a, p. 5). However, 'violent crimes have grown at more than twice the rate of the CCI and almost three times the rate of property crimes since 1952' (California, 1994a, p. 5). The FBI Crime Index for California, which includes in addition to the six offences in the CCI the category of larceny theft, estimates 2,033,430 crimes were committed in 1993 for the seven crimes measured by the Index. This represented a decline over the previous two years.

The use of recorded crime figures supplied by the law enforcement agencies can give a misleading impression. This is due to factors such as the difference in the propensity of victims to report crime, the definitions used to classify crime, and the procedures for recording and publishing crime data. These factors change over time but, more significantly for this research, they vary across jurisdictions. For instance, the California figures are based on six felony offences which are used to measure crime trends across the years, but this selective portrait is not so helpful in assessing the differences in the crime picture across jurisdictions.

A more helpful way of comparing the crime situation between countries and jurisdictions is to look at the result of victim surveys, and use this to contrast the statistical chances of becoming a victim. The reliability of this type of comparison is improved if a single offence category is used, so reducing the likelihood of distortion due to the variations in the perceptions as to what constitutes a crime.

International victim surveys try to develop common categories of measurement. An international victimisation survey conducted in 1988 and 1991 shows that the approximate percentage of the population who were burglary victims within a 12 month period was, 0.5 per cent in Finland, 2.5 per cent in England and Wales, and 3.5 per cent in the USA (van Dijk *et al*, 1991).

The report on the results of the international victim surveys of 1988 and 1991, based on a range of criminal offences, has the USA amongst the countries with a high rate of victimisation. England and Wales is categorised as a medium risk jurisdiction, but above the average for Europe. Finland is below the European average and classified as having a low victimisation rate. 'The only exceptions are in respect of bicycle theft and assault, in respect of which the rate in Finland is somewhat higher than the average for Western European countries' (Joutsen, 1995, p. 33).

Penological esperanto and sentencing parochialism

Ideas that start with universal or wide acceptance amongst policy experts about the way forward for penal policy take a variety of forms when introduced into different criminal justice systems. Sentencing experts use a common language of universally shared assumptions and meanings; a version of penological esperanto. An inspection of penal practice across jurisdictions reveals diverse and more parochial influences shaping sentencing policy in practice.

This book compares sentencing reforms in California, England and Finland that sought to introduce or expand the use of community sentences. Using focus groups with criminal justice officials, this cross-cultural study explores the similarities and variations in response to community sentences and examines the contrasting assumptions about punishments other than imprisonment in these three jurisdictions.

The final chapter of this book endeavours to identify those factors that explain the convergent and divergent influences on sentencing policy and the way similar policy directions in different jurisdictions result in marked variations when put into practice. An illustration of the convergence in thinking between policy experts in different jurisdictions is provided by policy documents on sentencing in Britain and California that have led to the recommendations in both jurisdictions that there should be a development of non-prison forms of intermediate sanctions.

An example of universalism - the case for intermediate sanctions

There have been three distinct rationales used to justify the introduction of community sentences. Firstly it was argued that the range of sentences was being extended to meet the wider range of offenders before the courts. Thus the introduction of probation in England and Wales in 1908 was justified in terms of offering a new sentence to meet the needs of the courts to deal with individual offenders. The new sentence was an addition to the choices available to the courts for dealing with offenders when the rehabilitation of the offender was the main aim of the court.

The second rationale is that community penalties can be an alternative to imprisonment. In Finland the experiment that started in 1991 with community service was explicitly justified as a way to reduce the use of imprisonment. A formula was provided to ensure that community service was used only instead of imprisonment, with a precise measure between hours of community service and days in prison: for most offenders one hour community service was equivalent to one day of a prison sentence. The community service order, introduced in Britain in 1972, was justified by the argument for community sanctions as alternatives to prison. This was used by the growing number of experts who subscribed to the prison reductionist's viewpoint, predicting an end to the institution of imprisonment on grounds that it was simultaneously inhumane and ineffective in preventing crime. However, other forces, to be discussed in Chapter 5, were at work, for about the time the penological experts were declaring an end to incarceration and detailing the failures of prisons as institutions, the use of imprisonment started to grow steadily in Britain and California, although its use has continued to decline in Finland.

In the UK the 1990 Home Office report was arguing that community penalties could not be an alternative to imprisonment as, 'no penalty can place the same restrictions on liberty as a custodial sentence...so there can in reality be no alternatives to it, only other ways of punishing' (Home Office, 1990, p. 18). The government proposed to restructure community sentences for adults and young offenders to reflect the concept of graduated restrictions on liberty, that are related to the seriousness of the offence.

Despite the declared failure, by penal experts, of prison and the prediction towards decarceration, the prison population in Britain and California continued to grow despite the occasional periods when the populations in prisons went down for a while. In 1981 the UK, where no new prison had been built between 1918 and 1958, the government announced a building program of 16 new prisons. In California, where no new prison had been built for 20 years, a plan to add 9 new prisons, plus making expansions to its existing prisons, was revealed in the early 1980s. It was apparent that prisons were serving some needs, even if the penological experts could not identify what they were in the 1970s and 1980s. Thus imprisonment was to remain as the most severe institutionalised form of punishment in most jurisdictions around the world, except in those where the death penalty was available.

It was in this context that the third rationale for community sentences was heard, as intermediate sanctions, that is a punishment that in terms of severity is between prison and probation. The principle underlying this role for community sentences was given by the philosophy of just deserts, the guiding criterion being that the penalty should reflect the seriousness of the offence. Thus a continuum of penalties is needed by the court to correspond to the range of criminals and crimes that require a sentence. Hence, community-based intermediate sanctions would settle into the tariff of sentences for those offences or offenders that were too serious to justify a fine or routine probation but not sufficiently serious to deserve a custodial term.

The intermediate sanctions role for community sentences was the universal theme heard in two reports in California and Britain in 1990 that focused on the problems of penal overcrowding and sentencing policy. The common message of both reports was the need to introduce more sentencing options in the form of more demanding community sentences that were tougher than routine probation. The Blue Ribbon Commission on *Inmate Population Management* started work in the summer of 1988, and presented its report to the governor and the California legislature on January 29, 1990. In February 1990, the Home Office in London presented its White Paper entitled, *Crime, Justice and Protecting the Public.*

The role of intermediate sanctions was not the only topic covered in these two far-reaching reports on the state of penal and sentencing policy in these two criminal justice systems. But there was a shared orientation towards the benefits of developing intermediate sanctions.

The two reports show a convergence in penal thinking and illustrates a common nine-fold logic that led to the recommendation in both reports to develop and extend the use of community-based intermediate sanctions with adults.

1. Problems of an expanded penal system: The growth of the prison population is a cause of concern in terms of cost and overcrowding in Britain and California. The White Paper makes it clear that the criminal justice system has grown over the decade and is very expensive to run. 'A price cannot be put on justice, but it is not without its costs', states the report, before revealing that the criminal justice system in England and Wales costs £7 billion annually, and 'has increased by 77 per cent in real terms in the last ten years' (Home Office, 1990, p. 47).

The Californian Commission described a penal system that had undergone dramatic change in size, with the prison population quadrupling over the decade from 22,500 in 1979, to 86,000 in 1989. The Commission identified a number of problems facing the criminal justice system, the first and most obvious being the overcrowding in penal institutions. Overcrowding results in the early release of sentenced offenders because of litigation over unacceptable prison conditions that do not meet the legal standards for housing inmates. It adds to the security and safety problems for staff and inmates.

The belief in the need to minimise the use of incarceration was evident in the Blue Ribbon Commission report. 'Paramount emphasis should be placed on those areas that will significantly lessen the numerical impact on prison and jail populations' (Blue Ribbon Commission, 1990, p. 123). In London the prison reductionists' message was also apparent. The White Paper described its proposals as likely to result in 'a significant reduction in the numbers of offenders in custody' (Home Office, 1990, p. 48).

2. Impact of imprisonment on offenders: The effectiveness of imprisonment in reducing crime is limited in the case of inmates incarcerated for short periods of time. The Blue Ribbon Commission argue that public protection would be greater if offender's behaviour could be modified. Behaviour modification is more likely, 'if offenders are kept in the community', because, 'these offenders retain their ties to family, jobs, and the community, thereby ultimately enhancing the likelihood of a successful reintegration into the community' (Blue Ribbon Commission, 1990, p. 119).

The California Blue Ribbon Commission's report came to the conclusion that intermediate sanctions would be preferable for the large number of inmates who go through the expensive State prison system for relatively short periods of time of less than six months. The Commission took the view that public safety would be enhanced by less use of imprisonment for short-stay inmates if there were highly structured intermediate sanctions: 'Such sanctions should function as a punishment, as well as provide the offender with the opportunity through programs, training and work to change their criminal behaviour' (Blue Ribbon Commission, 1990, p. 114).

Explicit recognition is given in the White Paper to the idea that imprisonment has a limited role to play in penal policy. The report states:

> It was once believed that prison, properly used, could encourage a high proportion of offenders to start an honest life on their release. Nobody now regards imprisonment, in itself, as an effective means of reform for most prisoners...however much prison staff try to inject a positive purpose into the regime, as they do, prison is a society which requires virtually no sense of personal responsibility from prisoners. Normal social or working habits do not fit. The opportunity to learn from other prisoners is pervasive. For most offenders, imprisonment has to be justified in terms of public protection, denunciation and retribution. Otherwise it can be an expensive way of making bad people worse. (Home Office, 1990, p. 6)

In what was regarded by some as a change of direction in the UK, Michael Howard, the Home Secretary, told the Conservative Party Conference in October 1993: 'Prisons work. It ensures that we are protected from murderers, muggers and rapists - and it makes many who are tempted to commit crime think twice.' Very similar views about the incapacitative and deterrent role of imprisonment were expressed by the Republican Governor of California, George Deukmejian. However, this does not constitute a threat to the argument for intermediate sanctions. On the contrary, it strengthens it, as not all criminals are murderers and muggers and the problem remains of what to do with the large numbers of property offenders in the system in Britain and California.

3. Need for a systems approach: The solution to the problems identified above cannot be solved by the prisons at the back-end of the criminal justice system but requires a comprehensive or 'systems-wide' approach that includes sentencing policy and practice.

The White Paper argued that prison overcrowding cannot be solved in isolation from sentencing policy, 'there is still too much uncertainty and little guidance about the principles which should govern sentencing...The Government is therefore proposing a new and more coherent statutory framework for sentencing' (Home Office, 1990, p.1). 'To achieve a more coherent and comprehensive consistency of approach in sentencing, a new framework is needed for the use of custodial, community and financial penalties' (Home Office, 1990, p. 5).

Demands for a more extensive systems approach are made in the Californian report. The problems of correctional overcrowding is an issue requiring a comprehensive and systematic re-evaluation of the entire state and local criminal justice system; from prevention through discharge of jurisdiction. The Blue Ribbon Commission comprehensively described the problems of a system which had expanded with unprecedented speed, without the benefit of a systematic evaluation of what it was doing, other than acting to placate the desire 'to get tough on crime'. The report's major findings conclude that :

> State and local corrections must be viewed as a system in developing corrections policy. Prison overcrowding is contributed to by probation underfunding and jail overcrowding and underfunding. The corrections system is presently lacking sufficient integrated strategies to manage probation, jail and prison populations. (Blue Ribbon Commission, 1990, p. 4)

To help reduce the prison overcrowding problem, the Commission recommended a comprehensive approach to the problem, 'involving changes in sentencing practices, adoption of a Community Corrections Act, changes in corrections practices such as parole revocation procedures, and additional construction of prisons, jails, youth facilities and community corrections facilities as necessary' (Blue Ribbon Commission, 1990, p. 123).

4. Public attitudes to crime: The public expects to be protected and has demanded stronger responses to crime in the 1980s, which includes the recognition that criminals should be punished in terms of just deserts, and that sentencing is not a private dialogue between judge and criminal but is of interest to victims and the general public.

The terms punishment and just deserts had been noticeably absent from official documents for many decades in the UK. While using the term punishment, the authors of the report recognise that punishment has a limited role in reducing crime, and crime reduction is the 'ultimate objective' of the criminal justice system.

The White Paper refers to the public's less tolerant attitudes towards violence and the expectation that violent crimes would be punished more severely. 'On the other hand, there is a growing awareness that prison is usually not the best way of dealing with many less serious property crimes' (Home Office, 1990, p. 10). In California the Blue Ribbon Commission concluded, 'It is questionable as to whether long-term public safety is being served or enhanced by certain non-violent new commitments or parole violators going to state prison for less than one year' (Blue Ribbon Commission, 1990, p. 45).

5. Just deserts philosophy: The Blue Ribbon Report makes no secret of the need for a punitive element in sentencing. In England the White Paper stated:

> The first objective for all sentences is denunciation of and retribution for the crime...This approach points to sentencing policies which are more firmly based on the seriousness of the offence, and just deserts for the offender. (Home Office, 1990, p. 6)

The logic of just deserts and proportionality requires that penalties be differentiated depending on the severity of the crime and the degree of individual culpability of the offender and that this should be reflected in the common currency of punishment measured in terms of the degree of restriction on the offender's liberty.

The comment of the Blue Ribbon Commission that imprisonment is not the only form of punishment is echoed in the White Paper. The loss of liberty is the common currency of punishment and that can be done by degrees of supervision and surveillance that do not require incarceration except for the most serious of crimes. Both these official publications showed that the hunt was on for a secondary sanction, which would not replace imprisonment but would provide a step in the hierarchy of penalties available to the courts, which would function as an intermediate punishment.

In the White Paper four of the nine chapters are given to explaining the role of community penalties. 'A new approach to punishment in the community' (Home Office, 1990, p. 18) is based on the assumption that the punishment element is provided by the restrictions imposed on the offender's liberty.

6. *Continuum of sanctions*: Imprisonment should not be regarded as the only form of punishment. The dichotomy between custodial and non-custodial sentences, the binary gap, has been a focus of concern in sentencing debate in recent years. These two reports make a similar point, that a wider range of sentencing options should be available to provide a continuum of penalties that allow for an adequate tariff of punishments.

The White Paper argued that imprisonment should be retained as the means of punishment for the most serious offences, and fines for the least serious offences. Intermediate punishment is to be achieved through the degree of 'loss of freedom of action'. The report clarifies this point, 'Liberty under the law is highly valued by all of us'. The extent to which a sentence restricts freedom of action provides the continuity of logic between the different types of sanctions:

> The deprivation of liberty through custodial sentences is the most severe penalty available to the courts and the proper punishment for the most serious crimes. But other measures also place significant restraints on liberty. A probation order can place some restrictions on an offender's freedom to live as he chooses. A community service order may require demanding and unpaid work carried out over many months. (Home Office, 1990, p. 7)

The rationale for intermediate sanctions found in the Blue Ribbon Commission report did not concentrate exclusively on the problems of the prisons and the lack of rehabilitative facilities. It took the view that intermediate sanctions would improve the sentencing options available to the trial judge. This suggests a refinement to the 'binary system' of punishment, with more choice for judges to choose sentences that are neither perceived as 'getting off' nor require 'doing time'. There is room in the sentencing tariff for tougher community sanctions, i.e. intermediate punishment.

The Blue Ribbon Commission's report recommended the expansion of punishment options. The report described the potential advantages of expanding the use of intermediate sanctions.

> These sanctions would provide a continuum of choices for judges and parole authorities, as well as provide options which are both substantially more restrictive and structured than present day routine probation. They would also provide several choices that include close surveillance in community settings. (Blue Ribbon Commission, 1990, p. 49)

7. *Sentencing goals*: Sentencing policy should reflect the multiple purposes of punishment and that, in addition to the protection of the public and just deserts for the offender, there is concern to help compensate the victim of crimes and when appropriate seek to rehabilitate those who commit crimes. The Home Office document declares that the primary objective for all sentences is the denunciation of and retribution for the crime. However, other objectives of sentencing play a role. 'Depending on the offence and the offender, the sentence may also aim to achieve public protection, reparation and reform of the offender, preferably in the community' (Home Office, 1990, p. 6). The White Paper makes clear the need to further improve the position of victims of crime. It cites the growth of volunteer victim support schemes and the priority given to ordering the offender to pay compensation to the victim in every suitable case. The Californian Commissioners do not envisage a 'move towards a wholesale relaxation of incarceration as a punishment option'.

The Blue Ribbon Commission recommended that community corrections legislation should be introduced with the following aims:

> To enhance public safety by encouraging the development and implementation of highly structured intermediate community sanctions between traditional probation and incarceration. Such sanctions should function as punishment, as well as provide the offender with the opportunity through programs, training and work to change their criminal behaviour. (Blue Ribbon Commission, 1990, p. 114)

8. Intermediate sanctions - rehabilitation with surveillance: A common emphasis that adequate supervision in community settings is possible both to achieve more demanding sanctions and promote the possibility of behaviour modification is found in both reports.

> There are increasing indications that adequate control and supervision outside of confinement is not only possible but can be more cost effective and purposeful for certain offenders. Highly structured programming incorporates both accountability and possibilities of behavioural change for the offender. (Blue Ribbon Commission, 1990, p. 48)

The White Paper identified the following three aims for intermediate sanctions:

> Effective supervision is more than simple surveillance; more than just keeping a check on an offender's whereabouts and activities. Its aims are: protecting the public; prevention of re-offending; and successful re-integration of the offender in the community. (Home Office, 1990, p. 35)

An intermediate sanction should not only operate as a form of punishment determined primarily by the severity of the offence but should seek to rehabilitate, and require supervision and surveillance of the offender in the community. Rehabilitation as a penal goal should require criminals to be held accountable for their crimes and that non-custodial sentences should be demanding and should not be regarded as a soft option. They should involve surveillance, more than is usually associated with routine probation, and impose restrictions on the offender's liberty such as home curfew and electronic monitoring.

Both documents retained a commitment to the goal of rehabilitation, but do not rely on an exclusively rehabilitative rationale for intermediate sanctions. They referred to a rehabilitative approach based on accountability and confronting the offender with their crime.

In language similar to that in the Blue Ribbon Report in California, the White Paper talks of the need to confront the offender with their behaviour, 'to enable offenders to see the damage and pain they have caused to their victims, their families and friends, and themselves; and to encourage offenders to develop more responsible attitudes' (Home Office, 1990, p. 36).

What would the new more demanding community penalty look like? In England, according to the White Paper:

> The main option for adults would be a probation order; a probation order with additional requirements such as attendance at a day centre or other activities; community service of between 40 and 240 hours; and a new combined order which would link community service and probation with or without additional requirements. There will be a new curfew order, which could be used by itself or with other orders. Sentencers would be able to select the precise form of punishment in the community best suited to each offender, relating the severity of the punishment to the seriousness of the offence. (Home Office, 1990, p. 19)

The curfew order is not intended, 'to keep people at home for most of the day', but is to be used 'to keep offenders away from particular places, such as shopping centres or pubs, or to keep them at home in the evening or at weekends...The aim is to enable them to go to work, to attend training courses or probation centres, to carry out community service or to receive treatment for drug abuse' (Home Office, 1990, pp. 22-23).

9. Target population for intermediate sanctions: Hence more demanding or tougher community-based sentencing options should be used for offenders, who in terms of the tariff would have been previously given a short prison terms, i.e. the target population of offenders should be those convicted of non-violent property offenders. Both reports targeted prison-bound inmate populations, focusing on property offenders, and effectively highlighting the issue of what to do with persistent thieves and burglars if we do not send them to prison.

The White Paper states, 'The aim is to ensure that the more restrictive, and usually more expensive, community sentences are used for more serious offenders, such as persistent thieves and non-domestic burglars, and not for those who have committed minor offences' (Home Office 1990, p. 19). The report is really addressed towards the issue of what to do with the persistent property offenders. There are, the reports states, 'About 10,000 of those in custody sentenced for burglary, theft, handling, fraud and forgery, who have three or more previous convictions' (Home Office, 1990, p. 21).

Similarly, the Blue Ribbon Commission identified non-violent property offenders as the primary target group for intermediate sanctions,

'The community corrections target population specified above should be further limited to non-violent property offenders including drug abusers. Emphasis should be on first-time offenders and those without a significant criminal history' (Blue Ribbon Commission, 1990, p. 114).

Both reports stressed the distinction between property and violent offenders when the courts were sentencing. In the UK the twin track approach was promoted such that violent offenders could expect a sentence of imprisonment, and that the development of community sentences could be focused more on property offenders.

The Finnish situation: Alternatives to custody?

The similarities between the logic of the two reports produced in Sacramento and London in 1990 were not found in the policy statements that led to the Finnish Community Service Act of 1990. In Helsinki the intermediate sanctions rationale for community sentences was not evident in the official documents and the experiment was very much based on the idea that the sentence would be an alternative to custody. Whether this was to prove acceptable amongst Finnish officials was one of the purposes of the research which is reported in Chapter 4.

Despite the difference in objective used to justify the introduction of Finland's first community sentence, there are some similarities with the nine-fold rationale outlined above. Thus, although the prison population is not such a problem in Finland, with its declining prison population, the logic of curtailing the costs associated with prison building and operations was a consideration in the search for a non-prison form of punishment as an alternative to imprisonment. The harmful consequences, in rehabiititative terms, on an offender were also part of reasoning behind the introduction of community service. Property offenders were identified as the most likely target population for community sentences in all three jurisdictions, with the addition in California and Finland, of drunk drivers.

The major difference resulted from a deliberate attempt to avoid net widening. The Finnish experiment only allowed for those who were sentenced to unconditional imprisonment to be given a community service sentence. However, there were those who felt the need to have a sentence in addition to a suspended prison sentence, between the fine and imprisonment, i.e. the need for additional steps in the ladder of the sentencing tariff. The formulation which made an hour of community service equivalent to a day's imprisonment seems to contradict the severity scales that are necessary for a sentencing system based on proportionality.

The just deserts logic plays, and has always played, a part in the principles of sentencing in Finland. This was not so much in terms of a more get-tough-on-crime approach as a logical result of the commitment to proportionality and equality in sentencing objectives based on proportionality. Punishment has always formed an aspect of the *Penal Code*. The Finnish sentencing rules of 1976 state the importance of the link between the seriousness of the offence and proportionate sentences. There is no attempt to identify the type of continuity pointed to in the Home Office report of 1990 about the gradations in the loss of liberty that supposedly provide a link between community and custodial types of sanctions such as to constitute a continuum of loss of liberty. The existence of open and closed prisons with a qualitative difference in terms of the inmates' experience of prison meant that quantity was not the only variable by which to measure the pain of imprisonment.

The Finnish innovation starting in 1991 provided a major focus of contrast with the situation in California and England. Would the Finnish criminal justice officials find an alternative to custody rationale persuasive at a time when the policy documents in California and England were rejecting rationale for community sentences in terms of alternatives to custody and were arguing a case for new forms of intermediate sanctions? The results of an empirical inquiry to examine the response of key criminal justice officials to these policy initiatives in these three jurisdictions is presented in the subsequent chapters of *Penological Esperanto and Sentencing Parochialism: A Comparative Study of the Search for Non-Prison Punishments*.

Content of the book

In Chapter 1 the methodological difficulties of comparative research and analysis is explored and the case made for making use of focus groups to minimise some of the difficulties associated with comparative study. Chapter 1 also outlines the stages and practical issues involved in conducting focus group inquiries with officials with regard to feedback on policy developments. The responses of the officials in California is given in Chapter 2, the views of magistrates in England in Chapter 3, and the attitudes of officials in Finland in Chapter 4. From the inquiries conducted it was apparent that there were marked similarities in the policy developments in the different jurisdictions, with common themes and policy reforms being proposed using similar arguments and rationales to support change in sentencing policy. It was also evident that the way the officials responded to the policy direction recommended by policy documents revealed another set of influences that led to considerable divergence in receptiveness to the ideas for change. In Chapter 5 these influences that lead to convergence and divergence in sentencing policy between jurisdictions will be examined.

1 Comparative Analysis of Criminal Justice

MALCOLM DAVIES

This book starts from the proposition that law is a cultural phenomenon. That is to say that the law is a special form of regulatory institution that requires human agency to interpret and apply the rules or norms enacted by legislation and to implement the recommendations of policy documents. Hence, the law does not have an impact or significance as a body of regulatory norms by the fact of its enactment, but achieves an impact and significance through the meanings given by the participants involved in the interpretation and implementation of the law. The implications of this perspective means that law is not a series of rules that are self evident outside of the cultural context of a given society, e.g. the significance of loss of liberty through imprisonment is not the same in all cultures or for all groups in society. Thus we start from the proposition that to understand the way the law works we need to understand the perspectives provided by the implementers and receivers of law.

This is the reason we chose to use focus groups as the primary means to collect data in the three empirical investigations to explore the cultural assumptions and perspectives in respect to the use of community sanctions with adult offenders.

Comparative analysis takes many forms. Firstly, it can be similar to the work of cultural anthropologists and involve case studies of exotic places. Some texts on comparative law and criminology do not make comparisons between systems so much as describe a number of discrete and different systems. Secondly, it can take the form of identifying cross-cultural movements that simultaneously influence a number of jurisdictions, e.g. Islamic fundamentalist law, or the back-to-justice movement. Thirdly, there are studies of one specific feature of the criminal justice process as it operates in multiple jurisdictions, e.g. rules governing police interrogation, or, the selection of jurors in Toronto, Florida and Edinburgh. Fourthly, there are studies of the contrasts in the role of a criminal justice agency which compare operations between jurisdictions. Julia Fionda's

(1995) work, contrasting the role of the prosecutor in England and Wales, Scotland, Holland and Germany is a good example of this. Fifthly, there are systematic cross-jurisdictional studies of one, two or three variables in an attempt to account for variations in one aspect of the system, e.g. the variations in prison population. Mike Maguire comments on a common problem with this form of comparative research:

> Figures from numerous different countries - usually derived from official government statistics - which purport to measure a phenomenon like 'homicide', or 'suicide', or 'isolation', or indeed 'crime', are subjected to regression analysis with independent variables deemed to represent anything from the level of 'modernization' to the level of sophistication of the criminal justice system in each country. The researcher picks out significant correlations and perhaps tries some speculative explanation of the results. To take a crude example, it might be found that, when other variables are held constant, countries where Catholics make up a high proportion of the population tend to have higher murder rates than those predominantly Muslim. Some explanation might then be sought in the precepts of the two religions. However, not only is the accuracy of the data often questionable, but no account is taken of the different social meaning of apparently similar phenomena in different countries. (Maguire, 1988, p. 557)

Finally, there are cross-cultural tables that make numerical comparison of different countries. This comparative index approach contrasts performances in different jurisdictions. This might compare crime-rates, or the ratio of police to public, or the number of people incarcerated in different countries or jurisdictions. The 1990 Home Office report, *Crime, Justice and Protecting the Public* recites the widely quoted figures on imprisonment rates between jurisdictions. 'In England and Wales there were 100 people in prison for every 100,000 in the population; the figure in other countries in 1988 were 81 for every 100,000 in France, 85 in West Germany, 109 in Canada, and about 350 in the United States of America.'

This form of comparative analysis seems potentially misleading as it provides a numerical indicator of the apparent performance of criminals and judges in different countries without providing any way of knowing whether these comparisons are meaningful. Are these league tables based on accurate data which measure the same phenomena?

The Council of Europe's league table of rates of imprisonment in European countries has the UK at, or near, the top of the countries compared in terms of the use of custody per 100,000 of population. Ken Pease comments: 'National differences so calculated are impossible to interpret. They could be attributed, *inter alia*, to country differences in age profile, crime rates, clearance rates, conviction rates, judicial severity, parole differences, or any combination of these or other factors' (Pease 1994, p. 316).

This type of decontextual comparative statistic simplifies what are quite important differences in the culture, communities, criminal justice systems and the patterns of crimes in those different countries. Lucia Zedner (1995, p. 14) writes, 'unless we can develop some satisfactory mechanism for allowing for variance in meaning then cross-national statistical surveys may tell us very little of worth. At very least some account needs to be made of the social and cultural context within which laws are formulated, crimes recorded, convictions dealt out and sentences passed.'

When interpreting data from other jurisdictions the first problem is to know if they are all measuring the same thing. Thus, do prison population figures include those held in police cells as they often do when quoted in England and Wales? In the USA do the figures for those incarcerated in a particular state, such as New York, include those held in local county jails as well as state prisons? How are Federal prison populations broken down to allow an estimate of the number of New Yorkers sent to prison in a given year? Do they include those held on pre-trial detention, or remand prisoners in England? Do the figures include those returned for violation of parole conditions? With perseverance these figures are obtainable.

The collation of accurate data to make cross-jurisdictional comparisons is possible if done carefully. For instance, note that the Californian data of rates of arrests are based on the population at risk, i.e. all those between 10 and 69 (Table 2.1). The Californian rate of incarceration in Table 2.3 is based on adult incarceration and measures it in proportion to the adult population of those aged 18-69. Most European-based tables use the general population data.

However, more fundamental when making this type of comparison is the problem of interpretation and knowing what sense to make of the statistics. There are two vital dimensions to any criminal justice system which must be taken into consideration. The first variable is structural, the second cultural.

First, a major quality of any criminal justice system is the interdependencies between the agencies that constitute that system. This is a consequence of differences in criminal procedure and the historic development of distinctive agencies with unique roles such that their work and the division of labour varies between jurisdictions. For instance, California counties have sheriffs who have a responsibility for law enforcement and jailing. There is no equivalent functionary in England or Finland.

The significance of the interdependencies of criminal justice agencies should be understood in another sense in that each agency operates in response to the other agencies in the system. Most obviously, the prison population, at the back end of the criminal justice system, will depend on the work of the criminal courts and the decisions of juries and sentencers who in turn depend on the operations of the police and prosecutors. But more than simple number flows are at work here. Also influencing events are the perceptions of the officials as to the purpose of the system, its guiding principles, and at a more detailed level definitions of crime in the criminal law.

How do those who implement the law interpret these principles and laws? The way the police interpret the adversarial system of justice is likely to have a major impact on how they respond to reports of crime from citizens. The police might perceive their duty to focus on crimes that can be successfully prosecuted. In an adversarial system of justice, the prosecution requires corroborative evidence that can withstand cross examination in the courts. This can affect police perceptions of priorities and influence the type of cases that receive the most attention. Thus, the expectation of the probable decision at a later stage of the process, either by the prosecutor or the courts, will shape the response of the police as front line definers of crime.

These expectations constitute the culture of the criminal justice system. The criminal law does not implement itself but requires officials who interpret the law and implement its operation. These arrangements and procedures that affect the operation of criminal justice reflect the specific histories that have created their own culture of criminal justice.

Thus the second vital dimension to take into account when undertaking a comparative study of criminal justice systems is the meaning and significance attached to decisions, events and procedures of those involved in that system be they officials, victims or criminals. The differences in the criminal law and procedure will reflect a history of specific concern about the need to censure certain types of behaviour and the subsequent debates about the best methods of intervention. The cultural variable is crucial to the study of differences between jurisdictions and requires a culturally sensitive methodology to gain access to the ways of seeing and doing things in different countries and the importance of certain actions and the responses to these actions. What type of illegal behaviour is tolerated and what is reported? Do the agencies have the same set of priorities as the citizens? And can we assume everyone thinks in the same way about events and behaviour? Clearly they do not and hence the need to understand those factors that shape cultural outlooks and filter into everyday consciousness of the participants in the system of criminal justice.

In order to understand a criminal justice system a number of formal and informal cultural factors should be examined. Formally, the aspirations and concerns of a jurisdiction will be embodied in the legislation regarding criminalised behaviour and the principles embodied in policy statements that indicate the way that the law should be enforced. Just as vital are the informal factors that shape the working cultures and ideologies of those involved in criminal justice. Obviously, this includes the officials and the citizens caught up in criminal procedure as victims, witnesses and criminals, but a researcher would also want to know the saliency of crime issues amongst the public and the extent of interest shown in these issues by the press and politicians.

The people who are at the centre of these competing pressures are the criminal justice officials who have primary responsibility for implementing the law within the limitations imposed by economic, administrative, political and cultural factors. Thus it was to these officials that we turned to seek information about the likely success of new policy initiatives in each of the three jurisdictions in our study. They were best placed to appreciate the conflicting pressure of societal expectations and the constraints set by the reality of the interdependencies and the limits of the criminal justice system.

We chose to use focus group methodology for this cross-cultural empirical inquiry, on the grounds that it was a method which allowed for the participants to relate their views in the company of equally well informed respondents and provided the opportunity to explore the assumptions about the views expressed in a way that allowed for clarification and more detailed and tempered statements of complex expressions of opinion. That is, to recognise that focus groups are a culturally sensitive way to conduct consultation.

We sought respondents who were in a position to comment in a knowledgeable way, firstly, about the influence of the contextualising criminal justice system, and secondly, appreciate the meaning and significance of the data presented to them for comment.

It was for this reason we chose to use focus groups with criminal justice officials to explore their receptiveness to the introduction of, or application of existing, non-prison forms of punishment. It was our belief that criminal justice officials would bring together an understanding of the complexities and interdependencies of the criminal justice system, and would be aware of the competing views and arguments on the topic. Criminal justice officials, with knowledge and experience of the particular topic under study, will be aware of the system implications of reforms as suggested by the policy initiative to increase the variety of community-based sanctions given by the courts.

This chapter looks at the theoretical and practical application of focus groups as a means of consultation on governmental policy developments in the field of criminal justice policy. The particular focus of the inquiry discussed in the following three chapters is the views of officials about the use of community sentences in California, England and Finland. Focus groups were set up with senior criminal justice officials in these three countries between 1990 and 1995 to provide feedback on policy statements that sought to change sentencing policy with regard to the use of imprisonment and community penalties.

Why use focus groups?

Focus groups as a means of consultation have many of the advantages associated with the interactionist analysis of social life. This allows for the context of the situation to be fully developed; involves using respondents in a situational encounter; provides an opportunity to explore the tacit and explicit assumptions of respondents; and allows for a more accurate reflection of the ambiguities and complexities in the responses given by the participants on topics where there is no simple answer to the questions posed in the focus group. As such it more accurately mirrors the real life situation of policy makers than other means of assessing responses to policy developments via opinion polling or the more overtly political response from professional interest groups and single-issue pressure groups. Where focus groups involve key decision makers they can provide important insight into the practical and political problems associated with the achievement and implementation of policy reforms.

A focus group is an in-depth group discussion on a pre-defined and limited topic by a small group of between five to eight respondents, under the guidance of a moderator. The session is referred to as a panel. The responses of the panellists are recorded as data for analysis. The comments are transcribed and a report is produced based on the views of the panellists.

Focus groups were initially developed as a research strategy in marketing. New products were discussed with potential consumers at various stages in the development of a new product. Political campaigners in the USA soon became aware of the advantages of testing out new slogans and key words on voters. The movie industry recognised their importance for testing the likely popularity of different endings to a film.

They are a qualitative research device in which the success of the research depends on the quality of the insights given by the panel, rather than the ability to be able to arrive at general statements about the views of a wider collectivity. This is a limitation and strength of the approach. They are not a cheaper form of social survey. The aim is not to reach a generalised or representative statement of opinions, as with the survey. The quantitative survey requires that the questions be asked in a form which generates straightforward and limited response categories. Thus, reaching generalised conclusions precludes asking questions which are complex. Focus groups have a number of advantages when compared to the survey. They are cheaper, more flexible, they can be set up relatively quickly, and the data derived is straightforward in the sense of being immediately available for use. They are particularly good for probing the insights, perceptions and assumptions that underlie attitudes.

The more natural and relaxed setting of the focus group discussion, allows respondents to make comments in their own words, while being stimulated by the thoughts and comments of others in the group. Some see the naturalness of the group discussion as a major advantage of the focus group as a qualitative research technique:

> There is a minimum of artificiality of response, unlike survey questionnaires that ask for responses expressed on five-point rating scales or other constrained categories. Participants can qualify their responses or identify important contingencies associated with their answers. (Stewart and Shamdasani, 1990, p. 12)

The assumption of focus group methodology is that opinions are not always readily available, perfectly formed, or immutable and are open to influence by others, in an interactive setting. A focus group can be used to probe the underlying assumptions that give rise to particular views and opinions. The introduction of stimuli such as new information, or a rephrased question, or a speculative supposition, in a group discussion permits the researcher to observe when opinions shift, and under what circumstances. The moderator can seek clarification in the case of apparent ambiguity, and observe non-verbal gestures which might well provide a more subtle interpretation of meanings than is possible through a reliance on just the spoken word. A relaxed and natural setting also means it is less threatening for the timid and diffident respondents. It also means that groups who would not normally participate in interviews and surveys, such as children or adults with literacy problems, might feel more comfortable in a group discussion.

The usefulness of a research technique requires an understanding of its logic and appropriateness for certain types of inquiry. An understanding of the limitations of the focus group helps to determine whether it is inappropriate for certain types of inquiry.

The limitation of small group discussions, even when they are duplicated and involve many participants, is that they cannot be regarded as representative of the wider population. Hence generalisations cannot be drawn from the results. The presence of the other panellists is intended to stimulate the comments of a respondent. One problem is when the respondent becomes overawed by an opinionated panellist, or by the comments of a moderator. The balance between setting the agenda and leading opinion is not always clear cut. The advantage of having readily available responses in the panellists' own words becomes the data-analyst's nightmare, as some sense has to be made of the wide-ranging information generated by the open-ended and unstructured nature of the recorded data.

Undue reliance on 'live' data has its problems as Stewart and Shamdasani explain, 'The live and immediate nature of the interaction may lead a researcher or decision maker to place greater faith in the findings than is actually warranted. There is a certain credibility attached to the opinion of live respondents that is often not present in statistical summaries' (Stewart and Shamdasani, 1990, p. 17).

Evidence from focus group interviews, Krueger, R. (1988, p. 23) writes, 'suggests that people do influence each other with their comments, and, in the course of a discussion, the opinions of an individual might shift. The focus group analyst can thereby discover more about how that shift occurred and the nature of the influencing factors'. Listening to others can be a stimulant, as Alan Hedges explains:

> First, most human problems have a social dimension. People are to be understood partly through their relationships and interactions with others, as well as through their own internal workings as individuals. Interviewing people individually can minimise the impact of this because it encourages the participants to look in on himself rather than out at his relations with others. Groups provide an essentially social context. It is of course an *artificial hothouse* society created for the purposes of the research, but it still obliges participants to take account of other people's views in framing their own responses. (Hedges, 1985, p. 72)

In utilising the focus group methodology in California, England and Finland the 'artificial hothouse' was avoided by reconstituting existing groups of people who met regularly in other circumstances, or who knew each other through their professional roles. Groups of strangers are used in group research to observe the process of group formation and dynamics. Simulated, or shadow jury research does this, and it is appropriate as a real jury is made-up of strangers. They have had no previous interaction or relationships. The advantage of using a pre-constituted group is that they have their own protocol and established balance and hierarchy, i.e. they are already established as a group.

In Finland and England the panels were not pre-existing groups, but in most cases the panellists knew each other, discussed similar matters between themselves, and were knowledgeable of some aspects of their common mission.

The research designer will avoid the use of existing social groups in those inquiries where extant power relations and existing dynamics might discourage less influential panellists from expressing their honest opinions. But in policy discussions with influential policy implementers there is a bonus in having access to those with influence as they will help to shape the response to a policy initiative.

However, policy research is not merely technocratic, in the sense of simply finding out what people say and collating these views. Bulmer makes the point that it is not unusual for government-sponsored research to be presented as merely an exercise in data gathering. But even the most straightforward of opinion testing involves more than simply collecting the facts. The world is wide, comments Bulmer (1982), with many nuances. In complex policy deliberations, the selection of facts to discuss, and the criteria of selection for the purpose of sifting through the views to be included in the report that follows the content analysis, is clearly an exercise in interpretation.

Furthermore, one purpose of academic inquiry is to unravel the views and world-taken-for-granted assumptions that underpin the comments in the discussion. We do this so that we have a better understanding of the subjective interpretations of the panellists who contributed to the discussion. This should not reduce qualitative research to the level of simply recording opinion, although this aspect of appreciative research is also important. But as Silbey points out, 'The goal of social research is not to take the perspective of the actor as the standard of inquiry but to make that perspective and epistemology the subject of inquiry. This distinction emphasizes the difference between technocratic and critical research' (Silbey, 1989, p. 27).

Research is conducted at times for primarily technical purposes, which might involve an assessment of whether officials are supportive or hostile to a particular policy. If all that is required is a summation of opinions for and against, it would seem to me to be a waste of time conducting a focus group to establish the position of officials. A telephone or mail survey would suffice. The point of using focus groups is that they are an excellent way of analysing how people construct the social world. To use focus groups to collect opinions about a topic is a misunderstanding of their potential use. The focus group is a very effective way of getting behind opinions so as to bring out the way in which personal or professional experience has influenced those opinions. It permits the moderator to probe the panellists' background assumptions about the objectives of the system and how it works, their perceptions of other officials, criminals, the public and the sources of crime. That is, it is a means of exploring how participants come to perceive and understand the world.

One advantage of focus group methodology, according to Krueger, is that it 'taps into human tendencies'. In identifying the way our attitudes are influenced by other people, Krueger reveals an assumption about social analysis that is shared with the symbolic interactionists:

> Attitudes and perceptions relating to products, services, or programs are developed in part by interaction with other people. We are a product of our environment and are influenced by people around us. A deficiency of mail and telephone surveys and even face-to-face interviews is that those methods assume that individuals form

> opinions in isolation.... People may need to listen to opinions of others before they form their own personal viewpoints. While some opinions may be developed quickly and held with absolute certainty, other opinions are malleable and dynamic. (Krueger, 1988, p. 23)

Whether the purpose of the research is primarily technocratic or critical, it is my contention that the use of focus groups with reconstituted social groups with influence over policy implementation is the most apposite form of empirical research technique for symbolic interactionist analysis of public policy. How the world-taken-for-granted assumptions of key decision-makers are constructed is a vital ingredient for understanding the social world for those who believe that human beings have some authorship of the world - whatever the limits are to that authorship.

To understand the extent of human authorship of the world, and the ability of any group or individual to change the social arrangements by which we live, it is important to understand the perceptions of social actors in terms of what they see as open to change and their perceptions of the limits to change. To do this requires listening to what people say. This type of information seeks to discover a person's reflective experiences. It is rarely available through a social survey or de-contextual attitude assessment scale.

Ellis Sandoz argues for a version of how the personal and the empirical inter-relate that challenges the opinion poll style of inquiry:

> I am not interested in terms of propositions, dealing with this or that doctrine, or teaching. Rather, I wish to speak in a common sense and persuasive way that goes to our common experience of humanity. Ultimately, the question that underlies any philosophical discussion is always Socrates' question: Look and see if this is not the case. This question does not mean ring doorbells and knock on doors to take a public opinion poll as a validation test. Instead, Socrates means for us to consult the content of our own personal experience; consider the matter with our reason; consult with those whose opinions are worthy of consultation; and honestly ascertain, as far as we can, whether or not what is asserted truly conforms with the realities. These, then, compose the facts of our own experience, and to that we can give a rather strong name and speak of existential truth. This designates the truth of human existence as empirically ascertained, i.e., as sifted and winnowed through the process of a person's reflective powers and honestly confronting

experienced reality. (Sandoz, 1990, p. 3)

To examine 'reality as experienced' rather than as conceptualised by theorists and policy makers, the method of research needs to be able to probe in a reflective way the assumptions and view of those who are responsible for implementing decisions on a regular basis. This preference for grounded theory (Glaser and Strauss, 1967) based on real participants and examining the perceptions and assumptions of those involved is consistent with a symbolic interactionist view of human engagement. While symbolic interactionists would not claim there is any one method of collecting data, in the field of policy analysis, it seems to me that focus group methodology is more consistent with the tenets of interactionism than other methods of collecting data.

Symbolic interactionism is a theoretical perspective that recognises that an individual's perceptions are not only winnowed through the process of self-reflection about experienced reality, but is additionally filtered by our interaction with others. Attitudes are not fixed in stone and they can be influenced by those we talk with and listen to. The symbolic interactionist sees a world influenced by social processes in which social action is shaped by many factors - a world where people are not propelled by deterministic forces, but where people drift into various lifestyles, where contingencies can affect life-opportunities, and where the symbolic and expressive aspects of motivation and mobilisation are recognised.

In Britain and the USA symbolic interactionism made most inroads into policy debate in the field of criminal justice and welfare studies with the development of the labelling approach to the study of social deviancy. Arthur Brittan (1981) argues, 'A powerful objection to labelling theory is that it tends to focus on the victim or the stigmatised person...hence, there are literally hundreds of participant observation studies of deviance, of working class crime, but a relative paucity of studies of the powerful'. Ken Plummer, a leading exponent of symbolic interactionism, explains the predisposition of the labelling school to look at the powerless because deviancy is the study of devalued groups. Plummer (1979) sees no reason why symbolic interactionism cannot be adopted as an approach for the study of any social group including powerful groups, in an attempt to understand the group process, dynamics, and contents of their interaction.

The use of focus groups to evaluate the arguments about, and influences upon, policy formulation is appropriate when the group involved has some influence on subsequent policy decisions. This same group might be entirely inappropriate if you were to pursue inquiries about the impact of particular policies, where you would want to hear the views of those who deliver the program and those who receive it. Clearly, the selection of panellists to discuss policy analysis will depend on whether the purpose is to understand the formulation, delivery or impact and consequences of a policy. But at the policy-formulating stage there are usually a limited number of key actors. While recognising they are not the sole determinants of policy, nonetheless their views will carry considerable weight in the balance of decision-making.

Where public opinion is clear and the electorate has given the administration a clear mandate, the analysis of policy formulation is relatively straightforward. But many decisions in government will not be guided by a public mandate. The outcome of policy deliberations on these issues will not be so easy to predict. Complex policy decisions will be shaped by many factors, and at an abstract level these can be conceptualised as representing the interplay of structural realities and human agency. This human agency will take many forms, but one crucial dimension will involve the subjective interpretations of opportunities, concerns and values of those office-holders representing political, professional and bureaucratic interests who have access to the decision-making process.

This research strategy is open to the claim that it is an elitist approach. To an extent this claim is correct. The extent depends on the assumptions made about the power of a particular group to solely determine the outcome of policy decisions. The criminal justice system has many external determinants of policy; electorate, politicians, media, administrators, professional and ideological interest groups. But there are also key internal actors, who are the post-holders in key institutions. It seems to me pointless to deny that many decisions are made by those in key institutional positions, albeit in conjunction with other key players. These key actors make decisions sometimes after consultation but not always. Even after consultation they will have the last say as spokesmen for their agency. Any other assumption is not based on a desire to understand 'what is', but to redefine, 'what ought to be'.

Accepting the existence of elites as part of the decision-making process, does not lead me to believe that we can reduce all aspects of power to the influence of an elite. Molm points to three different conceptions of power found in the research literature. The different definitions and assumptions can be seen as complementary forms of analysis rather than competing. However, distinctive research strategies are required to tap into the different levels at which power is manifested.

Molm writes:

> Social scientists have conceptualised power in various ways: as a structural potential (Bierstedt 1950; Wrong 1968; Emerson 1962), as a process of behavioral or tactical influence (Rubin and Brown 1975; Michener and Suchner 1972; Tedeschi and Bonoma 1972), and as the successful outcome of influence (Dahl 1957; Mayhew, Gray and Richardson 1969; Simon 1957). I argue that a complete analysis of power must include all three facets. Understanding the relationship among them requires integrating concepts at micro and macro levels of analysis. The macro level of power is the structure of control that provides the opportunities and constraints within which the micro level of power, the strategic behaviour of actors, operates. Together, structure and action produce outcomes of consequence for actors and relationships. (Molm, 1990, p. 427)

Molm's threefold and complementary conception of power implies that any one level of analysis is unable to complete the whole picture of power and influence. An obvious weakness of elite studies is that, firstly, they tend to focus on participants and play down the impact of interaction with other key notables. The great men of history, or personality, approach to power is unrealistic because they are decontextual accounts which focus on key players and disregard the dynamics of political manoeuvring and inter-personal influence.

A second criticism of an exclusively elite focused analysis is that the contextual and defining influence of structural and cultural factors is left out. While recognising that elites influence policy decisions, it is important to appreciate that they do not do so in a political, economic, social or cultural vacuum.

A limitation of the symbolic interactionist approach is that it is not well equipped conceptually to deal with the macro-level aspects of culture and social structure. However, it does not totally ignore this dimension of influence, but argues that culture and structure do not exist in a distant and concrete form independent of human reflection. Culture and structural dimensions of power require translation into conceptual representations if they are to have an impact on the process of deliberation. Once defined and legitimised, 'the world taken for granted' exercises an influence on social actors through the assumptions they make about the social world and their perceptions of the possible and the impossible.

An empirical, as distinct from an abstract, approach to power requires an understanding of how concrete and cultural factors interlink, and how key actors define, and so limit, the world which they inhabit. Meta-theoretical conceptions of power and influence can be interesting but lack the empirical credibility of those theories which start from 'what is'. Symbolic interactionism starts with the actual participants in real situations.

Criminal justice policy: Consultation using focus groups

How could we move beyond documents and data to make sense of the sentencing policy developments in the three jurisdictions in our comparative study? To provide an insight into the meaning and significance of developments in California, England and Finland, focus groups were used with panels of criminal justice officials. These officials were selected because they were in a good position to appreciate the goals and procedure of, and the constraints within, the criminal justice system. They would also be aware of the wider cultural and political influences shaping the responses to the policy developments in question. In our case, would the public and the professionals regard community sentences as a credible form of punishment.

In California, a series of focus groups were held during the summer of 1990, to assess the views of criminal justice officials about the recommendations of the Blue Ribbon Commission on *Managing the Inmate population* of state prisons. This was an official report jointly sponsored by the state legislature and executive, but without the status of a departmental report and not therefore having a direct legislative impact. Its recommendations thus do not commit the administration to action.

The focused discussion was about the form, role and credibility of community sanctions. 'I have made a list of studies done in the last 30 years which have contained recommendations similar to those of the Blue Ribbon Commission,' wrote Jim Rasmussen, the Head of the Bureau of Criminal Statistics in Sacramento in 1991. 'There have been seven [in California]. We have taken the first step many times but never seem to be able to move on'. (Davies, 1993, pp. 101-2).

To see if the idea of community sanctions was to progress beyond the stage of being a good idea, a focus group inquiry was set up to ascertain the support for and views of criminal justice officials about this proposal. Subsequently, similar research was conducted on the same, limited topic, with magistrates in England and criminal justice officials in

Finland. Using focus group methodology for policy consultation had three obvious advantages in that they promoted an awareness of police developments, provided feedback about these developments and encouraged a systems awareness amongst criminal justice officials.

Awareness of policy developments

The publication in January 1990 of the Blue Ribbon Commission's report provided the stimulus to invite criminal justice officials to take part in focus group discussions about the recommendations made in the report. In promoting discussion about the report, and the future direction of reform of the criminal justice system in California, focus groups have a number of advantages. In England, a similar opportunity was provided by the publication of the Home Office policy document *Strengthening Punishment in the Community* in February 1995.

An invitation to participate in discussions about a newly published policy document can help to extend an awareness about the document. One police chief in California had not heard of the Blue Ribbon Commission's report so was sent a copy, and all panellists were sent a summary. A judge at the end of a session volunteered the information that he had not read the report but would now, having been stimulated by the panel discussions. A second judge, in the evaluation questionnaire sent afterwards to all panellists, wrote, 'I was unaware of the report and its conclusions before being asked to attend'.

In California most of the panellists had heard of the report and read summaries of it prior to their invitation to participate in the focus group. However, the invitation to participate in a focused discussion on one aspect of the report encouraged a closer reading of the report by panellists. Also it might have encouraged some panellists to probe their colleagues' attitudes about the report and to generate discussion about its recommendations. After the meeting, a clearer picture of the implications of the report might have acted to stimulate further discussion.

There were 132 pages in the Blue Ribbon Commissions's report. It covered many aspects of the criminal justice system in California and the focus group provided an opportunity for panellists to clarify aspects of the report they felt unclear about.

Feedback

A focus group meeting provides the opportunity to discuss proposals in the context of a relatively non-judgmental group, and to explore ideas and listen to what others have to say.

This is provided by listening to the responses of particular audiences to policy proposals. As Krueger (1988, p. 14) states, 'Focus groups ...are particularly effective in providing information about why people think or feel the way they do'. By getting officials together to hear comments about policy innovation, problems can be avoided in terms of the aspects of policy which are acceptable or not, or require clarification, or amendment. Where officials are influential decision makers, their response is vital for the subsequent decision whether to progress with innovations. Their response will also influence the likelihood of the reform being successfully introduced and implemented. Whatever the reason and impetus for reform, if utopianism is to be avoided it is important to understand the culture of those who are to interpret the reform and implement it.

Systems awareness

Another potential advantage of using focus groups, is that they could be used to help build system-awareness among criminal justice officials. This is of particular relevance to the criminal justice system in California. The Blue Ribbon Commission's report highlights the need for a more systematic and comprehensive approach to the problems facing criminal justice and correctional agencies.

Evaluation: Did the participants find it useful?

How did the criminal justice officials who participated in the focus groups feel about this method of consultation? In California and England an evaluation questionnaire was sent to each panellist after the meeting, the overwhelming majority said they thought it was a useful experience and would attend another focus group, if the topic was of interest to them. An evaluation questionnaire was not used in Finland.

In California the questionnaire was sent to all of the 73 panellists who took part in the focus group panels. Replies were received from 66 (90 per cent). The questionnaire sought information about the convenience of the location, the duration of the session, the number of sessions, ways of improving the conduct of the meeting, the size of the group, and the suitability of the introductory, stimulus and support material. We also asked whether they would attend another panel. The questionnaire asked,

'Given an appropriate topic of interest to you and your agency, would you attend a future meeting, or recommend a colleague to do so?' Out of the 66 who responded, 59 said yes, one said no, and six people did not respond to this question.

Of the 66 panellists in California who responded, 48 agreed that it was useful, four panellists did not find it useful, and 14 made other comments or did not comment. The panellists were asked to explain their comments on whether they found the focus group a 'useful way of expressing your views?' Many took this as an opportunity to continue the debate and made further points about the substantive topic. Some commented on the process. A favourable view was expressed by a judge: 'Rarely is there any type of forum to explore these issues with other agencies that are in a position to influence change'. A sheriff wrote: 'There are limited opportunities available for expressing views that have state-wide implications'. A public defender answered: 'All who were there have direct knowledge of the problems, and work with it everyday so we could speak with first hand information and share our own concerns with each other'. A superior court judge wrote, 'There was a good interplay of ideas'. One panellist offered the view during the discussions that the focus group meeting was a good opportunity to let off steam.

In England a similar evaluation questionnaire was sent to the 58 magistrates who took part and 55 replies were received (95 per cent response rate). The evaluation questionnaire sought the panellists' views about the arrangements and organisation of the focus groups. We asked the following questions about the arrangements of the meeting. Was the meeting held in a convenient location? Was the length of the meeting appropriate? Given an appropriate topic of interest would you attend a future meeting, or recommend a colleague to do so? Of the meeting you attended, was one meeting sufficient for the topic discussed? What did you feel about the size of the group you attended? Should we have invited anyone else from other agencies to participate? How could we have improved the conduct of the meeting? Who should be sent a copy of our final report?

We also sought comments regarding the usefulness of focus groups as a method of consultation. Asked if they found the focus group a useful way of expressing their views, 54 said yes and only one did not comment. Asked to explain the main benefits, most expressed the view that it was very useful to listen to and hear the views of other magistrates and to air frustrations they had felt. Some also felt it gave them the opportunity to think about policy developments and to clarify their views about developments. The list of comments made by the magistrates about the utility of using focus groups can be found in the appendix at the end of this chapter.

Using focus groups: Practical and methodological considerations

Why use focus groups?

The starting point of any research investigation is a clear statement of what it is you seek to understand, and an appreciation of the data that will provide you with the information to arrive at an explanation of that phenomenon. Once you have clarified this, the next question is more readily answered and that is, 'what is the most appropriate data collection method?' Quantitative data is required for an understanding of society at large and sometimes secondary data is suitable. When you are more interested to find out the details of what people think, then more qualitative methods can be employed.

The focus group is most relevant to those inquiries where the purpose is to get behind opinions and assertions and to try to discover the assumptions and perceptions which influence the way people think. Some topics are particularly influenced by inter-group dynamics. In this case the focus group is likely to yield helpful data. In another study in England, using group discussion with magistrates and focusing on intermediate treatment, Mike Nellis and Tony Bottoms commented 'it seemed to us to be essential to gain some understanding of the relevant issues from the magistrates' point of view. The group interviews were, by and large, in our view, a successful mechanism for achieving this aim.' (Nellis, 1993, p. 306)

Using a focus group approach requires an understanding of the advantages and the limitations of this approach. These have been outlined above, but briefly the focus group would not be much help if the purpose of the research was to reach generalised and representative conclusions about what society or any large sub-section of the population thought about a particular topic. Of course, the other consideration is that some social investigations will evolve in stages, and the focus group may be used at a primary stage to test out a question for a larger survey; or used at the final stages to test the clarity of a final report.

Explaining why a focus group approach is the most appropriate for a particular study will help because it offers a legitimation of the research strategy, which should aid recruitment of the panellists, as it should make clear the reason for collecting the data in the form of focus group panels.

The Topic

In addition to explaining the mode of inquiry it is important to set out the importance of the topic of the inquiry. The rationale should cover the reasons why data should be collected in the way you envisage and the importance of the topic of inquiry. A well-chosen topic is crucial in gaining the cooperation of potential panellists. Panellists are more likely to participate if they consider the project to be worthwhile. This is the key which determines the motivation to participate. Is it topical, relevant, regarded as important, and is it likely to have an impact? In this respect government-sponsored projects have an advantage.

If you are considering the use of focus groups, another consideration is whether the topic is worthy of in-depth discussion. Has it not been discussed before? What is it about these discussions that is likely to guarantee something new will come from the discussions?

It is worth explaining the source of the topic of inquiry. Topics can originate from a number of sources: academic, government policy, organisational or professional demands, from political sources and from lobby group concerns. In the case of the Californian inquiry (Davies, 1990) the topic originated from the Blue Ribbon Commission report. The research topic was convincingly presented as being of immediate policy relevance, put on the agenda of public debate by a prestigious report in response to the pressing and practical problems caused by correctional costs and overcrowding. But the recently published report was a lengthy document, and so another point of interest was to clarify its conclusions and recommendations. What does it say? What needs to be clarified? What are its implications?

You have to decide early on in the study the intended outcome of your research. Is it to produce a publication or a report? Where is it to be published? Who is the report to be circulated to? Is it intended to be for a purely academic audience, or for policy-makers? This will help panellists make up their mind whether they wish to participate. Panellists will be more willing to participate in focused policy discussions if they think it will be fed back into the policy-making process.

To avoid utopianism in research design, make a clear inventory of the resources you have available and the constraints and limitations you are working under. In California, policy makers prefer concise reports produced quickly and preferably released to coincide with a staged event in the politico-legislative calendar.

Planning tasks and the resource implications

The manpower required for a focus group is determined by the distinctive tasks that need to be completed and the availability of different people to carry out each task. There are eight distinctive tasks that have resource implications. They are:

1. Oversight of the project by a research director/coordinator. They will be involved in all the planning decisions, most crucially deciding on the topic for focused discussion, selecting the panellists and writing the final publication.
2. Recruiting the panellists. A covering letter should be sent to recruit the panellists and an acceptance form designed. A confirmation of arrangements letter will have to be written and sent to confirm the details of the meeting. If background discussion material has to be sent to the panellists, this will need to be selected or written, and mailed to the panellist in advance of the session.
3. Preparation of meeting stimulus material for overhead projectors, videos, tapes, posters, etc.
4. Meeting planning and preparations. Someone will have to organise the details of the meetings and plan for rooms and refreshments as appropriate. On the day of the focus group you will need someone to welcome panellists, organise the seating arrangements, set-up the recording equipment and be responsible for changing tapes.
5. Deciding on the questions and writing the introductory commentary for the meetings.
6. Moderating the meeting. The number and timing of panels might determine the number of moderators you will need.
7. Selecting, transcribing and editing the recorded data. Transcribing is a tedious and time-consuming activity, which is best done by a trained audio-typist. Furthermore, the mass of transcribed material is more readily processed if some initial thought is given to the categories to be used in the contents analysis, and the likely format of the report to be written.
8. Writing the draft and final versions of the report or publication.

The minimum number of personnel for a small-scale focus group inquiry would be a director, administrator, moderator and an audio-typing secretary. If you were to hold a series of focus group panels across a number of differing locations you might need more than one moderator. It helps to have the back-up of a large organisation, with facilities for meetings, telephone and message services, an art and media resource to produce brochures, letters, posters and other stimulus material for the meetings.

You will need the following specialist equipment: a tape recorder with multi-directional microphones, a portable overhead projector, a portable easel to hold a poster-size note-taking pad, and an audio-typing machine with a numerical indicator. Funds might be required for room hire, the provision of refreshments and for payment of panellists, or to cover the travel costs of panellists.

In terms of the logic of the inquiry, the decision about the best method of research to utilise must be affected by three factors. Will it provide the data to answer the questions that the project sets out to explore, what resources do we have available, and under what other non-pecuniary constraints are we operating. Money translated into resources, and time determined by deadlines, are the major constraints on any research project.

Who to invite as panellists?

The decision on whom to select as panellists will depend on three factors: suitability in terms of the logic of the inquiry, the status of other invited panellists, and the practical limitations set by the availability of the panellists.

The logic of the inquiry generates the most important of the three criteria of selection of the panellists. Are the people selected the most appropriate to answer the questions? The guiding rule, Axelrod writes, is to 'Concentrate on those population segments that are going to provide the most meaningful information', (Axelrod, 1975, pp. 10-11).

The status of those invited is of importance in recruiting panellists. One of the questions panellists will ask is, 'Who else will be there?' Key local figures might influence the decision of others to attend and to take the research seriously. Sackman wrote about his experiences with Delphi studies (1974), 'Top names in the field under investigation lend prestige to the study and acts as a magnet to attract other participants'.

In the Californian study of 1990 only agency heads were invited, such as the chief of probation, the district attorney or the sheriff. If the sheriff sends an assistant then the district attorney is likely to do the same. Our introductory letter asked those who could not attend, if they could suggest another appropriate person to invite. We were not willing to let the person substitute one of their staff assistants or secretaries to take notes. Despite these precautions, this happened on two occasions and the substitutes did not take part in the discussion.

Passive participation can be avoided if the influence of group size is appreciated. For discussions with knowledgeable policy shapers, a group of six will keep the discussion going for two hours. It is tempting to invite a few more to ensure you have included everyone, but if the group is too big it might encourage 'social loafing' (Latane *et al*, 1979), i.e. poor participation by some panellists.

You should also make it clear that you do not want panellists who can attend only part of the session. Two consequences are likely, both unhelpful. Either the person sits near the door, and contributes little, or they come in, barnstorm the meeting and having delivered their lecture they leave. Both scenarios prevent the exploration of background assumptions and prevent the possibility of probing the comments made.

In California a few of the invitees suggested substitutes. They offered the name of someone whom they regarded as more appropriate for the topic of discussion. Several Presiding Judges of the Supreme Court suggested that the Judge in charge of the Criminal Calendar would be more appropriate, given the topic of the discussion.

A recruiter who is not the moderator is an advantage. They will have to engage in active calendar negotiations if named individuals are selected from the recruitment panel. A recruiter can engage in the art of persuasion and the details of timetabling with a persistence that might colour relations with the moderator.

Panellist recruitment will involves two stages. First, is there an objective panellist frame. In England, all the magistrates in the local area, called a 'panel', were written to from a list provided by the Clerk to the Justices. In California, the State Government holds a register of county officials, so lists were readily available in the California Attorney General's Office of chief probation officers, district attorneys, public defenders, chiefs of police. There is also a list of Judges and Presiding Judges in each county. Other sources include membership registers of professional and county government organisations. In England, the Clerk to the Justices provided a mailing list of all magistrates.

The second stage may involve informal contacts and direct liaison with some of the panellists or their secretaries, and other local informants to discover if a key actor at the local level has been omitted. At this second stage you are looking for named individuals to invite. Once either formal or informal contact has been made about the purpose of the project, details of the availability of those you have chosen to attend should be sought.

Practical details that will influence acceptance to attend will include: where and when the meeting is, the identity and number of other panellists likely to attend. You need to talk with secretaries, assistants or administrators to get details of their weekly diary. Meetings held in the lunchtime or afternoons, later in the week, would improve the chances of the judges attending in California.

The status of the project as a whole will be enhanced if it has the sponsorship of a reputable organisation. Credibility is a vital ingredient for high-level policy analysis involving influential and usually very busy officials. Sponsorship and a professional style of contact and liaison will help to encourage participation. An initial letter of contact explaining the purpose of the study and a covering letter from the sponsoring or cooperating agencies should enhance the legitimacy of the research.

The use of local contacts as an informal sounding board to ensure that you have contacted all the key players should not result in the panellist list being decided only on the basis of that source of information. In California the local officials would say, 'There is no point inviting the district attorney as he is opposed to the policy'. The views of all the key players should be sought and not just those officials with sympathy for the project. It is of course easier, there are fewer refusals, and it is faster to recruit panellists who are known to the research director, or their sponsoring agency. But there can be a problem with this, as Sackman (1974), points out, 'Expert panels are often selected from accessible experts, and this accessibility is largely covert'. The danger Sackman points to is that it can result in a panel selected with 'similar views who think along similar lines'. This is to be avoided for, although you cannot claim to be gathering a representative sample of opinion, you do want to encourage the widest range of views as possible.

Where, when and how long?

It is vital to get the organisational details of the meeting correct. If possible choose a convenient location, which is centrally located and within short travelling time for the panellists. You will need a small conference or committee room, not too big and not too crammed, and which will comfortably accommodate up to 12 people. In addition to the five to nine panellists, you will need space for a moderator and a research assistant.

There should be sufficient space to allow for an overhead projector and screen and an easel for a notepad and poster display. Facilities for coffee and food are essential for lunchtime meetings.

A letter confirming the time and location of the meeting should be sent a week before the meeting and telephone calls made a few days before to check that the details have been received and understood. You need to book a room, with time to set up the recording and meeting materials. If lunch or coffee is to be provided, the logistics should be worked out in advance.

The duration of the meeting has to be carefully considered to accommodate the schedules of the panellists, but also to provide sufficient time for a focused discussion. One hour will usually be insufficient time. In the California and English studies a two-hour meeting allowed for sufficient discussion, while not taking up too much of the officials' day. Longer sessions, even all-day discussions, are possible but will depend on the availability of the panellists and the elasticity of the topic.

Pre-meeting planning stages

This will require the identification of the stages and tasks and a standardised checklist to include:

- the dates the initial letter of invitation was sent out to the panellists
- dates of receipt of reply cards
- follow-up telephone calls to non-repliers
- a list of the original invitees with the panellists' names, addresses and telephone numbers
- a list of substitutes and final panel names
- the date for mailing the background reading material and questions
- the date and time of the meeting
- the contact points for room booking and confirmation of room booking
- the location of the room and telephone number of room booking contact
- details of refreshment requirements and contacts
- date the confirmation letter was sent out
- name of the moderator with contact information
- the date of receipt of moderator report and meeting tapes
- the date the tapes were sent for transcription; and the date they were returned.

The day before the meeting a further checklist is required to ensure that the following equipment and meeting material is ready: list of panellists with individual name-cards for the seating arrangement, the introductory commentary script, audio recording machine, multi-directional microphones, batteries, extension lead, clean cassettes labelled in advance with the meeting date and location, prepared overhead projector diagrams, pre-printed flip charts, flip pad and a portable overhead projector and overhead projector pens, and a lightweight tripod for holding posters and writing pads.

Moderator

The skills you would require of a moderator are the skill of chairing a meeting, with knowledge of the topic under discussion. This required an understanding of the criminal justice system, and an awareness of the policy developments in the field.

The moderator should have no obvious ideological predispositions or affiliated interests, hence academics without known prejudices can be of use here. Avoid moderators with known stands on the issues discussed or with a high political profile. It is better if moderators are seen as not having an interest in the outcome of the discussions. The moderator should adopt a stance of passionate neutrality, and having introduced the topic discussion they might say, 'so how are we to solve this problem?'

The moderator should attempt to create a non-combative mood in the meeting. The discussion should be informative and relaxed, where views in response to the question are welcomed. However, you do not want an uncritical consensus, but an exchange of opinions and arguments and probing of those opinions and arguments.

A focus group discussion is not a multiple-item agenda meeting, nor is it an academic seminar, but a more directed, and narrowly focused discussion than typically found in a meeting or seminar.

The moderator is more than a meeting facilitator. The moderator will need to give firm and clear leads as to the focus of the discussion, and keep the panellists in tune with the topic. In England, the magistracy are chosen, not because they are professionally trained, but to act as representatives of the lay public. It therefore follows that not all magistrates will be familiar with technical terms in sentencing theory. The moderator will have to be able to diplomatically explain some definitions and curtail discussions that do not focus on the point of discussion. In California most of the officials had considerable experience and strongly felt views on the topic of discussion. Elected officials such as the District

Attorney and the Sheriffs had an added authority to express their opinions cogently. Some will want to use the meeting to further the argument from the viewpoint of their particular agency.

It is an advantage if there exists a cadre of trained moderators. In California, there were staff trained in the state agencies as facilitators, known as transfer-of-knowledge-facilitators. Their background experience in government and their training as meeting facilitators, make them an ideal cadre of instantly available moderators.

Conducting the panel

In the introductory comments the moderator should outline the reasons for the meeting, setting the parameters of the session, and clarify what will be happening, welcome the panellists and ask them to identify themselves. The transcription of the recorded tapes is made easier if voice recognition of the different speakers is established early in the meeting. Then, with the help of stimulus material, introduce the topic of discussion.

It is preferable to have an assistant at the meeting in addition to the moderator. Their role is to help set out the room and the material for the meetings. Extra sets of background documents are often requested by the panellists. They should help to set up the overhead projector, the recording equipment, refreshments and organise the room. They should welcome panellists and check attendance and deal with latecomers, by showing them where to sit. They should take responsibility for the recording of the meeting, by ensuring the equipment is working and changing and labelling the tapes. They should take notes in case of a failure of the recording, and to help with voice recognition at the transcription stage.

Background material and information should have been sent prior to the meeting, as should the questions for discussion. These topics and questions will provide an agenda for the meeting. The pre-meeting material should not be too intensive, complex or lengthy so as to avoid spending too much time clarifying the meaning of the background material.

The prepared material and questions should provide the agenda, not the script for the session. A steered conversation is what you are ideally looking for. The questions sent to the panellist will set the framework for the discussion, but be prepared to adapt to the flow of conversation.

Stimulus materials in the form of charts, statistics or policy statements are useful. The stimulus material should be used flexibly so as to help the flow of the discussion. In the UK, Nellis and Bottoms used group interviews to discuss the views of magistrates about intermediate treatment. Sentencing statistics showing proportionate changes in the use of particular disposals throughout the 1980s were used as stimulus material to focus discussions on changes in sentencing patterns in their area.

The questions for discussion should be as specific as possible. This helps the panellist to understand the scope of the panel's discussion. Furthermore, the responses to the questions can then act as one guide to categories used in the content analysis of the session. Remember, the advantage of this mode of inquiry is that it allows for a more natural flow of discourse, in which the conversation is not forced into pre-set response categories. Hence post-discussion structuring is required, which is time consuming. However, the open-ended nature of the question and the subsequent flow of conversation provide for a more natural setting for exchanging views. The open-ended questions used in focus groups, writes Krueger (1988, p. 23), '...allow the respondent to determine the direction of the response....The answer is not implied and the type or manner of response is not suggested'.

Evaluation questionnaire

In California and England, although not in Finland, we sent an evaluation questionnaire to all panellists within a week of the focus group meetings. We sought their views on three matters.

Firstly, the organisation and administration of the focus group meetings, to ascertain if we could run them more effectively. We asked about the timing and location and whether a different mix of panellists could have had any advantages.

Secondly, we used a follow-up questionnaire in England in order to quantify some of the views from the panels. Where there was a very specific proposal that had been aired in the discussions we sought to clarify the degree of support for it. Thus we found that there were no magistrates opposed to the idea of weekend custody and the overwhelming majority thought it was a good or very good idea.

Thirdly, we used the same questions in California and England to probe the benefits of focus groups by asking all panellists to response to the question: 'Did you find the focus group a useful way of expressing your views?' and, 'In what other ways did you find the meeting useful or not useful?' The overwhelming majority in California and England took the opportunity to express the view that the experience was rewarding and made the point that there is very little opportunity to discuss issues in detail in such a way as was provided by the focus groups.

Producing a report

The final report will be based on the transcribed tapes and the moderation notes of the meeting. The report will usually be in the form of a narrative summary with quotations from panellists to illustrate viewpoints.

After each meeting you should have about two hours of tape plus whatever notes were taken by the research assistant. You should also ask the moderator to write an assessment of the meeting. This should include matters of substance regarding the opinions offered in the discussions, as these will provide a guide to summarising and editing the material recorded on the tape.

The next stage is to decide on the transcription procedure. You should read the meeting notes made by the moderator and the assistant. Take the recorded tapes and check that they are complete. A recording failure must be dealt with immediately by use of the notes taken at the meeting, and by asking the moderator and assistant to recall as much as they can.

Prior to transcribing, editing can be done to remove irrelevant material on the tape, such as noise, repetition, non-relevant material. Continuous talk is difficult to transcribe as there is often confusion about who is talking as well as redundancy, repetition, and conversations to do with the arrangements rather than the topic of discussion, such as, 'where's the coffee?' Pre-transcribing editing should reduce the length of the tape to be transcribed by as much as a third. If an assistant is available for the meeting, they should take notes, indicating the order of speakers, the time every five or ten minutes, and the topic under discussion at the time. This helps to identify speakers on the tape.

Listen to the tape and then re-listen to the tape. A straightforward transcription is not worth much and is very costly in time. An alternative is for the moderator and researcher to listen to the tape, make notes, and make a selection, for which you will need a playback machine with a numerical indicator. In this way a 50-page transcription can be reduced to a smaller number of pages, with the relevant material already sifted out. This is a speedier and cheaper way to transcribe the tape.

The next stage in producing a report requires a content analysis of all the focus group panels. This is not easy as the advantage of the focus group is to provide relatively unstructured verbal data based on a more natural setting of a group discussion, free from the artificiality of the survey questionnaire's pre-coded response categories. Hence, the real challenge to the researcher is to provide a summary without the help of predetermined categories. However, this is not done in a vacuum, as there is a structure determined, firstly by the questions sent in advance to the participants, and secondly, by the moderator's guidance of the meeting.

Bulmer (1982) comments that policy research sponsored by government is often regarded as a simple matter of fact gathering. But this is too simple, as a researcher is also engaged in structuring the inquiry and in interpreting the data. This is most vividly seen in the selection of data from the transcript. Content analysis, as Walker (1985) points out, involves 'fracturing' the data into 'lumps of meaning', followed by a subsequent restructuring of the data, and an interpretation of the links between the data. How do we fracture the transcribed verbal data into lumps of meaning and restructure it for the research report?

The key to successful content analysis of qualitative data is the generation of appropriate categories for coding the transcribed conversations, and the determination of criteria used to select the coding categories. There are both internal and external categories.

Internal categories emerge from the topic of the research and the responses to the questions discussed. Clearly, one should remain faithful to the views expressed in the focused discussions and use the categories that emanate from the recorded data to provide the categories to cluster the material. There are those categories that emerge naturally from the responses to questions, that flow from the topic and the reason for the inquiry. The internal categories are given by the questions chosen for discussion and these will provide one set of headings for clustering responses.

A second set of external categories can be imposed externally upon the material by theoretical and policy considerations. They can emerge from the theoretical ideas that underpin responses in the focus group discussions. For instance, discussions about sentencing policy will often depend upon the respondents' assumptions about the causes of crime and the degree of accountability or social determinism that is attributed to criminal behaviour. Another source of external categorisation for clustering the data comes from the public policy agenda and the relevance of panellist responses to current policy debates.

Therefore it is possible to identify three types of categories for the content analysis: source-related categories to provide the opportunity to accurately summarise the discussions in the panels; policy-related categories to reflect the salient policy issues that relate to the topic of inquiry; and theoretically-related categories that allow for a wider analysis of the assumptions and logic of the topic from a theoretically informed viewpoint.

Conclusion

How useful is the focus group as a part of the process of consultation on matters of policy? I would conclude that it is one additional element that can be fed into the policy-formulating process. It is not the only element, but it is one where opinions have a chance to take shape in a discussion of the wider context of influences and constraints on policy by those who have to put them into effect. This approach has an advantage over an opinion poll approach to policy making in that the complexities of issues can be more readily addressed. Furthermore, focus groups might be capable of identifying the problems of implementation as perceived by key officials or participants and they can be used to help to build a consensus for reform, in contrast to the inputs into the policy-formulating process from single-issue pressure groups or interest groups.

In the sensitive field of sentencing reform, if good ideas are to be translated into practice then two constituencies must be satisfied that these reforms are practical and acceptable. The two key constituents whose views are vital in this respect are the officials who will translate the reforms into action, and the public in whose name the system is supposedly working in a democratic society. This paper has been concerned to describe the use of focus groups to provide feedback about policy developments amongst criminal justice officials.

The substantive focus for this study in comparative criminal justice was the search to find non-prison forms of punishment. In particular, the start of the inquiry was based in policy statements since 1990 that have recommended the greater use of community sentences as intermediate sanctions. The specific issue of the study was the way that key participants in the criminal justice systems in different jurisdictions have responded to these policy initiatives, in terms of the credibility of this proposal in their opinion.

The methodological problems associated with this type of comparative study are set out in the beginning of this chapter. It was the view of those who conducted these studies that are reported in the next three chapters that the use of focus groups would minimise the difficulties outlined and provide useful insights into the substantive concerns of those who have a key role in implementing community sanctions and influencing their likely success as credible intermediate sanctions.

Appendix: Comments about the utility of focus groups

The following are the comments made in the evaluation questionnaire sent to the 58 magistrates who participated in the nine focus groups held in England in 1994 and 1995. They were asked the following:

Did you find the focus groups a useful way of expressing your views?

In what way other ways did you find the meeting useful or not?

Panel No.1

'I was surprised at the overall dissatisfaction with community penalties.'

'Too little opportunity to do this usually. Good to have non-magistrates/non-clerks involved.'

'Helped me realise that I am not alone in my concern with regard to community punishment.'

'Helpful to have the opportunity of a small bench meeting on sentencing issues.'

'Particularly helpful so soon after the Bench amalgamation as several others present were not known to me.'

'Thoughtful experience.'

'A relaxed but confidential environment.'

'It may possibly influence future sentencing policy.'

Panel No.2

'Possibly the only opportunity to hear and express views I've been given so far.'

'Everyone has ample opportunity to express their views and was made to feel their views were of value.'

'One gets an inside version of how your fellow magistrates approach justice and penalties for wrong doing.'

'It is very difficult to find time when on the Bench to discuss fully the whole subject.'

'It was very enlightening to hear other members at the Bench give their opinions.'

'More useful to listen to the others.'

'It was useful, though disturbing, to find out how little confidence colleagues have in community sentences.'

'We rarely have occasion to talk with each other in this way. It could well be a possible focus for future meetings.'

'In looking at how we dispense "justice" and realising that we are very straight jacketed on our bench.'

Panel No. 3
'Open forums allow expression of interest of all participants.'

'Hearing other opinions expressed and points raised which had not been previously considered.'

'Interesting (as a team opportunity) to hear views of colleagues in a formal discussion.'

'There are limitations on magistrates' comments. Obviously through the groups is one way of having your voice heard.'

'Insight into magistrates' reluctance to send people to prison.'

'Good way to air frustration.'

Panel No.4
'An opportunity to discuss matters of concern with fellow magistrates. We see little of each other normally.'

'Whether useful or not will depend on the way the varied opinions are reported.'

'Greater insight into some of the issues involved.'

'Just magistrates from our Bench in front of unknown moderator and assistant. Could say what we felt in relaxed surroundings.'

'I do feel that it should lead to some positive action, hence my opinion we circulate the report.'

'The moderator ensured that all participants had floor-time. It was useful to hear fellow JPs' views and confirmed that we all felt frustrated although when sitting one gets on with the job.'

'The feeling that maybe, in a minute way, we might influence social justice.'

Panel No.5

'I have never had to consider what exactly happens and express an opinion before.'

'Better this way than in a small or larger forum.'

'The informality of discussion facilitated the chance to clarify in expressing one's views.'

'It was good to hear the views of other magistrates on such a vital topic - and a reliable interchange of ideas took place.'

'I thought the moderator was responsible for helping to draw out individual members' views and make them all feel they had contributed by the excellent way she summarised the focal points during the discussion.'

'Small group discussion provided a focus which enabled me to voice my views without feeling intimidated.'

'A further meeting would be useful.'

'We were all given adequate opportunity to express our views.'

'With about 8 members it encouraged forceful discussion.'

Panel No.6

'It is not often one gets the chance to air views on criminal/sentencing topics in such a structured, focused way. A valuable insight, too, into the minds of one's bench colleagues.'

'It focused my ideas. It was also beneficial to hear the other views of magistrates I do not normally sit with.'

'Well 'moderated' discussion away from training environment.'

'It was good to explain views and then discuss the implementation of realistic ideas.'

'There is very little opportunity for actually expressing concerns and views - we attend many training sessions, lectures, meetings where we are in the main listening and training. Very few occasions involve or seek the opinion of magistrates before enactment.'

'It was a comfortable and pleasant forum with everyone being given equal opportunity.'

'I feel certain things need to be said and acted upon, also when one is sitting in court there is not always time to hear and discuss how other magistrates feel about certain aspects of punishment - so it is good to hear and discuss their views and vice versa.'

'We were all able to express our ideas and opinions, compare and contrast and conclude with a sensible decision.'

'It demonstrated to me the different views held by my colleagues on community sentences.'

Panel No.7

'I liked the freedom to express personal views and the chance to hear those of others. If this could be enlarged to other areas of the country, we would get a better idea of what JPs really think - not what their representatives think they think.'

'Very interesting to become aware of the attitudes and prejudices of colleagues.'

'Interesting to hear how other magistrates (especially those with whom we rarely sit) feel about specific issues. The meeting allowed for candid opinion to be expressed without appearing judgmental.'

'It was a rare occasion to hear the opinions of one's colleagues and their reactions to one's own.'

'New ideas regarding the type of community sentences or relating to offenders were voiced which I had not previously considered.'

'It was interesting to hear the views of other magistrates in a larger group. Normally there are 3 present when discussing cases.'

'To hear colleagues' views and to be able to compare with one's own views'.

'It provided a good forum to make and develop ideas.'

'It was useful but as mentioned in the discussion group I think members of the general public should be able to express their views on sentencing and how they view the legal system, magistracy and sentencing generally.'

'It was interesting to discuss community punishments with someone outside the local magistracy. Whether or not it was useful will become apparent if it achieves any results particularly in view of the lack of extra funding.'

Panel No.8

'It made me review my ideas on community sentencing.'

'It was useful as a contribution to the debate. However the judiciary and police cannot provide all the answers - other areas must be considered and involved. Lack of adequate parenting, education - unemployment must all be considered - also the need for all of us to be aware of our responsibilities and other peoples' rights as well as our own rights.'

'I feel that there are some magistrates who are less interested in these issues and it is a pity therefore, that they were absent. Perhaps more informal discussion would generate interest/awareness.'

'I hope that this and other meetings will be a serious attempt to do something about the rise in crime and the people who conduct these meetings will not view this as a series of just exercises, but will push to take this forward, and take our views into consideration.'

'Having listened to other opinions it helped to increase our understanding of the subject in a wider context. It encompasses a training element in the process.'

'It is always interesting to hear colleagues views in general, but not in a social setting - i.e. when they have to state their views.'

Panel 9

'I found the focus group extremely interesting but was very depressed to learn there would no further funds available. I'm sorry to say that I felt 'what's the point of it!.'

'I am interested in learning your conclusions from the various group discussions.'

'Having visited working parties on several occasions over the years, I am impressed that the attitude to the 'job' has become more serious and less of a pastime.'

'I would like to have the views of the Probation Service in relation to more positive ways in which work would be introduced e.g. cleaning up graffiti/collecting litter and clearing rubbish from canals/rivers etc.'

'The public are losing confidence in the judiciary. Their views should be sought and considered, in particular those of victim support groups.'

'Thank you for giving me the opportunity to join the debate. I thoroughly enjoyed it. More please.'

'I am glad that perhaps people in high places (Home Office) will at last listen to the people who try to administer sentences with one hand tied behind their backs.'

2 Responses in California to Community Sanctions

MALCOLM DAVIES

Sentencing policy and trends

From indeterminate to determinate sentencing, 1917 to 1976

Indeterminate sentencing was introduced in 1917 in California. In the year following its introduction the California Supreme Court stated in support of the reform:

> It is generally recognised by the courts and by modern penologists that the purpose of the indeterminate sentence law, is to mitigate the punishment which would otherwise be imposed upon the offender. These laws place emphasis upon the reformation of the offender. They seek to make the punishment fit the criminal rather than the crime. They endeavour to put before the prisoner great incentive to well-doing in order that his will to be well should be strengthened and confirmed by the habit of well-doing. (Davies, 1985, p. 3)

In 1944 the system became fully indeterminate. The sentences laid down by law for the common felonies such as robbery, burglary and rape referred only to a minimum and maximum term (e.g. one year to fifteen, five years to life) depending on the crime. On conviction, the judge sentencing could indicate that the length was 'for the term prescribed by law'. The actual time spent in prison would be decided not by the judge but later on by the parole board (the Adult Authority established in 1944), which in reality determined the amount of time the inmate served.

The indeterminate system had a number of advantages. It shielded elected officials, such as the district attorneys and the judges, from public pressure and the high maximum made the system appear more punitive than was actually the case, so appeasing the public who elected them. It provided a means for ensuring conformity in inmates, who were led to believe that if they did not behave their release date would be extended. It provided a safety valve for regulating prison population levels - when prisons got too overcrowded the Adult Authority would grant parole earlier than usual.

This system was not without its problems however and by the late 1960s there was growing disquiet about the assumptions, operation and effectiveness of this approach to sentencing, which was based on the goal of rehabilitating offenders:

> First, a growing number of penologists came to regard its implicit ontological views on human behaviour as ethically objectionable. Secondly, the operation of indeterminacy led on occasions to considerable disparity in actual time served by offenders committing the same offence in similar circumstances. Furthermore, the discretion required for the system to work also provided the opportunity for injustices, as personal, racial or other biases came to influence the staff's attitude towards inmates. Thirdly, questions began to be asked about the effect of rehabilitation. By the early 1970s statistical studies all tended to the same general conclusion that correctional treatment programmes had no significant affect on inmate recidivism. (Davies, 1985, p. 3)

Indeterminate sentencing principles were abandoned with the Uniform and Determinate Sentencing Act 1976. It came into force on 1 January 1977 and stated boldly that, 'The purpose of imprisonment for crime is punishment' (Section 1170a of the *California Penal Code*). 'This is best served by terms proportionate to the seriousness of the offence with provision for uniformity in the sentence of offenders committing the same offence under similar circumstances.' To achieve uniformity prison terms for each offence category were to be fixed by statute, and discretionary parole was abolished except in the case of life sentences. Life imprisonment remained the sentence for murder. The multiple aims of sentencing remained, but the purpose of imprisonment was punishment.

The new law of 1977 indicated three possible base terms for each category of felony. The sentence for burglary, previously one to 15 years became 16 months, two years and three years, the middle term being the normal term with the longer and shorter terms being used in the case of aggravating or mitigating circumstance. Rape which previously attracted a sentence of three years to life became set for periods of three, four or five years. These base terms for rape were increased in the 1980s. The base terms could be enhanced if particular circumstances were involved. Enhancements, an additional period of imprisonment added to the base term, can be given in the following circumstances: if the offender had previous convictions, carried or used a gun, caused injury, or stole more than a certain amount of money. Initially, two additional years could be added for each category.

The judge when sentencing had a choice and could give a fine, probation or sentence the offender to county jail for a shorter period than a term in the state prisons. There were some offences where legislation made imprisonment mandatory or barred the use of probation. These were to increase in the 1980s.

In California the Superior Court and the Lower Court are responsible for sentencing. The Superior Court has trial jurisdiction for felony cases - a crime which is punishable with death or by imprisonment in the state prison. The Lower Court is the trial court for persons accused of misdemeanours and some felony offences. They may also sentence certain felony offences. Misdemeanours are defined as crimes punishable by imprisonment in a county jail for up to one year.

Sentencing Trends

The most obvious fact about criminal justice policy in California in recent times has been the magnitude by which the population of those incarcerated and those under state supervision has grown (Table 2.1 and 2.2). The Blue Ribbon Commission, an official state commssion set up to examine the difficulties associated with the rapid rise in the prison population, commented:

> In 1975 state prison represented about 18 per cent of all Superior Court sentences and had increased to about 34 per cent by 1988. Sixty-six per cent of all felons sentenced by superior courts were retained in local jails or on probation. Probation with jail was about 50 per cent of all dispositions in 1975 and had increased to almost 60 per cent by 1988. Of those granted any form of probation by the court, the percentage who have jail as a condition had increased from 56 per cent to 86 per cent during that period. For the same period, grants of probation without jail decreased from about 22 per cent to about 6 per cent. (Blue Ribbon Commission, 1990, p. 25)

In 1992 the Lower Court sentenced 88,361 convicted criminals and the Superior Courts 111,758 (Table 2.3). The numbers sentenced by the Superior Courts have doubled in less than ten years from the 52,335 offenders who were sentenced in 1984. Not only are the courts sentencing more offenders (a total of 206,119 in 1992), but the use of more severe sanctions has increased (Table 2.4). Sentencing distribution figures for 1992 show that the Lower Court gave a fine in only 1.4 per cent of all sentencing decisions, and the Superior Court in less: 0.1 per cent of cases sentenced by them (Table 2.4). The differences in the use of the fine is one of the most pronounced differences between the sentence dispositions given out by Californian criminal courts when contrasted with its frequent use in the courts in England and Finland.

The Lower Court cannot sentence a person to state prison but can send offenders to county jail. In 1992, 11.2 per cent were given a jail sentence and 69.8 per cent of all those sentenced by the Lower Court were given probation with jail. In the Superior Court, of all those sentenced in 1992, 37 per cent were sent to state prison; 54.8 per cent were given probation with jail and 0.8 per cent jail (Table 2.4). The use of prison reached the highest proportion ever for sentencing dispositions by the Superior Court, while the use of jail with probation has remained relatively stable. The use of probation on its own has fallen as a proportion of all sentences given in the Superior Court from 9.7 per cent in 1984 to the 5.5 per cent figure in 1992 (Table 2.2). In the Lower Court it has similarly fallen from 24.1 per cent in 1984 to 15.4 per cent in 1992.

The trend in the Superior Court between 1975 and 1988 has been to make far less use of straight probation and more use of state prison and probation with jail. It was therefore not surprising to see the subsequent phenomenal rise in the prison population in California, which is the largest state prison population across the USA. The federal prison population accounts for only 10 per cent of those incarcerated in the USA.

The population of incarcerated adults in state prison in California rose from a daily population of 25,606 in 1968 to 134,511 on October 29, 1995 (California, 1995b). In city and county jails over a similar period the numbers increased from 26,308 in 1968 to 68,706 in 1993 (Tables 2.1 and 2.2). In total in 1993 there were 558,633 adults under supervision by correctional agencies in California, 209,178 by state agencies in state prisons and camps or on parole; and 349,455 under county supervision in jails or on probation (California Department of Justice 1994a, p. 158).

Not surprisingly, there has been a major prison-building programme with consequent increases in employment. In the period from 1982 to 1995 the number of prisons has risen from 12 to 31 (California, 1995). California has undertaken the largest prison building programme in the United States - probably in the world - spending $5.27 billion on prison construction since 1982. In 1970 there were 17,000 full time employees working in correctional agencies in California and in 1993 there were 50,300 (California Department of Justice, 1994a, p. 167). One state prison, Vacaville, holds over 8,000 inmates and must rank amongst the largest of prisons in the world. The number of people sent to state prison as a proportion of the population of Californian residents was 107 per 100,000 in 1973 compared with 440 per 100,000 in 1990. As a proportion of its population, California imprisons four times as many citizens as does the UK.

Explaining the growth in the prison population in California

To explain such a sustained and rapid increase, a number of factors has to be examined. First, the amount of crime and the number of people arrested for crime. The number of felony arrests rose steadily to almost 2 million people in 1990, since when it has gone down to 1.67 million (Table 2.3). The trends in arrests will also reflect trends in the volume and pattern of crime.

An official measure of the incidence of recorded crime is the California Crime Index (CCI). It is based on the number of cases reported by the public of the felony categories of wilful homicide, forcible rape, robbery, aggravated assault, burglary, and motor vehicle theft and is expressed as the proportion of offences per 100,000 people.

The CCI rose steadily between 1952 and 1980 from 1,000 per 100,000 to 4,000 per 100,000. The rate then dropped and has remained relatively stable between the years 1988 to 1993 at 3,500 per 100,000. The general trend in the CCI is shown in Table 2.4. The rate at which recorded crime has changed since 1980 would not seem to be the major explanation of the growth in the use of imprisonment over the same period. Joan Petersilia comments: 'In sum the CCI figures reveal a mixture of results suggesting that overall crime rates in California have remained relatively stable since reaching a high point in 1980, that property crime has actually declined, but that violent crime (with the exception of rape) shows recent increases.' (Petersilia, 1992, p. 13). This trend in recorded crime is confirmed by the victimisation studies produced by the federal government's National Crime Victimisation Survey (NCVS) published by the Bureau of Census in Washington.

Another factor thought to play a part is the growth in the role that drug abuse has in enlarging the prison population. Drugs have an impact in terms of criminal offending and because of the large numbers of parole violators returned to state prison because they have failed drug testing, a condition of their parole. 'Drug use detected by urine analysis is a primary factor in over 50 per cent of all revocations. The felon parole population increased from approximately 9,000 in 1978 to in excess of 55,000 today and is projected to increase to almost 97,000 by 1994.' (Blue Ribbon Commission, 1990, p. 24). 'According to the Board of Prison Terms data, in fiscal year 1988-89, drug charges were a known factor in 56 per cent of all revocation actions, with drugs as a contributing factor in over 64 per cent of parolees returned to custody for parole violations'. (Blue Ribbon Commission, 1990, p. 71).

Drugs and crime were put on the agenda in the 1980s by the government in Washington. Petersilia wrote 'one significant explanation could be the Reagan and Bush administrations' war on drugs' (Petersilia, 1992, p. 17). However, Petersilia does not offer this as a full explanation and to this effect, quotes Patrick Langan's US study, 'Change in drug arrest and imprisonment rates only explains about 8 per cent of the growth in prison populations since 1974'. (Petersilia, 1992, p. 18).

While the drug war played its part in affecting the prison population growth, the extent to which parole violations, especially linked to drug use, contributed to the increase was also noted. In 1977 the total number of parole violators returned to prison was 788. Ten years on that number had risen to 25,207 in 1987. It rose to 41,334 in 1991 and fell to 34,932 in 1992 (Department of Corrections, 1995, Table 43). Of receptions of new prisoners into the state institutions in 1992, there were 40,158 sentenced as convicted felons by the courts, and 55,775 parole violators sent by state parole officers (Department of Corrections, 1995, Table 4A).

Another set of factors external to the criminal justice system that penologists would consider as influential would be the social and demographic variables and their influence on rates of incarceration. Referring to their findings in *The Scale of Imprisonment*, Zimring and Hawkins comment:

> There is no automatic linkage between the rates of imprisonment and social indicators such as the crime rates, unemployment, the age structure of the population, and trends in drug arrests. Using rates of imprisonment for the US as a whole, none of these factors is a strong explanation of rates of imprisonment since 1950. (Zimring and Hawkins, 1991, p. 221)

Factors more directly related to policy decisions were also influential in enlarging the prison population of California. As sentencing policy moved, under the influence of public pressure, towards tougher sentencing, California introduced more mandatory prison terms, longer prison base terms for some offence categories, longer periods for enhancements, and longer terms for life imprisonment, including life without the possibility of parole. The 1981 Beverly Burglary bill denied probation to offenders convicted of residential burglary. From 1983 all residential burglaries were to be punished as first degree burglary. So the first offender, who would previously have been sentenced to jail or probation or both, was now sent to state prison.

Prison terms were lengthened on an *ad hoc* basis for rape, using a gun during a crime, drunk driving and domestic violence. The 1986 Domestic Violence Laws classified domestic violence as felony. In March 1994 another policy change saw the introduction of the 'three strikes and you're out' policy whereby a felon convicted for an offence would on the occasion of a third offence be given a life sentence.

In California the tougher sentencing mood has been unleashed by the move to a just deserts sentencing policy. The determinate sentencing law was passed in California in September 1976 as a result of the efforts of prison reform groups, the Prisoners' Union, and other liberal organisations, in coalition with more conservative pressure groups. The former were happy to see certainty replace indeterminacy. The latter were happy to see punishment replace rehabilitation. But the question was yet to be clarified of who should set the tariff under a just deserts approach. In California the opportunity afforded by the shift to a just deserts approach allowed the public to have a greater role in the determination of sentences and they choose to have tougher penalties. The elected district attorneys and judges swept along by this mood respectively demanded and granted more jail and prison sentences. The use of imprisonment went up. At the same time, the system of discretionary parole release was abolished with the removal of the Adult Authority and with it a pragmatically useful safety-valve with which to cope with prison overpopulation.

Did the move to determinate sentencing cause the huge prison population expansion in California? Zimring and Hawkins cite the Blumstein study (1983) which indicates that the expansion in California was a continuation of an existing trend. But they comment on the indirect effects of the sentencing law reforms of 1976:

However, the movement towards determinacy may have had two delayed effects that contributed to increasing prison population in the 1980s. First, the reallocation of power to set prison terms to legislatures may over time result in more or larger upgrades in punishment than in states with sentencing commissions or non-determinate sentencing systems...

Second, the parole board's release power with its safety valve function may not have been very significant in controlling prison population growth in the late 1970s and early 1980s. However, the lack of that power in the late 1980s when imprisonment rates reached an all-time high meant the parole board's ability to react to fluctuations in prison population no longer existed at a time when it may have been employed. (Zimring and Hawkins, 1991, p. 170-1)

Table 2.1 State institution inmate population

Number and rate per 100,000 of population at risk

YEAR	NO.	RATE	YEAR	NO.	RATE
1993	121,954	582.9	**1972**	17,758	139.2
1992	111,338	538.9	**1971**	18,391	146.6
1991	103,563	508.7	**1970**	22,399	181.5
1990	99,145	495.0	**1969**	24,403	209.3
1989	89,171	458.4	**1968**	25,606	224.5
1988	78,102	413.6	**1967**	23,668	212.1
1987	69,176	376.4	**1966**	23,563	216.7
1986	62,128	347.0	**1965**	22,766	214.4
1985	52,747	301.9	**1964**	22,822	221.3
1984	45,685	267.4	**1963**	22,936	228.3
1983	41,642	248.4	**1962**	21,086	216.5
1982	37,600	229.1	**1961**	21,845	230.7
1981	32,966	205.0	**1960**	21,660	237.4
1980	27,916	176.9	**1959**	19,299	-
1979	25,527	166.6	**1958**	19,202	-
1978	24,068	161.4	**1957**	16,918	-
1977	22,127	152.9	**1956**	15,532	-
1976	23,641	167.9	**1955**	15,230	-
1975	22,723	165.9	**1954**	15,376	-
1974	27,479	206.0	**1953**	14,149	-
1973	24,984	191.7	**1952**	13,169	

Tables 2.1 and 2.2 are compiled from: California Department of Justice (1994) *Crime and Delinquency in California, 1993*, p.158.
The rates are based on the adult population at risk (18-69 years of age).
The data on the institutional population is based on a one day count.

Table 2.2 Adults on parole, probation and in jail, 1963-1993

	Parolees/outpatients		County and city jails		On active probation	
Year	**No.**	**Rate**	**No.**	**Rate**	**No**	**Rate**
1993	87,224	416.9	68,706	328.4	280,749	1341.8
1992	87,867	425.3	74,131	358.8	302,754	1465.3
1991	84,207	413.7	71,682	352.1	315,421	1549.4
1990	72,223	360.6	74,257	370.8	305,700	1526.4
1989	61,211	314.7	74,016	380.5	285,018	1465.3
1988	52,587	278.5	67,021	354.9	265,643	1406.6
1987	43,390	236.1	63,767	347.0	242,529	1319.6
1986	35,304	197.2	57,887	323.3	220,614	1232.3
1985	32,020	183.3	51,053	292.3	210,449	1204.7
1984	28,000	163.9	47,329	277.0	197,413	1155.6
1983	22,797	136.0	42,211	251.8	176,555	1053.2
1982	18,209	110.9	39,085	238.1	157,009	956.5
1981	15,431	95.9	33,652	209.2	152,563	948.6
1980	16,002	101.4	30,054	190.4	151,085	957.5
1979	15,865	103.5	26,993	176.2	150,566	982.6
1978	16,895	113.3	26,938	180.6	153,133	1026.5
1977	22,006	152.1	26,546	183.4	149,587	1033.7
1976	21,759	154.5	28,201	200.3	152,242	1081.2
1975	23,517	171.7	24,992	182.5	153,140	1118.2
1974	21,128	158.4	25,217	189.0	158,887	1191.1
1973	23,120	177.4	24,391	187.2	150,292	1153.3
1972	14,848	116.4	26,995	211.3	143,183	1122.2
1971	15,808	126.0	27,629	220.3	132,078	1053.0
1970	14,927	121.0	27,694	226.6	117,095	948.9
1969	13,028	111.8	27,669	237.3	102,042	875.3
1968	11,833	103.8	26,308	230.7	93,282	818.0

These rates are based on the adult populations at risk (18-69 years of age) for each year.
Source: *ibid* see Table 2.1.

Table 2.3 Sentencing in California, 1985-1992

Numbers sentenced

YEAR	1985	1986	1987	1988	1989	1990	1991	1992
LOWER COURT								
Sentenced:	**76,971**	**78,256**	**81,018**	**75,674**	**80,688**	**77,314**	**89,519**	**88,361**
Prison	N/A	N/A	N/A	N/A	N/A	N/A	N/A	1,626
CYA[1]	3	1	2	5	1	-	3	3
Probation	17,949	14,839	14,862	12,895	13,855	13,711	15,342	13,626
Probation with jail	45,043	49,865	53,271	50,448	53,556	52,227	62,201	61,716
Jail	11,574	11,484	11,113	10,807	11,630	9,994	10,486	9,915
Fine	2,118	1,871	1,628	1,391	1,430	1,221	1,293	1,230
CRC[2]	N/A	N/A	N/A	N/A	N/A	N/A	N/A	26
SUPERIOR COURT								
Sentenced:	**63,562**	**70,034**	**72,582**	**77,997**	**86,939**	**92,029**	**106,280**	**111,758**
Death	16	21	25	34	33	33	26	40
Prison	21,421	24,218	25,029	25,887	29,056	32,265	37,288	41,573
CYA[1]	225	171	125	168	149	98	92	111
Probation	4,978	4,434	4,128	4,818	5,344	5,915	6,476	6,096
Probation with jail	35,197	39,529	41,671	45,455	50,221	51,498	60,030	61,203
Jail	950	912	830	760	776	770	793	860
Fine	20	28	21	28	46	54	103	85
CRC[2]	678	721	743	833	1,170	1,252	1,354	1,768

Tables compiled from: California Department of Justice (1994), *Californian Criminal Justice Profile 1993*, p. 16.

The Tables represents the sentence disposition of adults arrested for and convicted of felony offences.

1 Californian Youth Authority
2 Californian Rehabilitation Centre

Table 2.4 Sentencing in California, 1985-1992

Percentage distribution of sentencing dispositions

YEAR	1985	1986	1987	1988	1989	1990	1991	1992
LOWER COURT								
Sentenced:	**100.0 0**	**100.0 0**	**100.0 0**	**100.0 0**	**100.0 0**	**100.0 0**	**100.0 0**	**100.0 0**
Prison	N/A	N/A	N/A	N/A	N/A	N/A	N/A	N/A
CYA[1]								
Probation	23.3	19	18.3	17	17.2	17.7	17.1	15.4
Probation with jail	58.5	63.7	65.8	66.7	66.4	67.6	69.5	69.8
Jail	15.0	14.7	13.7	14.3	14.4	12.9	11.7	11.2
Fine	2.8	2.4	2.0	1.8	1.8	1.6	1.4	1.4
CRC [2]	N/A	N/A	N/A	N/A	N/A	N/A	N/A	N/A
SUPERIOR COURT								
Sentenced:	**100.0 0**	**100.0 0**	**100.0 0**	**100.0 0**	**100.0 0**	**100.0 0**	**100.0 0**	**100.0 0**
Death	-	-	-	-	-	-	-	-
Prison	33.7	34.6	34.5	33.2	33.4	35.1	35.1	37.2
CYA[1]	0.4	0.2	0.2	0.2	0.2	0.1	0.1	0.1
Probation	7.8	6.3	5.7	6.2	6.1	6.4	6.1	5.5
Probation with jail	55.4	56.4	57.4	58.3	57.8	56.0	56.5	54.8
Jail	1.5	1.3	1.1	1.0	0.9	0.8	0.7	0.8
Fine	-	-	-	-	0.1	0.1	0.1	0.0
CRC[2]	1.1	1.0	1.0	1.1	1.3	1.4	1.3	1.6

Table compiled from: California Department of Justice (1994), *Californian Criminal Justice Profile 1993*, p. 16.

1 Californian Youth Authority
2 Californian Rehabilitation Centre

Table 2.5 Total arrests, 1957-1993

Number and risk per 100,000 of population at risk

	Total	Adult	Juvenile
1993	1,667,522	1,412,431	255,091
1990	1,979,355	1,736,828	242,527
1985	1,716,040	1,485,079	230,961
1980	1,542,850	1,260,324	282,526
1975	1,439,857	1,068,907	370,950
1970	1,340,072	957,137	382,935
1965	1,017,198	739,549	277,649
1960	856,869	674,154	182,715
1957	792,553	647,575	144,978

Rates are based on population at risk (10-69 years of age).

Table 2.6 California Crime Index

Number and rate per 100,000 population of the state

	Number	Rate
1993	1,068,996	3,367.80
1990	1,017,665	3,443.00
1985	828,461	3,172.60
1980	928,297	3,922.10
1975	739,766	3,434.90
1970	580,551	2,897.10
1965	351,291	1,873.00
1960	228,668	1,441.80
1955	125,147	960.10

Tables compiled from California: Department of Justice (1994), *Crime and delinquency in California 1993*, pp. 108 and 120.

The research in California

Policy context: Impact of penal expansion on the criminal justice system in California

In California the criminal justice system operates through 58 separate counties. In 1988 all senior officials in the counties were invited by the California Attorney General's Office in Sacramento to take part in a survey to help identify the problems associated with the expansion of the system. All chief probation officers, district attorneys, police chiefs in large cities, public defenders, sheriffs and presiding judges of the Appeal Court, Superior Court and municipal courts were sent a questionnaire about the growth of the criminal justice system in California. The 294 replies (70 per cent completion rate) formed the basis of two reports published by the California Attorney General's Office in 1988.

The limitations of the current system and the exacerbation caused by the rapid expansion, as seen from the perspective of criminal justice officials in the counties, were documented. The local officials described a system lacking funding for their vastly enlarged caseloads. In addition to inadequate resources they described a system which had become overly complex in terms of, what it had to do, and how it had to do it. Local senior criminal justice officials in California described a system lacking planning, consultation and balance.

The problems associated with a rapidly expanding penal system were recognised, reluctantly, by the Republican Governor, George Deukmejian and in response he accepted a proposal from the state legislative bodies to establish a commission of inquiry. The Blue Ribbon Commission on *Inmate Population Management* was given statutory authority by Senator Robert Presley's Senate Bill 279, and introduced into the California legislature in 1987. The Commission started work in the summer of 1988, and presented its report to the governor and the legislature on January 29, 1990. Despite the narrowness of the title which was chosen to focus upon the management of the incarcerated, the 132 page report provided a broad vision of an entire criminal justice system which in a decade had experienced rapid and unplanned expansion.

Recommendations of the 1990 Blue Ribbon Commission

In presenting the Commission's report, its chair, Grover Trask II, the district attorney from Riverside County wrote, 'The Commission has come to the predominant conclusion that the criminal justice system in California is out of balance. Additional punishment options must be expanded to reduce overcrowding while protecting public safety.'

The Blue Ribbon Commission comprehensively described the problems of a system which had expanded with unprecedented speed, without the benefit of a systematic evaluation of what it was doing, other than to placate the desire 'to get tough on crime.' The report provided a picture of a criminal justice system under considerable pressure from numbers.

The commission's description of the system as 'out of balance' did not imply an interpretation that they sought a swing of the pendulum away from tough to softer approaches to crime. It recommended that we look at corrections as a part of, and at the end of, the criminal justice system, and proposed that to overcome the problems of prison overcrowding there was need for a comprehensive and systematic re-evaluation of the entire state and local criminal justice system; 'from prevention through discharge of jurisdiction.' (Blue Ribbon Commission, 1990, p. 4)

The Commission identified a number of problems facing the criminal justice system, the first and most obvious being the overcrowding in penal institutions. Overcrowding results in the early release of sentenced offenders where inmates litigate over the unacceptable conditions, which do not meet the legal standards for housing inmates. It adds to the security and safety problems for staff and inmates. It concentrates the mind of administrators on the mundane operational tasks of transportation, feeding and bedding, and leaves little money, energy or space for programs to help those inmates who might choose to re-evaluate and redirect their lives.

New construction resulted in an additional 40,000 prison beds and 25,500 jail beds between the years 1982 and 1990, and continues. A five-year projection included in the report, estimated that the daily average population of incarcerated offenders would be a quarter of a million by 1994. But despite the growth, the Blue Ribbon Commission concluded, 'by the time the current expansion program is constructed in 1994, the projected population will be more overcrowded than it is today.'

The California Blue Ribbon Commission's report came to the conclusion that intermediate sanctions would be preferable for the large number of inmates who go through the expensive state prison system for relatively short periods of time of less than six months. They took the view that public safety would be improved by less use of imprisonment for this group of inmates and more community based sanctions. The high turnover of offenders and parole violators who stay for relatively short periods of time in the state prisons offers little by way of an incapacitating effect because of the limited duration of their stay and does not allow for the development of structural programmes to reduce the chances of repeat offending.

Half of the inmates admitted to state prisons from the courts in 1989 were released in less than a year according to the Commission's report. In 1988, there were 5,000 who served three months or less in state prison and 8,000 who served six months or less. In addition, half of the admissions to state prison in 1989 were parolees. The Blue Ribbon Commission reported that in 1988, of the parole violators returned to the Department of Corrections, 15,000 served three months or less and 23,000 served six months or less.

The population of short term prisoners and those returned as parole violators reduces the role of the state prison. 'The largest set of revolving doors in the history of incarceration', is the words of Brian Taugher, the commissioner representing the attorney general on the Blue Ribbon Commission describing the situation of Californian prisons.

The Blue Ribbon Commission raises a number of important questions related to cost effectiveness. Is it cost-effective to spend money on imprisoning offenders given a number of failures of the system in this respect, when the incapacitative effect of imprisonment with this population is reduced to a few months a year? They also pointed to the failure of the system in deterrent and rehabilitative terms as evidenced by the numbers of prisoners who are returned to prison as parole violators. Of those paroled in the first six months of 1987, 67 per cent were returned to prison. The parole violators rate had risen from 15 to 70 per cent since the determinate sentencing legislation came into effect in 1977.

They describe a penal system with few programs in prisons to attempt rehabilitation; where offenders are bounced between different agencies in the system in their short but persistent involvement with the system, with little continuous authority and surveillance to control and supervise their behaviour.

The Blue Ribbon Commission concluded, 'it is questionable as to whether long-term public safety is being served or enhanced by certain non-violent new commitments or parole violators going to state prison for less than one year.' The Commission recommended that 'the prison and jail overcrowding problem should be (resolved) through an approach involving: changes in sentencing practices, adoption of a community corrections act, changes in corrections practices such as parole revocation procedures, and additional construction of prisons, jails, youth facilities and community corrections facilities as necessary. Paramount emphasis should be placed on those areas that will significantly lessen the numerical impact on prison and jail populations.' (Blue Ribbon Commission, 1990, p. 123)

Thus a key recommendation from the report was the need to encourage and develop, 'highly structured intermediate community sanctions between traditional probation and incarceration. Such sanctions should function as punishment, as well as provide the offender with the opportunity through programs, training and work to change their criminal behaviour.' (Blue Ribbon Commission, 1990, p. 114). Greater use of intermediate sanctions was to be encouraged through the adoption of a community corrections act. This recommendation of the Blue Ribbon Commission, to make greater use of community-based intermediate sanctions was to provide the focal point for discussions in the focus group panels with California criminal justice officials.

Methodology

In 1990, eleven focus groups met in nine counties across California: Contra Costa, Los Angeles, Napa, Riverside, Sacramento, San Francisco, Santa Clara, Solano and Sonoma. The panels were made up of senior criminal justice officials in the counties. Six key local officials were invited to attend: chief probation officer, district attorney, presiding judge of the superior court, presiding judge of the municipal court, the public defender and the county sheriff. Where appropriate, chiefs of police were invited and the head of the local department of corrections. In other counties, members of the board of supervisors and representatives of the county executive's office were invited because of an expressed interest in the topic. In one county, a director of the pre-trial services unit was invited; in another, the county drug program administrator.

Seventy-three panellists attended the eleven groups. Typical attendance was six or seven panellists, with a range of four to nine panellists. A letter of invitation was sent with a brochure explaining the background of the project. They were asked to reply indicating their willingness to participate. Substitution was not encouraged but allowed when a person could not attend or thought that there was a more appropriate person in the agency. Presiding judges of the superior court, in some cases, suggested that the judge in charge of the criminal calendar would be more appropriate.

All panellists were sent a summary of the Blue Ribbon Commission's report along with the list of questions to be discussed. These questions were intended to be a guide to discussions rather than an agenda to be rigidly followed. The questions asked about existing community programs which could be expanded and what new programs could be introduced. The questions asked about the potential advantages of community sanctions and what would be acceptable to the public and the best way to achieve public and professional support for the introduction and expansion of community corrections as intermediate sanctions. Finally the questions asked about the features that panellists would like to see if there was to be a Community Corrections Act and what should be the main features of community correctional centres.

All the panellists were sent a copy of the report on the findings of the focus groups and after the sessions they were asked to complete an evaluation questionnaire about the organisation and conduct of the panels. They were also invited to make a comment about the utility of focus group discussions. The favourable nature of these comments has been discussed in Chapter 1.

Criminal justice officials' views of community sanctions

Attitude to the conclusions of the Blue Ribbon Commission's report

There were 38 recommendations in the Blue Ribbon Commission report. For the purposes of this research, the focus groups agenda was confined to those recommendations concerned with the expansion of punishment options. In effect, this became a discussion on the possible form, role and acceptability of intermediate sanctions. Most panellists agreed with the report about the problems described and that the commission had clearly spelt out the complexities and problems the California criminal justice system was facing. The description of the system and its problems was consistent with the realities as the majority of panellists saw them.

Several panellists frankly expressed their disagreement with some of the assumptions and conclusion of the report. Four district attorneys doubted the implication in the report in terms of the efficacy of the use of imprisonment for the short termer. However, prosecutors seeking convictions for felonies, as one judge explained, are unlikely to see the use of prison even for short terms as a problem, 'as the one thing the district attorney is usually concerned about is getting another "prison prior" on the person.' This would build the offender's profile as a previous offender with a prison record, which will be used by the prosecution, should he be convicted in the future for another offence.

The majority, which included those district attorneys who were critical of some of the assumptions made in the report, saw no problem with intermediate sanctions in principle. The problem of expanding their use would come, firstly, from how to finance the expansion, secondly, identification of the target population and, thirdly, their acceptance by the public.

One critic focused on the economic motives behind the proposed reforms. A County Director of Corrections commented:

> The pendulum is beginning to swing the other way, not driven by altruistic views about rehabilitation or what is most appropriate, but rather its cost driven....I think in California there is a jaundiced view about the state's purpose here....the goal seems to be to reduce cost, not to improve effectiveness. I think the criminal justice system statewide, through the legislature, needs to get clear what it is trying to do, what are our goals and set performance objectives that are not driven strictly by dollars.

There was only one panellist, a chief of police from Los Angeles, who took the view that the report was fundamentally wrong in its analysis and conclusions. He interpreted the report as an about-face, whereas what was needed, in his opinion, was more of the same:

> I think those projections are just as clearly wrong as they possibly can be. They are based upon a state that did not do anything for several years. All through the sixties and the seventies, we did very little. We were letting them out of jails. We had probation subsidy, all these phoney systems to deal with the criminal element. Now we have finally gotten tough in the eighties and start putting them in prison. We are basing all our projections on failure at the beginning and not our successes, and we think it is going to continue on forever and it's not. The criminal element out there is not infinite. It's finite. This view that it is going to go on forever [costs of prisons and custody] through the nineties and into the next century with billions and billions of dollars spent, I don't believe that. I think there is a point where it is going to start levelling off. We are going to have to find that point. I read this report and what it says is that the criminals have us just exactly where they want us. We

> are on the run again. We are going to back away from the approach that has been working. I can show you now where it is starting to level off in my city, substantially levelling off in my city, even though the population is increasing, even though some of the social problems have increased and gotten worse. What I am saying is that our tough policy has begun to pay off. Now we want to back away from that because we are going to spend too much money. I look in here and it says we are spending 6 per cent on corrections. That is the first order of business for government to make sure people are safe.

A more typical response was made by an official from the same county as the chief of police quoted above in support of the recommendation to make greater use of community-based intermediate sanctions:

> I have to believe that the thrust of things in the Blue Ribbon Commission is the wave of the future. I believe we will see support for legislation. I believe we have the opportunity, if we work together and understand what we are trying to do, to provide something we are not now providing; truth, sanctions and an opportunity for rehabilitation. We could do it through the use of intermediate sanctions.

Imprisonment, sentencing options and the role of community sentences

The comment of the Blue Ribbon Commission that imprisonment is not the only form of punishment suggests the need to identify other forms of punishment within a retributive framework. Thus the recommendation for judges to have sentencing options available that are properly regarded as severe without requiring imprisonment. A refinement of the tariffs of punishments is possible. A gap exists between 'getting off' and 'doing time'. This gap in this binary system of sentencing provides a potential role for community sanctions to be developed as intermediate punishment within the principles of proportionality, so that the level of severity of the punishment relates to the level of the seriousness of the offence.

In the context of sentencing policy in California, there was little support for community penalties as alternatives to custody. They simply have no credibility as an alternative, and hence as an equivalent to imprisonment in the eyes of the public or the officials in the focus group study.

If the rationale of community sentences as alternatives to custody is no longer acceptable and most panellists were convinced it was not, then what justification and role can be found for community sentences? There was acceptance that community sentences could play a role as an intermediate sanction, that is, as a punishment option, located on the tariff of penalties between probation and imprisonment. A district attorney commented:

> We have to expand the punishment options to widen this and to get the public to understand this is not an alternative. This is not letting somebody off from doing his time. What we are doing is providing a system of more accountability and more control and the only difference is now we are dealing with some of these people locally as opposed to spending a lot of money sending them to prison through a revolving door.

Community sanctions, intermediate or not, can be multi-functional. The panellists felt that for intermediate sanctions to be effective and acceptable such that the public has confidence in them, then they should combine the characteristics of punishment, surveillance and rehabilitation. That is they should be recognised as an attempt to achieve multiple purposes within a primary logic defined in terms of just deserts. Then, if rehabilitation is not successful, the punitive element will have served just deserts purposes.

Furthermore, the surveillance element gives some assurances that the offender who is released back into the community will have some degree of monitoring. A chief probation officer describes the importance of surveillance and sanctions for failure to comply with intensive probation supervision:

> They are watched seven days a week, 18 hours a day in this county. If they violate this probation, it goes back to the court; and nine times out of ten, that individual is on his way to the state penitentiary or county jail.

If community sentences are to be used with a population of more persistent offenders the role of monitoring and surveillance becomes vital in assuring the public that they are being protected. In recent years, more effective means of surveillance in community settings have been developed, e.g. 24-hour reporting systems and electronically monitored home confinement. Sentences and correctional officials may have been tempted to see custody as the only means of achieving appropriate control over and supervision of the offenders.

A multi-purposed community sentence should provide for multiple elements, i.e. restitution, community work, fines, and electronic monitoring, as considered appropriate by the judge. Some of the elements that constituted a community-based intermediate sanction would be directed at rehabilitation. The logic for rehabilitative aspirations was put by a sheriff. He commented, 'The fact is the people in our jails don't come from somewhere outside the area. They all come from our community, and we are going to turn them right back into the community. We at least should not turn them back worse off than when they came in.'

The comments of a county analyst reflect the view of those who have sympathy for more rehabilitative efforts with this group of inmates, but think it is unlikely to gain public support if it involves release into the community: 'I don't think it's going to be easy to sell intermediate sanctions in the community right now. It might be easier to bring the services to the inmates because I think the public still wants the inmates locked up.' But some panellists saw the attempt to change behaviour of felons as futile. If resources were available for programs, it should go on primary or secondary preventative work for those at-risk groups in the community who had not yet come in contact with the system, or had only marginal contact.

Panellists seemed aware that prisons did little to improve the future behaviour of people sent to them and were in the main aware of the dysfunctional consequences of incarceration in terms of enhancing rather than reducing criminal tendencies. For those whose crime does not require a prison sentence in terms of public protection or punishment the sentence given should attempt to reduce the future likelihood of re-offending. However, this conclusion provides a reason to limit the use of imprisonment to those situations where punishment or incapacitation are paramount.

The predominant view of the panellists about the purposes of community sentences was that they should be multi-purposed. Given that the target population envisaged by the Blue Ribbon Commission is some of those offenders who would otherwise be going to jail and prison, community sanctions, although not an alternative to prison, should be structured to provide an element of punishment. This did not prevent them having a rehabilitative role, so long as the punishment and surveillance aspect was incorporated.

Rehabilitation

The Blue Ribbon Commission argue that public protection would be greater if offenders' behaviour could be modified. This is more likely, the Blue Ribbon Commission report suggests, 'if offenders are kept in the community, these offenders retain their ties to family, jobs, and the community, thereby ultimately enhancing the likelihood of a successful reintegration into the community'. But ironically, many panellists felt that the community was the source of criminality in terms of the influence of peer pressure, drug subculture, family and housing problems.

The style of rehabilitative intervention, identified by the Blue Ribbon Commission, differs from the behaviour modification techniques associated with the 1960s. They talk of holding offenders accountable; and while recognising the need for services for groups who have multiple problems, insist, while excluding the mentally abnormal and children, that offenders should be held responsible for their acts.

The comments from the California panellists in the focus groups would suggest the following elements of a fully developed rehabilitative program of intermediate sanctions: recognition of the low success criteria; long-term follow-up; multi-purpose programming and comprehensive service provision; more flexibility and discretion for handling offenders on these programs; additional surveillance and sanctions for failure.

Panellists were concerned that this type of community program should not be perceived by either the inmate or the public as a soft option. While the offender is still under surveillance and punished, if he or she does not respond to the programs offered, then there should be the flexibility in the system to remove the offender from a particular community-based program. Flexibility was considered important during the correctional period so that phased de-scaling of surveillance was possible, depending on the offender's progress.

Panellists felt that past programs aimed at rehabilitation were sometimes unsuccessful because it was easy for an offender to get lost in the system. The system processes the arrestee-offender-inmate through many stages. So in addition to a long-term strategy of behaviour modification, greater continuity of supervision was required as the offender proceeded through the system. Continuity is a key quality required if community sentences are to succeed as a form of intermediate punishment.

It is also required for the rehabilitative element, in that there must be a comprehensive and wide range of service providers whose tasks are coordinated so that offenders with multiple problems can be helped in a way which is likely to achieve life-style changes. This cannot be done in a piecemeal way.

Given the target population of offenders, many of whom have already gone through community corrections as a result of past offences and parole violations, some panellists were very dubious about the likelihood of success and thought money could be better spent on preventative measures at the primary or secondary level, i.e. with younger target populations and at-risk groups rather than with persistent offenders who would constitute the intermediate sanctions target population.

Proponents for and against the idea of adopting a rehabilitative role for community sentences both agreed that the success rate was bound to be low. A more critical comment was made by a chief of police:

> I can remember the same failure rate with probation that we have today, and the same failure rate with parole that we have today. It hasn't changed one bit. We keep doing it. We have a failure rate that private industry would look at and say we have to go out of business because with that failure rate, we can't make a buck.

A public defender commented, 'They don't have the Rhodes scholars on probation or parole. It is a success, if 5 per cent of them make it.' Others, like this judge, thought rehabilitation should not be the primary concern of the sentence:

> My own personal feeling is that rehabilitation is a by-product of the system working appropriately. I don't think you focus in on rehabilitation. I think if you put someone in a situation where he is paying back the community for what he has done by work or whatever then that allows him to get his dignity back.

Causes of crime: What programs and services are needed?

Many of the comments of the panellists as to the way to deal with criminal behaviour came from their assumptions about the causes of crime. Should crime be regarded as an issue of personal responsibility and accountability or does it have its roots in social conditions or personal characteristics. This was a debate not resolved in the focus groups. But these assumptions underpinned many of the comments of the panellists, as seen in this statement made by a judge:

> One of the reasons we have so much recidivism in these young offenders is that they have no family, never gone to school, they are uneducated, have no job skills, the can't fill out an application, and they have never learned to get up in the morning. If they do get the job, they get fired because they don't report or get there on time. You have got to recognize you are not only dealing with the offender. You can take offenders and put them out in the desert and with all the supervision and training and you could do a lot with those people, but turn those people back into the communities where the houses are dilapidated and rundown, with no electricity, (we have lots of homes where they haven't paid the gas and electricity bill for six months), the bathrooms don't work; it's terrible. You put these people back in the environment and time after time these defendants will tell me 'there is nothing I can do to help myself judge'.

If a rehabilitative logic was to be part of the role of community sanctions then there was a need to provide a comprehensive range of services to achieve offender behaviour changes, something that was evidentially not happening in the view of the panellists. The following were identified by the panellists as the major problems which contributed to criminal behaviour: alcoholism, drugs, educational and employment needs, family and domestic problems, immaturity and irresponsibility, literacy and social skills, mental illness and psychiatric problems, subcultural life-styles and underclass life opportunities.

The degree of surveillance would depend on the offender and their assessed risk. The array of programs would have to be related to offender needs. Programs would involve the delivery of services to offenders. A list of services for offenders for rehabilitative and surveillance purposes would include: family counselling, work training, employment opportunities bureaux, mental health services, literacy and educational courses, housing, welfare, social skills training, drug abuse programs and drug use monitoring. Funding costs could match and surpass incarceration costs if all these programs were applied in a comprehensive way in an effort to change offender behaviour.

The point being made by the officials is that if crime has its roots in the community, as claimed by the Blue Ribbon Commission, then the range of causally related factors are considerable, and subsequent programs could as a minimum require a recognition that the above list of problems would require tackling. With one or all elements being required, dependent on the problems identified for each of the inmates after the screening process had been completed.

A recognition that behaviour modification is not likely to be easy and that along with a low-success criteria goes the need to provide long-term follow-up with services and counselling.

The target population for community-based intermediate sanctions

The Blue Ribbon Commission identified a target population of those who would be eligible for community corrections. They include short-term new prison commitments serving one year or less, with emphasis on those serving six months or less, and parole violators returned to prison with emphasis on those serving six months or less. With younger offenders they identify some less serious non-violent offenders from juvenile courts, and also include technical parole violators and offenders in the last 120 days of their sentence with the Californian Youth Authority. They also see the target population including these in county jails, commitments and pre-trial detainees. They conclude:

> The community corrections target population specified above should be further limited to non-violent property offenders including drug abusers. Emphasis should be on first-time offenders and those without a significant criminal history. (Blue Ribbon Commission, 1990, p. 115)

The eligibility criteria were accepted by most panellists as appropriate. What concerned them most was the importance of screening the eligible population in terms of the risks and needs of offenders. The target population for intermediate sanctions has been identified by most theorists and policy documents as prison-bound offenders. In the American Correctional Association's Model for a Community Corrections Act, the first of eight components identifies: 'A clearly defined target group of prison-bound offenders.' The fear of some panellists, with respect to the use of intermediate sanctions, is that those offenders previously given a discharge, a fine, or routine probation will be swept up, not necessarily in a wider net, but a more demanding net which imposes more controls and sanctions on the offender. I would have thought this likely and even, in cases, desirable. Only if we think the past 'binary' system was working perfectly would there be no doubts that all offenders got what they deserved: that there was no inconsistent sentencing, no 'lucky' offenders, and above all no lack of appropriate sanctions.

Given the target population of offenders, many of whom had already gone through community corrections as a result of past offences and parole violations, some panellists were very dubious about the likelihood of success and thought money could be better spent on preventative measures while at the primary or secondary level, i.e. with younger target populations and at-risk groups rather than with persistent offenders who would constitute the intermediate sanctions target population.

A problem identified by the panellists was the concern about the efficacy of dealing with felony inmates who had already reached prison, and that it might be too late to do anything to change their behaviour. One chief probation officer took the view:

> The problem is once they are at a level where they have to be committed to state prison, it is too late. They need state prison. If we put the resources when they were first involved in the commission of crimes so that we had them adjusted to the community and had whatever resources, whether it's drug rehabilitation early in, we could prevent it. That's prevention. 80 per cent of the people going through felony hearings end up on probation now. If we would put a tenth of the money we put into state prison into making it a real sanction or punishment when they first get probation, we might be able to make an impact. If you address the issue in the community, it has got to be early. It's too late once they need prison.

The future of probation?

A dramatic shift in role is envisioned by several chief probation officers in California. Unlike their British counterparts, they have, in some cases, given up their individual welfare casework-oriented approach. They are ready to subscribe to a more surveillance oriented role, in which the casework, be it employment or social skills training, is handed over to specialist counsellors in public or private practice. The probation officer is being left with a screening and monitoring role in general and with supervision in some cases. The weight of numbers and the frustrations of failure have influenced this shift, along with the recognition of the declining public faith in probation as anything other than a token punishment. One chief probation officer who foresaw a new role for probation commented:

> Probation means more than half of the felons on probation are never seen...They are tracked only by computer. That's what it means. The other half get supervised in caseloads of 35 to 200. A lot of the felons that end up on probation should not be on probation, they need to be incarcerated.
>
> Probation should only provide the surveillance and sanctions. I don't believe probation officers should do the treatment or counselling. I believe there are specialists who are trained to do that. If I got the resources, I could provide the kind of supervision so that I knew what the probationers were doing. That's why I would want my resources doubled. The other resources would be to go to private or public agencies who are trained to do specifically drug counselling, job counselling, and all that. I don't believe the probation officer can be the counsellor to everyone.

Another chief probation officer argued the need for greater preventative efforts:

> An effective system in my view has to invest in preventing the circumstances and situations that result in crime. This does not necessarily mean, not incarcerating someone after they have earned their ticket, but to prevent the crime that earns them the ticket from occurring. We haven't done a very good job. In fact, we have done worse and worse. All of the community-based corrections programs and non-institutional programs have gotten worse and worse. We have 257,000 people in California that are there on the streets who are convicted, on probation, and supervised zilch.

A major problem for probation agencies is the negative public image and the lack of credibility for probation:

> Probation has a very negative connotation. We don't know what to call ourselves any more. We haven't come up with anything any better than what we have. Corrections also does not leave a very good taste in the mouth of the general public. Probation is even worse.

The general public's view of probation as getting off is confirmed by a judge: 'The public perception of me putting somebody on probation, is that the judge has given the person a break.' The poor public relations image of probation was recognised by one chief probation officer who commented:

> Many probation offices across the county are no longer calling themselves probation departments because the very reasons you hear talked about. They are becoming community corrections agencies or community safety agencies. They are no longer called probation. The public will never get over the perception that probation is equivalent to 'getting off'.

Community correctional centres

Many panellists thought there was a need for a new style of institution, a type of local jail with rehabilitative services and programs. These should, where possible, be based in communities so that community contacts can be built on for rehabilitative purposes. The idea of less secure, dormitory style institutions was regarded by most panellists as acceptable in terms of the cost advantage and the potential benefits. There is recognition that many offenders sent to custody are not a security problem and do not require the costly security conditions found in state prisons and the main local jail. The advantage of correctional centres is described by one district attorney:

> A community corrections program needs to develop some kind of confined setting because you are talking about felons with serious records who should not be directly out on the street in contact with the public. These individuals have been through the system many times and generally have been on probation one, two, three, four times and it hasn't worked. Supervision, even intensive supervision, won't work. For the purposes of accountability and punishment, there has got to be something at the local level that the court can use to house these people.

Concern was expressed by many panellists about the control and funding of these institutions. If they are desirable, went one argument, then with resources made available the sheriff could build them for locally held offenders, and there is nothing stopping the Department of Corrections doing the same for state prisons. This could be accomplished if the problem of siting could be overcome: a problem about which nearly all the panellists were pessimistic.

Senate Bill 2000, introduced by Senator Presley in 1990 but never enacted, provided for substance abuse community correctional centres for drug abusers. These would be built with state funds and operated on the basis of 50 per cent of the operational costs provided by the Department of Correction with use of 50 per cent of the bed space; the county paying the other 50 per cent of operating costs and having 50 per cent of the bed space. The state agency would pay all the construction costs of the facility, and the operational costs would be shared equally between the state and the county. Despite this, the county officials were sceptical about the long-term financial viability of such an arrangement.

Community-based correctional centres are not a new idea in California. In 1961 California Rehabilitation Centers were introduced for use with selected felons and others with drug addiction problems. In the early 1990s community-based facilites run by the Department of Corrections were renamed as California Correctional Centers, housing 5,911 offenders on December 31, 1991 (California, 1993 p. 1-3). These provide residential facilities for a maximum period of 18 months for selected newly sentenced offenders, parole violators and those on work furlogh programs for the last 120 days of a prison term. They provide pre-release and educational schemes and work crews for cleaning parks and streets, although the high profile projects involving offenders clearing litter from the state highways on the weekend are run by the counties.

Most of the panel discussions recognised the need for a more systematic and comprehensive approach to community sanctions so as to provide the continuity, follow-up and delivery of integrated services that is required to achieve offender behavioural changes and also allows for more thorough monitoring of the offenders' progress. The problem being faced by some offenders are monumental, and for a beneficial life-style change a concerted effort involving criminal justice and other community agencies is required.

For surveillance purposes, a more coordinated approach is required from the agencies in the system so as to reassure the public that the offender will not slip through the net of monitoring in the case where several agencies are involved. Equally important in rehabilitative terms is that the offender proceeds through the system with some 'continuity of authority' and avoidance of the feeling that he or she is bounced around from one ever-increasing caseload to another.

Public confidence in community sentences

Most panellists took the view that presentation of a new program in the context of a community corrections legislation was important. The problem with the term 'community' was that it was associated with the community treatment project of the 1960s.

A judge in Los Angeles commented though that public confidence in community sentences would be enhanced not by the use of electronic means of surveillance but by the inclusion of work as an element in community sanctions:

> The public is going to think that electronic surveillance or house arrest is a laugh. The public will never accept it as a form of punishment. It's not really a form of punishment, it's a form of accountability and tracking. The public likes the idea that the inmate is working.

A judge thought the public should be told, 'That we are overcrowded and busting at the seams and we don't have enough resources to accommodate those in the system.' A chief probation officer thought, 'People don't care, basically, the public wants the criminal justice system to put people away and forget about them. They don't want to be involved in all this. We are not hiding it. There are a lot of stories in the *Los Angeles Times* about overcrowding. The public doesn't care about that.'

A chief probation officer identified a similar public attitude when it came to trying to find a site for correctional buildings:

> The biggest stumbling block to community-based sanctions is that of understanding the local community resistance. People want to treat criminals like they treat their trash. They want to put it out by the curb and have someone come along to take it away.... I am trying to open up an office -not a facility - and the city is ready to sue me for moving into their city. It's just a probation office.

Public acceptability is a key to the success of community sentences. In a criminal justice system where some senior officials (district attorney, judges, sheriff) are elected, the support of the public for sentencing reforms is vital. Public reaction to community sanctions is manifested in a number of ways. It is made manifest in the objections to siting community-based offender centres or programs in urban neighbourhoods. More fundamental is the general credibility for this type of approach. The issue posed by a chief probation officer during the focus group discussions is: how are reformers who are keen to promote community sanctions going to convince the public that home confinement even with electronic monitoring is punishment when 'the bum is going to sit at home, drink beer, get welfare, watch television all night and get someone pregnant?'

Community Corrections Act

The pressure to introduce a Community Corrections Act is increasing in California. In part, this is motivated by the need to avoid some of the consequences of the expanded use of imprisonment over the last decade. These consequences are viewed from varying perspectives by senior criminal justice officials, who took part in this research. Some stressed the budgetary impact of the expanded penal system, others the overwhelming numbers in the system, and others the overuse of prisons which further criminalised those sent there.

But these views provide a potential rationale for making less use of imprisonment, they do not offer feasible or credible goals for a Community Corrections Act. Legislation in this field should proceed by offering specific objectives, which must be clearly explained if the public is to have confidence that those offenders, who by their actions are perceived as a threat to the community, should be allowed to continue to live amongst them in the community.

The 'balanced' and 'systematic' approach suggested by the Blue Ribbon Commission will enable the multiple goals of the system to be met in a way that maintains public and professional confidence in the system. Conveying. In this regard a balanced system should seek to avoid the impression of another 'swing in the pendulum' between 'soft' and 'tough' sentencing. The Determinate Sentencing law of 1976 and the subsequent expansion of the use of imprisonment in California since the 1980s, has not succeeded in alleviating public anxiety about crime any more than the previous system with its considerable emphasis on offender rehabilitation.

A Community Corrections Act should seek to establish goals, which in my opinion would require a composite sentence for intermediate offences, combining the aims of retribution, control, and rehabilitation. Retribution is required to ensure public confidence that this category of offender is held accountable in terms of the principle of just deserts. That punishment will be distinct for these intermediate categories of offences, from the token sanctions for the more trivial offences, and imprisonment for the most serious offences. Control and surveillance is required to provide some degree of public assurance that these previously prison-bound offenders convicted of fraud, theft, non-domestic burglaries and drug use, will not continue their criminal behaviour if left in the community.

Seeking to rehabilitate this category of adult offenders would be one of the goals of community-based intermediate sanctions. Rehabilitative efforts, previously a systems goal, should be concentrated on this category of offender. Rehabilitation will not be cost-effective or acceptable, either with lesser offenders, as there are too many, or with the most serious offenders, as it is too late. Correctional efforts, within the criminal justice system should be directed at achieving, where appropriate, life-style interventions with offenders convicted of intermediate level offences. To achieve this multi-purpose approach to community corrections, most criminal justice officials recognise the need for a more systematic and comprehensive approach to both sentencing policy and correctional practice.

Funding and systems implications

The Blue Ribbon Commission had recommended that money be made available from state agencies like the Department of Corrections to use in jail facilities to ease both state and local overcrowding, and also make programs available to inmates. This approach is based on the assumption that state agencies, especially Department of Corrections, had a relatively more stable and less threatened sources of funding. Hence, they saw this as a way of getting money to the counties. While most panellists approved of the expansion of intermediate sanctions if funds were available locally, they balked at the idea of money coming from state sources. A panellist commented: 'something which needs to be overcome is the county's suspicion that a partnership with the state is like tying your leg to an anchor and throwing it overboard'.

Examples were quoted of previous state-county arrangements, such as the mental health program, probation subvention, and trial court funding where the counties had entered into fiscal links with the state, which subsequently landed additional responsibilities on the counties. Concern with funding was a recurrent theme mentioned in the focus group.

The concern over financing took two forms. Firstly, that funding subsidies might start off high but would be reduced in subsequent years or not increased in line with inflationary costs. Secondly, that the state would mandate unacceptable conditions which would erode any financial gains made by the counties through state-imposed conditions and standards on institutional programs. A chief probation officer complained:

> The California Youth Authority comes in and sets up all these beautiful standards that we must meet in all our institutions. This county is one of the only counties in the state of California that has already spent over $10 million on putting 100 new beds on line. They had the audacity to come into this county last week and say they were going to decertify a brand new $20 million dollar facility because one unit was two kids over.

Another panellist explained his perspective:

> We are all parochial, county versus state; their money versus our money. I think in order to make the system work, with 46,000 inmates that spend less than one year in the prison system, we should take a portion of those individuals and deal with them in a more cost-effective manner at the local level. From a prosecutor's point of view, we have to develop detention facilities, a confined setting where they can be placed, and the court should have the option to do that at the local level.

Conclusion

The impact the Blue Ribbon Commission's recommendations had on sentencing policy and trends is not obvious. As the figures below show the prison population has continued to grow steadily. However, there are now also more people on community-based intermediate sanctions than before, especially as regards the increase in places in community correctional centres and those who are on electronically monitored home curfew. Unless this is entirely a result of net widening then it is likely that most of the latter population would have been incarcerated in county jails and state prisons.

It seems that the argument for the greater use of intermediate sanctions has had some success but the argument to bring down the prison population has not met with the same success, as there were 334,851 receptions into CDC institutions. In 1992, 40,158 were new felon admissions but more - 55,775 - were parolees returned due to violations of the condition of their parole.

The total population under the control of the California Department of Corrections stood at 253,359 on October 30, 1995 (California, 1995b). Of this total 93,368 were on parole and the rest were in state prisons, camps or community correctional facilites.

The officials who participated in the focus group study in California had little problem with the idea of community sentences as intermediate sanctions, if they could be made demanding and involved adequate supervision and surveillance. They did not see community sentences as an alternative to custody and did not envisage much support for a movement away from the currently high rate of imprisonment. Most were familiar with the existence and use of community sentences as intermediate sanctions. Their main concern was the funding and administrative responsibilities if new measures were introduced by a Community Corrections Act. Those who were more in favour of including a rehabilitative element were aware that this would be rarely achieved without the provision of more programs and resources for this purpose and greater concentration of effort on fewer offenders to achieve life-style intervention with those who would be the potential target population.

The trend in the use of incarceration in recent years in California does not make the case for intermediate sanctions any less valid in 1995 than it was in 1990 when the Blue Ribbon Commission presented its report. The reasons why the logic of that report has not had the effect of changing the direction of sentencing policy and practice will be explored in Chapter 5.

One major lesson to be drawn from the series of focus groups held in California in 1990 is that sentencing reforms will have to pass the test of public credibility. The democratic system in California has elected officials and a public that is vociferous about, and active in, matters of sentencing policy. While there was acceptance amongst many of the officials that prison was ineffective as a means of rehabilitation, it retains public confidence as a means of punishment and protection. In California the cost and non-rehabilitative influences of imprisonment are not regarded as being as significant as the impact prisons have as a credible means for punishing criminals. Community sentences and fines are not as culturally acceptable as punishments in California as they are in Europe. They are not seen as an alternative to imprisonment and it will take some time to see whether they come to regarded as credible intermediate sanctions.

3 Responses in England to Community Sanctions

MALCOLM DAVIES and JANE TYRER

Sentencing policy and trends

The major trend in sentencing in England and Wales over the last 100 years has been the declining use of imprisonment by the courts and the increased use of other types of sentences (Table 3.1 and 3.4). By the middle of the 19th century imprisonment had become the dominant penal sanction in England, having replaced transportation and capital punishment. However, by the end of the century new sentencing options were becoming available.

A hundred years after the Penitentiary Act 1779 introduced imprisonment as a new form of sanction, other types of sentences started to emerge, driven initially by offender-instrumental rehabilitative principles: conditional discharge (1879), probation (1887), borstal (1900), detention centres (1948), attendance centres (1948), suspended prison sentence (1967), community service orders (1972), partly suspended prison sentence (1982), curfew orders for young offenders (1982), the combination order (1991), and curfew orders and electronic monitoring of offenders aged 16 and above (1991).

The Summary Jurisdiction Act 1879 introduced a conditional discharge for younger and first time offenders. The court could order the imposition of conditions that required supervision. It was from this development that the role of the probation officer emerged, consolidated in the Probation of First Offenders Act 1887. This Act formulated the rehabilitative role of probation but did not provide for countrywide provision, which was later established by the Probation of Offenders Act 1907.

The fine was another sanction that was to grow in use dramatically in the 20th century, such that from 1950 onwards the fine was the most frequently used sentence even for the more serious category of indictable offences (Table 3.1). Physical punishments were to decline in use and finally be abolished: capital punishment in 1965, and whipping and hard labour by the 1948 Criminal Justice Act. This Act, originally introduced in 1938 as the Criminal Justice Bill, was delayed for a decade by the onset of war. The Act abolished penal servitude and introduced corrective training and new sentences aimed at the younger offender, namely the detention centre and attendance centre orders.

Sentencing is a task carried out by judges in the higher criminal courts and by magistrates in the lower courts. Judges sitting in the Crown Court (established in 1972 and replacing the assize courts and quarter sessions) sentence the more serious offenders convicted of offences that are triable on indictment. Magistrates' courts, presided over by three lay magistrates or a single professional stipendiary magistrate, deal with the less serious summary offences. Offences in the middle band, referred to as triable-either-way, can be tried in either court. If tried in the Crown Court the judge has greater powers of punishment as regards size of fine and length of imprisonment. Otherwise, the powers of the two courts, e.g. in the imposition of community sentences, are identical.

Judges and magistrates are influenced in their sentencing decisions by legislative, appellate and voluntary guidelines. Statutory maxima for a category of offence are always set out in the legislation. Occasionally there is also a minimum as in some driving offences, and in some cases a certain sentence is mandatory if a person is convicted, e.g. life imprisonment for murder. There are also statutory criteria for the imposition of custody and community sentences. The Court of Appeal, established in 1907, helps to shape the tariff through sentencing appeals. This influence has been enhanced since 1980 by the Court of Appeal giving special guideline decisions which act in effect as policy decisions for the lower courts. The court's role was further increased in this regard by the introduction in 1988 of the right of the Attorney General to refer unduly lenient sentences to the Court of Appeal for a decision. Before that time only the defendant could appeal against a sentence. Self regulation by the judiciary is achieved by the training sessions run by the Judicial Studies Board in the case of judges and by the Magistrates' Associations' published set of recommended guidelines.

Offenders coming before a judge for sentence at the beginning of the century had a strong likelihood of receiving a custodial sentence. In 1900, of all offenders convicted and sentenced by the higher courts 90 per cent received a custodial sentence and a fine was only given in 1 per cent of cases. Of those convicted of a summary offence and sentenced by the magistrates, 47 per cent received a custodial sentence and 27 per cent were fined (Halsey, 1972, pp. 288-9). In 1900, of all indictable offenders, 56 per cent were sent to prison. In contrast, in 1990 the proportionate use of custody for adults sentenced for indictable offences was 14 per cent (Table 3.1).

The most common sentence used in recent years is the fine. In 1993, of the 1.425 million offenders sentenced by the courts, over a million (77 per cent) were given a fine and 141,000 (10 per cent) were given an absolute or conditional discharge. An absolute discharge means no punishment will follow the conviction. A conditional discharge is followed by a penalty only if a new offence is committed within a specified period. In the same year 58,400 were sentenced to immediate custody and 114,800 were given a community sentence. The most frequently used community sentence were the probation order and community service order. In 1993 probation was given to 43,800 offenders and community service to 48,000, the attendance sentence order and supervision order being used less frequently with younger offenders (Table 3.4).

The use of custody by the higher and lower courts dropped dramatically in proportionate and absolute terms over the century. In 1894, the total number of convicted criminals sent to prison in that year was 156,466, which represented 526 persons per 100,000 of population (Ruggles Brise, 1922, p. 219). In 1994, the number given an immediate custodial sentence was 60,800 (Home Office *Statistical Bulletin* 27 April 1995, p. 5), representing 118 persons per 100,000 of population.

The number of receptions into custody fell dramatically between 1900 and the onset of World War I in 1914. The average daily prison population was then relatively stable between 1920 and 1940, from which time it started to increase generally upwards until 1985. The rate then fell until 1994 when it has begun to increase again. The increase was a result, in part, of the increase in average sentence length given by the courts from the 1930s onwards (Tables 3.3 and 3.4). It was also a result of increasing usage as the numbers of fines and convictions increased over the period from 1940 to 1990. On December 1, 1995 the population in custody was 52,540.

Tables 3.3 and 3.4 show how the number of receptions fell and average sentence lengths increased between 1913 and 1975. This is partly explained by the increasing use of non-custodial sentences from 1913, which meant that fewer petty criminals were sent to prison for short periods of time - thus increasing the average sentence length. The figures also include offenders of all ages, and are therefore affected by the growing use of borstal and detention centres for those under 21, and by statutory restrictions on sending younger offenders to prison. By 1975, over 28 per cent of inmates were serving lengths of imprisonment of over 12 months, compared with less than 1.5 per cent in 1913. Policies based on rehabilitation also appear to have led to longer prison sentences. The Report of the Commissioners of Prisons for 1925-6 stated:

> The short sentence remains an outstanding defect in our penal system and difficulty in prison administration. Repetition on this point is not amiss.
>
> The highest administrative and judicial authorities have taken the same view, and have drawn attention to the uselessness of the short sentence. The International Penitentiary Congress in August 1925 passed a resolution to the same effect. (Prison Commission, 1927, p. xiii)

In their annual report for 1949, the commissioners also exhort the need for longer sentences in the context of discussing the new Criminal Justice Act 1948. They argue, 'the purpose of the Act was not to provide some new form of training but to give the courts power to pass sentences long enough to enable the methods of training already developed in training prisons to be effectively applied'.

Rupert Cross wrote, 'It is the vast increase in the average length of sentence which took place between 1938 and 1959 which leads me to believe that there has been some regress rather than progress in penal reform during this century' (Cross, 1971, pp. 98-9). This came about 'due to the contemporary belief that prisons could be reformative if only the authorities were given enough time' (Cross, 1971, p. 102).

The May report of 1979 also noted these longer sentences and commented:

> However, confidence in the treatment model as it is usually called has now been waning throughout the Western world for some years. The drive behind the original borstal ideas has fallen away and there is now no belief that longer sentences may be justified because they make actual reformative treatment more possible. (Home Office, 1979, p. 63)

The Prison Commissioners noted in their annual report in 1951 that the population in prison as measured in terms of average daily population was the highest recorded since the Commission was established in 1877. This reflected, in part, shifts in penal policy and in particular the drive for longer periods for those sentenced to prison, but also the reality of a steady rise in the recorded crime rate from the 1930s, with rapid growth from the 1950s, which was to result in more offenders being brought before the courts. In 1994 the police recorded 5.4 million offences committed. This compares with half a million in 1950 and 2.5 million in 1980. It is not just the number of crimes that has increased, so has the crime rate. 'The number of crimes has risen from about 1 per 100 of the population in the 1950s to 5 in the 1970s and to 10.6 in 1992' (Home Office, *Digest* 2, 1993, p. 8).

However, the overall trend in this country for much of this century has been the decline in the use of prison and the increase in the use of other sentences, most notably the fine and community sentences. Much is made of the rising prison population and a continual message is heard from the penal reform groups such as NACRO, Howard League and the Prison Reform Trust for the courts to make less use of imprisonment, citing the apparent high custodial rate in this country contrasted with other European jurisdictions. The supposed high use of custody in England and Wales has been challenged by recent analysis of sentencing trends in the context of the amount of crime and the number of people dealt with in the criminal justice system. Chris Nuttall and Ken Pease comment: 'Prison use in England and Wales has declined in the period 1950-1990 relative to the presenting crime problem, to the number of crimes cleared, and to the number of people processed....this conclusion is an important corrective to charges of the country's comparative overdependence on prison as a penal sanction' (Nuttall and Pease, 1994, p. 316).

Nevertheless, the prison reductionist perspective, until very recently, has been very influential in the policy making forums, appealing to humanitarian, fiscal and penological arguments that have encouraged the search in the 20th century for non-custodial sanctions.

New non-custodial sentencing options

The first innovative non-custodial sanction that reflected the shift in the penal paradigm at the beginning of the century was the Probation of Offenders Act 1907, which formally gave the courts the power to appoint officers to advise, assist and befriend offenders. The role of the service has been expanded in subsequent legislation, but the predominant ethos has had an emphasis on rehabilitation. A gradual change in emphasis has been introduced since the early 1990s to seek to distance the Probation Service somewhat from this role.

The rehabilitation ethos embodied in the probation order was emphasised by its categorisation as an order instead of sentencing - a description removed only in 1991. The order was used in a variety of circumstances where courts perceived that help rather than punishment was required. Since the Criminal Justice Act 1991, a probation order is available for use with offenders aged 16 and above, and can be imposed for any type of offence, where the seriousness criterion is met. The 1991 Act formalised the powers of courts to impose probation with additional requirements such as attendance at groups dealing with alcohol or drug abuse or programmes aimed at specific offending behaviour or problems.

In 1967 the suspended sentence was introduced. When enacted it was aimed as an alternative to custody, specifically aimed at reducing the prison population. The Court of Appeal in 1969 emphasised its categorisation as a custodial sentence, this being legislatively confirmed in the 1972 Criminal Justice Act. Despite the limited effect of the suspended sentence in reducing the prison population, its varied appeal was such that the partly suspended sentence was introduced in 1982, but later abolished by the Criminal Justice Act 1991. The criteria for imposition of the suspended sentence were tightened by section 4 of the Act so that once the decision to imprison had been made, the sentence could only be suspended in 'exceptional circumstances'. Since then it has declined markedly in use.

In the 1960s a number of differing practical, philosophical and fiscal pressures had combined to create an urgent need to provide means of dealing with offenders other than imprisonment. Prison reductionists pointed to the unpleasant environmental conditions, overcrowding, and the growing feeling - in the light of rising crime figures - that prison did not work either to rehabilitate or deter.

In 1966, the Advisory Council on the Penal System set up the Wootton Committee to report on changes that could be made in the existing range of non-custodial penalties. The *Report of the Advisory Council on Non-custodial and Semi-custodial Penalties, 1970*, recommended that a new sentence - the community service order - should be made available. This would involve an offender being sentenced to do a number of hours of unpaid work for the community.

In reviewing the development of the community service order, 20 years after its inception, Oldfield suggests it is a penal measure with something for everyone, but points to the negative effects of this universal appeal: 'the ambiguous nature of community service leaves its use and value open to a variety of readings' (Oldfield, 1993, p. 30).

Roger Hood commented that the Wootton Report 'based its proposals for community service by offenders on the implicit ideological appeal of the scheme'. This appeal was based on the possibility of achieving several penal goals simultaneously by proving a 'punitive element', an opportunity for 'constructive service' and the 'possibility of a changed outlook on the part of the offender' (Hood, 1974). The equation of work with punishment without regard to its content or control has been a continuing issue in the development and perception of community service.

The Wootton Committee did not attempt to categorise the type of offender for which a community service order would be appropriate but felt it not suitable for trivial offences and expressed the hope that the community service order would be felt by courts to constitute an adequate alternative to a short custodial sentence.

Was the community sentence a sentence 'in its own right' or an 'alternative to custody'? The community service order was available only where a custodial sentence was possible. It was not necessary, however, that a custodial sentence was being considered in the particular case. This led to a diversity of approach. Courts were encouraged to specify in what sense the order was imposed, so that in the event of its breach, a subsequent court would be aware of the tariff envisaged for the original offence. The Court of Appeal indicated that a short community service order was appropriate where a prison sentence was not appropriate.

The community service order thus was introduced with multiple penological goals in mind. This unfocused approach led to many of the uncertainties relating to the place of the community service order in the sentencing spectrum, which still has an inheritance today, despite the structure imposed by the Criminal Justice Act 1991.

Since its introduction, increasing emphasis has been given to moving the community service order 'up-tariff', using it for more serious, repeat, or previously imprisoned offenders. To this end, national standards for the probation service were introduced for the first time in 1989, and these dealt with community service. The national standards were introduced to improve sentencers' confidence in the disposal after a period of decline in its use between 1985 and 1989. The standards provide a framework of rules for the implementation of community service orders, their management, and action on breach proceedings.

A green paper, *Strengthening Punishment in the Community*, was published in March 1995 with proposals for making the community service order and other community penalties more attractive to sentencers. This was closely followed by a new set of national standards with the same objective.

The combination order, introduced by the Criminal Justice Act 1991, and available in the same circumstances as the community service order, allowed for the combination of 40-100 hours community service with one to three years probation for a single offence. The intention was to provide for circumstances where both punishment and rehabilitation were sought. Again, the position of the combination order in the tariff was not clearly indicated in the legislation, though it is considered to be at the top end of the community sentence spectrum. The Act specifically does not impose a hierarchy of community orders but provides that restrictions on the offender's liberty should be commensurate with the seriousness of the offence, and that the order should be suitable to the offender.

Sentencing reforms in England and Wales have rarely been directly attributed to penological theories. However, shifting rationales can be discerned in the policy and official documents such as those published by commissions of inquiry, the Home Office and the Prison Commissioners annual reports up until 1964. Furthermore, contrary to the English tradition of avoiding 'bees in the bonnet' (Walker, 1977), the white paper preparing the ground for the Criminal Justice Act 1991 went further than most documents in referring to sentencing objectives of just deserts and denunciation as well as recognising the penological rationale for making restricted use of custody. It was the first comprehensive attempt to come to grips with the failure of offender-instrumental theories of sentencing - rehabilitation and deterrence - which until the 1970s had influenced the penal reforms since the Summary Jurisdiction Act 1879.

After a hundred years, the faith in rehabilitative thinking in England and Wales was to wane, 'a faith dashed on the rocks of the unprecedented rise in recorded crime in the post war years' (Davies *et al* 1995, p. 246). Rehabilitation fell out of favour as the search for criminal pathologies proved elusive and the espousal of the theory was seen to justify intervention of a type or duration not deemed to be merited by the offence.

Failure of rehabilitative intervention to solve the crime problem and the feeling that 'nothing worked' contributed to the rise of the justice approach where 'deservedness' was the touchstone in meting out a measured amount of punishment as befitted the crime in question. The 'just deserts' approach was given statutory authority in the Criminal Justice Act 1991 which attempted to impose clearly for the first time in England and Wales a structured theoretical approach to the sentencing decision. In this Act, as announced in the white paper that preceded it, 'The first objective for all sentences is denunciation of and retribution for the crime' (Home Office, 1990, p. 6).

Sentencing objectives of deterrence and rehabilitation had been identified a century earlier by the Gladstone Committee 1895, as the twin goals of the penal system. The 1990 white paper commented that deterrence was:

> a principle with much immediate appeal...(but that it was) unrealistic to construct sentencing arrangements on the assumption that most offenders will weigh up the possibilities (of apprehension and punishment) in advance and base their conduct on rational calculation. (Home Office, 1990, p. 6)

Rehabilitation of the offender was accepted as a principle that might be achieved but should not lead to a disproportionate sentence being passed as had previously occurred.

The primary principles of denunciation and retribution are translated into a measurement of sentencing by virtue of the 'seriousness' of the offence to be punished. The more serious the offence the more the sentence passed will seek to denounce and exact retribution. Neither aim seeks *per se* to achieve a change in offending behaviour: though this might result as a bonus, as might the dissuasion of others from similar conduct. The sentence primarily can and in the terms of the act should indicate the amount of disapprobation felt towards the offence.

The 1991 Act ranks offences into three bands of seriousness: so serious that only custody is justified; serious enough for a community sentence; not serious enough for a community sentence (referring to fines and discharges).

This notion of graduated penalties relies on the assumption that the sentences in the middle band - the community sentences (defined as probation, community service, combination order, supervision order, attendance centre and curfew order) - successfully bridge the gap between fines and prison. This is not an assumption shared by all sentencers as can be seen in the research findings below. The framework imposed by the Criminal Justice Act 1991 sought to bring the existing community sentences for the first time into a systematic theoretical hierarchy. Existing sentences had been introduced and developed on an *ad hoc* basis to meet penological or fiscal pressures increasingly dominated by a need to reduce the prison population.

The changing way of looking at crime and sentencing, together with the urge to reduce the prison population led to an increased dependence on non-prison and particularly community sentences (Table 3.4). This is the context for our research.

Table 3.1 Sentence received: Indictable offences, 1900-1990

Proportionate use of custody, fine or community sanctions for those sentenced (all ages) for indictable offences. Given as percentages.

	Custody	Community Sanctions	Fine	Other
		%		
1900	56	11	21	12
1910	56	10	17	17
1920	40	11	32	17
1930	44	20	24	12
1938	29	22	24	25
1950	29	13	39	19
1960	24	15	45	16
1970	14	9	51	26
1980	14	17	48	21
1990	14	21	39	26

Table compiled from: Walker, N., in Halsey, A. (ed.) (1972), *Trends in British Society Since 1900*, pp. 289-290, and also,
Home Office (1984), *Criminal Statistics England and Wales 1983*, p. 151.
Home Office (1993), *Criminal Statistics England and Wales 1992*, p. 155.

These figures refer to indictable offences only. 'Other' sentences will refer to the death penalty, whipping, absolute or conditional discharge, fully and partially suspended custodial sentences. 'Other' in 1900 includes 3218 whippings, a punishment which is accounted for under 'other' until 1938. Whipping was abolished in 1948. 1938 figures are given because of the unusual circumstances to do with the onset of World War II in 1939. The rise in the 'other' category in 1970 is caused by the introduction of the suspended prison sentence which is recorded under 'other'.

Table 3.2 Prison population, 1900-1994

	Receptions: Annual numbers of receptions of adults and young offenders	Prison population: Average daily numbers of adults and young offenders in custody
	Under a sentence of immediate custody	All prisoners
1900	149,397	17,435
1910	179,951	22,018
1920	35,439	9,683
1930	38,832	11,346
1940	24,870	9,377
1950	33,875	20,474
1960	42,810	27,099
1970	62,020	39,028
1980	68,300	42,264
1981	74,600	43,436
1982	77,800	43,754
1983	78,200	43,772
1984	78,800	43,349
1985	83,300	46,278
1986	72,900	46,889
1987	74,400	48,963
1988	72,100	49,949
1989	64,100	48,610
1990	57,600	45,636
1991	61,200	45,897
1992	58,000	45,817
1993	58,400	44,566
1994	60,800	48,800

Table compiled from: Halsey, A.(1972) *ibid* see Table 3.1, p.292.
Home Office (1988), *Criminal Statistics in England and Wales 1987*, p.158, Table 7.15.
Home Office (1992), *Prison Statistics England and Wales 1991*, pp. 22 and 39.
Home Office (1994a), *Criminal Statistics England and Wales 1993*, p.173, Table 7.15.
Home Office (1994b), *Prison Statistics England and Wales 1993*, pp.26 and 36.
Home Office (1995), *Statistical Bulletin 8/95*, Tables 2 & 5.

Table 3.3 Length of prison sentences, 1913-1993

(Prison terms given and includes those sentenced in default of fines)(percentages in bold and numbers in brackets)

	1913	1938	1948	1958	1968	1988	1993
Up to 2 weeks	**58.6**	**28.7**	**10.0**	**8.9**	**8.1**		
	[80,961]	[8,820]	[3,366]	[3,030]	[2,932]		
Over 2 weeks up to 5 weeks	**21.9**	**24.4**	**16.7**	**14.5**	**10.5**		
	[30,359]	[7,475]	[5,595]	[4,922]	[3,765]		
Over 5 weeks up to 3 months	**12.0**	**23.0**	**24.7**	**24.7**	**19.2**	**37.5***	**45.4***
*[1988/1993 up to 3 months]	[16,862]	[7,043]	[8,925]	[8,398]	[6,930]	[30,661]	[33,133]]
Over 3 months up to 6 months	**3.7**	**12.9**	**18.3**	**19.7**	**21.6**	**17.4**	**17.9**
	[5,070]	[3,947]	[6,447]	[6,710]	[7,801]	[14,236]	[13,107]
Over 6 months up to 12 months	**2.1**	**6.1**	**14.3**	**14.2**	**16.2**	**17.0**	**13.9**
	[2,873]	[1,881]	[4,775]	[4,843]	[5,858]	[13,924]	[10,156]]
Over 12 months up to 18 months	**0.7**	**2.3**	**7.1**	**6.3**	**8.8**	**9.3**	**6.5**
	[1,033]	[694]	[2,361]	[2,085]	[3,179]	[7,644]	[4,764]
Over 18 months up to 3 years	**0.5**	**1.9**	**7.4**	**8.5**	**11.3**	**12.8**	**9.4**
	[774]	[581]	[2,478]	[2,906]	[4,059]	[10,460]	[6,875]
Over 3 years to life	**0.3**	**0.7**	**1.5**	**3.3**	**4.3**	**6.5**	**6.5**
	[364]	[219]	[770]	[1121]	[1,545]	[5,286]	[4,031]

Table compiled from: Home Office (1977), *Prisons and the Prisoner*, p. 158; Home Office (1994), *Prison Statistics, England and Wales 1993*, p.36.

Table 3.4 Offenders sentenced for all offences by sentence, 1987-1993

[Thousands]

Type of sentence	1987	1988	1989	1990	1991	1992	1993
Fine	**1249.8**	**1248.3**	**1227.8**	**1192.7**	**1166.6**	**1183.8**	**1091.5**
Probation order	42.2	43.6	44.2	47.7	47.5	43.9	43.8
Attendance Centre order	9.7	8.5	7.7	7.9	8.2	7.2	6.8
CSO	35.9	35.3	33.9	38.6	42.5	44.1	48.0
Combination Order	-	-	-	-	-	1.3	8.9
All Community Sentences	**96.3**	**94.7**	**92.5**	**100.9**	**104.5**	**102.4**	**114.8**
Young Offender Institution	26.4	24.1	19.1	16.2	16.9	15.1	15.2
Partly suspended custody	2.8	2.8	2.2	1.5	1.1	0.6	-
Unsuspended Custody	45.2	45.2	42.8	39.8	43.2	42.3	43.2
Total Custody	**74.4**	**72.1**	**64.1**	**57.6**	**61.2**	**58**	**58.4**
Fully Suspended	29.2	30.9	29.8	27.4	28.1	22	3.8
Absolute discharge	19.0	19.0	19.5	20.4	21.5	23.8	25.9
Conditional Discharge	75.6	77.6	85.4	94.5	102	109.8	111.6
All Discharges	**94.6**	**96.6**	**104.9**	**114.9**	**123.5**	**133.6**	**136.5**
All sentences	**1554.8**	**1555.4**	**1534.1**	**1513.9**	**1503.9**	**1519.9**	**1425.0**

Table compiled from: Home Office (1988) and (1994), *Criminal Statistics in England and Wales 1987*, Table 7A and, *Criminal Statistics in England and Wales 1993*, Table 7.1.

The research in England

Policy background

Does the existing range of community sanctions offer a solution to the problems of reducing the reliance on imprisonment? Despite the reference to 'Punishment in the Community' in the 1990 white paper, there would seem to be a problem with the perceived credibility of community sentences as sufficiently punitive.

The Chief Inspector of Probation, Graham Smith, in the annual report of the Probation Inspectorate in 1993 acknowledged there were credibility problems with probation and that the Probation Service still adopted a primarily welfare approach and 'had not yet fully integrated the notion of punishment into its repertoire'.

> there was some evidence...that courts were not able to perceive attendance at a probation centre or an offending behaviour programme as sufficiently demanding and restrictive to constitute a punishment...
>
> No doubt some of this credibility could be enhanced by improving the wording of proposals in pre-sentence reports, of which there were only a few in the sample inspected that were felt to spell out sufficiently clearly the nature of an order's restriction on liberty. But it may be that there need to be some more fundamental changes to the content of probation orders, if they are to find an appropriate place in the sentencing structure, where hitherto they were much more freely available to be used 'instead of' passing sentence. Such changes would have to ensure that all offenders placed under supervision experience, are perceived to experience truly demanding programmes that both restrict liberty in tangible terms and tackle their offending behaviour. (HMI of Probation, 1993, pp. 42-3)

The Chief Inspector's report also commented that the Probation Service 'must listen to what the people who use the service want from them'. The magistracy is one group whose views are of importance for the future use of community sanctions, in that they are responsible for the imposition of approximately three-quarters of them.

In particular, the key question to be resolved by this research is whether it is possible to reconcile the two objectives of limiting the use of imprisonment and punishing the criminal. One potential way to reconcile these objectives is to ask magistrates what form of community-based sanctions they would regard as sufficiently punitive to mark public disapproval and so allow for punishments that do not require a custodial sentence.

The search for credible non-prison sanctions has been at the forefront of policy concern for many years. Recently the changing rationale of sentencing philosophy has allowed for a new approach to this issue, namely that sentences other than imprisonment do not have to be confined solely within the framework imposed by attempts to rehabilitate offenders. Rehabilitation takes its place since the Criminal Justice Acts 1991 and 1993 with incapacitation and restitution within a framework in which, 'The first objective for all sentences is denunciation of and retribution for the crime' (Home Office, 1990, p. 6).

Within this framework it is possible to search for sanctions that meet a denunciatory and retributive logic without the use of custody, which could also serve rehabilitative, restitutive and control purposes. However, if they are to be used by sentencers, a major concern must be the credibility of the sentence as a punishment with respect to the level of seriousness of the offence.

The Criminal Justice Act 1991 sought to provide a framework for sentencers by which the seriousness of the offence was to be the primary determinant of sentencing. The Criminal Justice Act 1991 clarified the point that community sentences are available to the courts in cases 'serious enough', but not 'so serious' as to merit custody. The degree of restriction on the liberty of the offender should be commensurate with the seriousness of the offence.

The relationship between offence and appropriate punishment is therefore a crucial one and depends to a large extent on the perceptions of sentencers as to the demands and restrictions placed upon offenders by various sentences.

The Criminal Justice Act 1991 sought to provide for a greater range of more demanding community sanctions. This development was made apparent in the Government's *Response to Consultation on Community Penalties and the Role of the Probation Service* published in 1992:

> The implementation of the Criminal Justice Act 1991 is an important task. It will require a co-ordinated and co-operative effort between all criminal justice agencies and many other organisations. This will provide an impetus for the development of partnerships. In

> particular the Act: creates a range of tough community sentences most of which are to be managed by the Probation Service and aims to ensure that there are wider opportunities for offenders to be dealt with in the community. (Home Office, 1992, p. 3)

In March 1995 the Home Office published a green paper, *Strengthening Punishment in the Community*. Its aim was to overcome the problems associated with the piecemeal development of community sentences, the perception that these were soft options and the problem of how different community sentences fitted in the framework of proportionality required by the Criminal Justice Act 1991. The report sought consultation so as to develop a 'comprehensive new framework for community sentences, which have been added to the statute book in a piecemeal way over many years'. The report states:

> Probation supervision is still widely regarded as a soft option. Although in many cases, this perception may be misconceived, it must be addressed. Both courts and the public have found some difficulty in squaring their concept of the probation order (with its additionally high social work content) with the notion of a punishment involving a significant restriction of liberty. (Home Office, 1995, pp. 11-12)

The 1995 green paper set out a number of proposals for consultation, including replacing existing sentences with a single integrated community sentence, allowing magistrates more discretion in determining the content of community sentences and providing more feedback on the outcome of these sentences to magistrates. Another proposal was to remove the requirement that offenders have to give their consent if a community sentence is to be imposed. This would bring community penalties into line with custody and fines where the convicted person's consent is not required. These proposals aim to allow for more flexible 'sentences with elements of both punishment and rehabilitation' and with the magistrates deciding how to balance the requirements for restriction on liberty, reparation and preventing re-offending. The green paper expressed, 'the view of the Government that the role of community sentences is poorly understood and - perhaps as a result - that they have failed to command the confidence of the public' (Home Office, 1995, p. 11).

Methodology

In the light of the framework set by the Criminal Justice Acts of 1991 and 1993, and the denunciatory-retributive principles implied therein, this research aimed to explore magistrates' views of community sanctions in terms of their credibility as punishment and to investigate where the magistrates would place the various community sentences in the tariff of penalties.

A pilot project was established to consider the opinions of lay magistrates on the use of community sentences with adult offenders. We were concerned with their view about those sentences between routine probation and prison (intermediate sanctions) to discover whether lay magistrates had confidence in them or whether additional disposals or elements were required by them in order to gain confidence. Magistrates were investigated rather than other participants in the criminal justice system because, as sentencers, they often deal with offenders where there is a real choice between a community sentence and imprisonment. They are responsible for approximately three-quarters of community sentences and, in providing a lay element in the sentencing system, should reflect the wider public view of sentences.

Whether magistrates have confidence in a disposal inevitably is affected by their intentions or aspirations for that disposal, and expectations might be affected by training, experience, input from other agencies and from policy makers as well as their past and current sentencing experience.

The logic of the Criminal Justice Act 1991 provides that in a just deserts framework of retribution and denunciation, sentencers need a range of disposals to adequately reflect the seriousness of the offence. In order to denounce and exact retribution for those offences where seriousness falls between probation and prison, a credible punitive disposal is necessary: this is most evident in respect of those offences which fall just short of custody, but is also an issue whenever a community sentence is considered.

A pilot project was carried out in two petty sessional areas in England in the Autumn of 1994 and Spring of 1995 and set out to examine the views of lay magistrates on community sentences to ascertain the sentencing logic applied by magistrates and to see whether there was, in their view, a gap in their panoply of disposals.

In order to ascertain the views of magistrates, focus groups were held with each of the two benches. The two benches chosen were:

- Central Buckinghamshire, which is a rural/semi-rural bench comprising 98 magistrates in total. The bench sits at three court centres after the recent amalgamation of three benches. Twenty-seven individuals, just over a quarter of the bench, took part in four groups in October 1994.

- Ealing, which is an Outer London magistrates' court. It sits at two court centres and has regular attendance by Stipendiary magistrates. There are 136 members of the bench and 31 of them, just under a quarter, took part in five groups in March and April 1995.

All magistrates from the two benches involved were invited to take part on the dates arranged. Participants indicated whether and when they would be able to attend. The groups were therefore entirely self selected.

Background papers and list of questions were sent in advance: the questions being designed to encourage deliberation, rather than act as a strict agenda for discussion. Magistrates were invited to attend one meeting lasting one and a half to two hours. Each group was chaired by a moderator and had no more than eight participants. The discussions were tape recorded with their permission. The tapes were transcribed and edited under various headings and a report formulated, which was subsequently sent to participants.

Between the focus group meetings and the preparation of the report a follow-up questionnaire to quantify the specific appeal of certain of the proposals canvassed, was sent together with questions seeking the magistrates' views on the value and appropriateness of the research methods used. The results are set out at Appendix 1.

Methodology using focus groups was chosen in order to explore concerns in depth, to avoid the oversimplifications inherent in some other methods, and to examine proposals as they arose from the discussions.

Magistrates' views of community sanctions

From the transcript of the recordings of each of the focus groups we have summarised the views expressed and given illustrative examples of comments made under the following headings: credibility of community sentences, implementation of community sanctions, objectives of sentencing, the use of imprisonment, the binary gap, sentencing policy, and specific proposals for the reform of community sanctions, including in the case of the later groups, discussion of the proposals set out in the 1995 green paper.

Credibility of community sanctions

Magistrates from both benches expressed reservations as to the ability of existing community sanctions to act as credible punitive disposals. The most commonly expressed concerns related to the implementation of community service.

Magistrates felt that offenders who did not comply with the terms of their community service orders should be dealt with more rigorously: they felt that breach problems were not dealt with soon enough or severely enough. The provisions of the *National Standard for the Supervision of Offenders in the Community* were referred to in some groups. The standards introduced in 1992 did seem to satisfy magistrates' concerns on this issue, and the revised standards of 1995 had not yet had an effect.

It was impossible to assess in the context of this research how accurate the perceptions of magistrates were and it may, moreover, be the case that changes effected by new National Standards may address some of these concerns. Nevertheless, a severe lack of confidence in the mechanics of the community service order was expressed even by those magistrates who expressed support for the principle of community service and who had welcomed its introduction.

The focus on rehabilitative goals was felt by many as impeding the ability of the Probation Service to oversee community service orders that were intended as punishment. Some went so far as to say that another body should be responsible for the delivery of community disposals; one participant voiced the view that the Probation Service was more concerned with 'diverting from prison than diverting from crime'.

Although many thought community sanctions could be useful, invariably they were regarded as a soft option by the magistrates. Community sanctions clearly had a credibility problem as a punishment with magistrates and, in their eyes, with the public.

> The punishment aspect is missing.

> I sit on one of the advisory sub-committees and therefore see new potential magistrates. When we discuss sentencing, community service is the one that strikes everybody as being a great idea. ...most of these potential new magistrates said, 'well, I'd prefer not

> to send someone to prison, it would be much better if they could do something for the community'. The concept is brilliant. It's just not being carried out properly.

> I still have this feeling that it's a bit of a jolly ... you can go along and you can take your girlfriend and your girlfriend can take her children and they will be looked after and you can play ping pong and you can all have a nice jolly time. [Comment on Probation Centre].

The magistrates overwhelmingly thought the public regarded community sanctions as a soft option.

> I think they [the public] equate it [community service] with probation which they also see as a let-off unfortunately.

> The public perception is not that somebody is being punished.

> You've got to satisfy the rest of the community, the public, that there is a punishment element in this because the trouble is the public are losing faith in the judiciary because they don't feel that they're getting justice and that people are being punished.
> [They] see community penalties and probation as being a very much softer ... they don't see it as a punishment.

Several magistrates commented that the view that community sentences were undemanding permeated down to the offenders:

> It's not taken seriously at all by the people that have been punished at that stage, which I think is wrong.

> Word gets around. They, offenders and their friends, say 'Oh don't worry about that'.

Some magistrates commented that their powers to pursue a retributive framework for punishment was weakened by the requirement for the offender's consent to community punishment. Indeed, some felt that the idea of consent undermined any notion of punishment. This was discussed, with later groups, in the context of the green paper proposal to abolish the need for consent.

Some magistrates regarded community sanctions as having limited punitive value because of the involvement of the Probation Service, with their commitment to a welfare and rehabilitative approach. Magistrates' views on the Probation Service varied. There were several magistrates who appreciated the difficult job they had to do with limited resources. However, there was near unanimity that the Probation Service operated with a very limited perception of their role in the criminal justice system, which emphasised the needs and concerns of the offender above most other considerations.

> The word punishment doesn't come up when you listen to probation officers.

> Probation officers.... You never get any tough recommendations from probation office on their reports.

> The underlying view I think of probation officers would not be to divert people from crime but to divert people from prison.

In assessing punitive value the magistrates did not subscribe to a simple equation provided for in the Criminal Justice Act 1991 that punitive value is determined by the amount of restriction on liberty.

When asked which the most restrictive of the community sentences was, magistrates considered it to be either the community service order or the combination order or in a few cases a probation order with other requirements. Restriction on liberty was assessed by reference to the number of hours taken up by the court order. However, perceptions of punitive value were also influenced by the content of the hours. A combination order with a high probation element was seen by many as not particularly punitive. Others referred to the nature of the task imposed under a community service order in assessing its level of punishment. Hence, the magistrates' perceptions were influenced by their perceptions as to the way community sanctions were implemented and how demanding they were for the offender.

Implementation of community sanctions

Magistrates accepted the potential value of community service, indeed many were enthusiastic in principle, and appreciated the difficulty of implementing this sentence within resource and other constraints. They accepted that in some cases community service work was well organised and seemed to help some offenders. However, nearly all the panellists had reservations about the implementation of community sentences.

Implementation concerns focused in particular on community service orders, and fell into four categories: information in the pre-sentence report; the nature of tasks provided; discipline during the community service order period; and attitude to breach.

Information in the pre-sentence report: some magistrates expressed a lack of confidence in the pre-sentence reports provided by the Probation Service on which they were called to make sentencing decisions. They felt that the Probation Service saw only the defendant's point of view and that, therefore, their advice on sentence was not based on the totality of the case as it affected victims and the public.

> We seem to get besotted by what we try to do here for the people who've committed the crimes and the people outside are ignored to a great extent.

Some felt the information in many pre-sentence reports was bland and pre-formulated.

> Quite honestly ... every report I read (is) one more that has been run off with a Xerox.

The nature of the tasks provided: There was a strong feeling that the tasks were insufficiently demanding. This was largely a complaint that the tasks were not physically rigorous; in Ealing in particular, many references were made to the primacy of painting and decorating as a community service task. Some magistrates, however, voiced their own approval of less physically demanding tasks, where the nature of the placement was in a caring situation, but all stressed the need for the work to be demanding. Many magistrates referred to the appeal of tasks which clearly were of benefit to the community.

> From my experience and I have been on visits...there is very limited choice of work in this area. For example, they could go round scraping the graffiti off the walls

> I wouldn't say it was terribly demanding necessarily, only the

> discipline of having to be there and doing it...I wouldn't think they'd break out in a sweat.
>
> ...painting and decorating seems to be about the limit.
>
> I think some of the tasks aren't really as punitive as they should be and they are soft options in the courts.

Discipline during the community service order period: some panellists expressed concerns related to offenders' attitudes to their tasks, their conduct during community service orders, and the acceptance by the probation service of reasons (seen by some magistrates as invalid) for non-attendance.

> To me it is not structured enough. They come and go as they please.
>
> On the occasions when I have visited this Saturday morning work, it has been very poorly supervised and terribly casual.
>
> When I went on a visit I was surprised to hear Probation Officers saying...'I allowed him to have that Saturday morning off because he was going to his cousin's wedding'.
>
> The discipline is lax I think probably one of the problems is really one of lack of resources.

Attitudes to breach: magistrates felt that offenders who did not comply with the terms of their community service orders should be dealt with more rigorously. They felt breaches were not dealt with soon enough or severely enough. The provisions of the *National Standard for the Supervision of Offenders in the Community* were referred to in some groups. The standards introduced in 1992 did not seem to satisfy magistrates' concerns on this issue, and the revised standards of 1995 had not yet had an effect. There were strong views that where breaches had occurred, return to court was dilatory.

> What do you do if the chap goes on turning up late? Or doesn't work hard enough. ...so you would breach him? That's what should be happening at the moment. I don't think it happens as it should do because I think perhaps it's in the wrong hands.

> There was one guy who came up; he'd been put on a community service order for 200 hours - he had done one hour in a year. And it had taken a year to bring him back and get him sentenced.

> I think they tend to lose credibility with me when we have breach hearings and you hear how often the administrator has really bent over backwards to accept their excuse.

It was impossible to assess in the context of this research how accurate the perceptions of magistrates were and it may, moreover, be the case that changes effected by new National Standards may address some of these concerns. Nevertheless, a severe lack of confidence in the mechanics of the community service order was expressed even by those magistrates who in principle supported community service.

Objectives of sentencing

Mike Nellis and Tony Bottoms, in their research into the views of magistrates about the use of intermediate sanctions with young offenders, point out that magistrates are not, as a rule, accustomed to engaging in strong theoretical discussions of issues of this sort. They quote a magistrate as saying:

> We don't spend a lot of our time actually discussing the theoretical basis of sentencing. We spend more time on practical alternatives...Whether or not we are being consistent. That's the aim of most of our training exercises...I honestly can't say that I've discussed it very deeply with anybody else. (Bottoms, 1993, p. 308)

In the follow-up questionnaire seeking magistrates' views on the conduct of the focus groups, many magistrates specifically referred to the lack of a forum to discuss the objectives of sentencing policy. However, some views were expressed as to the desired objectives of sentencing:

> What should be the main purpose of community based sanctions? I think ultimately it must be rehabilitation that is the most important, because that is going to stop people offending again and again.

> You have forfeited your rights when you offend and therefore society is going to have strict retribution for that offence.

> If they pay something back to the society that they have done wrong to that really ought to be one of the things that we achieve.

Most of the magistrates recognised the multiple aims of sentencing:

> You may have to punish, you may also at the same time want to try and do some kind of rehabilitation....It has to be a kind of multi-faceted approach for each person. For some people you may feel, well, the only thing we can do with them is punish this person. Rehabilitation just doesn't work.

> We have these three things we have to wrestle with. You punish, deter and reform.

When discussing the objectives of sentencing, many magistrates expressed a strong commitment to offender-instrumental strategies, such as deterrence and rehabilitation, aiming to bring about a change in the offender's criminal behaviour. Thus, despite contemporary policy statements, the notion of retribution and denunciation through the deprivation of liberty was not always the paramount concern of the magistrates in the focus group panels. Many comments reflected a view that they sought to reduce re-offending. Deprivation of liberty was seen as an attempt to achieve three objectives. First, to reduce the likelihood of re-offending by imposing constraints on the offenders' time. Second, to make the punishment uncomfortable to deter them from re-offending. Third, to bring about lifestyle changes in an attempt to rehabilitate offenders.

> Our purpose surely is to try to stop that individual in front of us from offending again. Because it's a waste of their life [and] it represents damage to society.

The deterrent aspect of sentencing was one that was referred to by many of the magistrates, though with mixed views as to the likelihood of achieving this aim.

> I can't honestly say that any of the sentences in the community side really leave me with the impression, 'well, I won't do it again because I don't like this sentence'.

> The majority of crimes that we see are traffic and there is an element of deterrence in the sentencing of them....Yet as far as burglary or any of the other crimes are concerned, they don't expect to be caught so how can they be deterred by a sentence if they're not expecting to be caught.

Magistrates were conscious of the difficulties of achieving retributive sentencing goals through the use of community sentences as they felt they lacked a punitive element.

> It's frustrating to be a magistrate because you feel that there is nothing you can give these people to punish them for what they've been doing.

> I sometimes wonder about the concept of the deprivation of liberty, though. I mean, those of us sitting round this table are the kind of people who are reasonably, I hope, well off, who have all kinds of opportunities and choices that we can make in our lives and lead fairly interesting and varied lives. To us, the total loss of our liberty is something quite serious. But I have a suspicion that to a lot of people, and possibly a lot of young people whose lives are already pretty bleak and deprived, lacking in variety of interest, the concept of the deprivation of liberty is not really quite so dreadful as it might seem to us.

Magistrates, with a few exceptions, seemed unfamiliar with the denunciatory aspect of sentencing identified, along with retribution, as the primary objective of sentencing in the 1990 White Paper, *Crime, Justice and Protecting the Public*. However, some implicitly subscribed to a denunciatory philosophy and made, or wished to make, an explicit statement such as '*this behaviour will not be tolerated*' when passing sentence:

> ...to mark the seriousness of the offence.

> I think that the expression should be used publicly again and again, not only by this court but by all courts. 'This is unacceptable behaviour.'

Use of imprisonment

With few exceptions, the participants revealed that they had personally been involved in few impositions of custodial sentences in the previous six months. Nevertheless, participants voiced a desire for a further non-custodial sentence to bridge the enormous gulf between the existing current disposals and imprisonment, to provide a demanding credible disposal. In Ealing, the most commonly cited offence leading to imprisonment was repeated drink driving and/or driving whilst disqualified. Particularly for those offenders a new disposal was sought. One proposal that gained much support was the concept of weekend imprisonment. This appealed to both groups of magistrates (96 per cent of all participants were either 'in favour' or 'very much in favour' of weekend custody).

A few magistrates shared the view, which they felt was prevalent amongst probation officers, that offenders should be diverted from custody. They felt that prisons were counter-productive and the use of custody should be kept to a minimum as it was not effective at reducing crime amongst those sent to prison.

> What are we sending them to prison for? It's certainly not to deter. It doesn't work.

> They ought...to do something about community service orders because we ought to stop sending so many people into prison. It's an absolute waste of resources.

> [Prison] doesn't do any good except introduce them to a criminal fraternity which may enhance their offending rather than anything else.

> You have to consider the person in front of you as a human being with family responsibilities, with work, which if they go to prison are going to be smashed to pieces and you may feel that you want to do something different from simply locking that person up.

In addition to those magistrates who were reluctant to impose custodial sentences, there were others who felt restricted in their use of custody and most indicated that they rarely imposed a custodial sentence. The following statements were typical of the responses when questioned about their use of imprisonment in the last 12 months.

> Not many...I think in my 6 years ... probably about 4 people.
>
> None in last 12 months and hardly any in 16 years on the bench.
>
> I can't remember any in the last 12 months.
>
> Two. One for a fine due to poll tax and the other for several breaches of his probation order.
>
> The last person I was involved in sending to prison would have been about a month ago and that was for repeat drink-driving. Very high readings and very little mitigating factors around.
>
> The only time I've [considered sending someone to prison in the last 12 months] is if it's violence against the person.

Some magistrates would have liked a tougher community disposal to use in borderline cases where they might consider a prison sentence. However, as magistrates made little use of imprisonment, their chief objective was not diversion from custody but a rather more credible and effective community sanction in its own right.

The binary gap

The combination order, introduced in 1992, was intended to fill the gap between community and custodial sentences by offering a tougher community penalty. Some magistrates felt it did. Others thought it was helpful in that it combined punitive and rehabilitative aspects, but most regarded it as less punitive than the existing community service order because of the limitation to only 100 hours of community service when used as part of a combination order. Magistrates were firmly of the view that a wide gap existed between the most demanding community sentence available to them and imprisonment.

> It is a tremendous jump between either probation or CSO and custody and it would be very useful to have something in between.
>
> I personally feel what is so lacking is the ability to remove the liberty of the offender but not with prison. I am a great believer that we should develop in this country what I call 'weekend loss of

> liberty' camps ... because that's what hurts them most ... it's not being able to enjoy their weekends.

> The straight community service order is more restrictive [than a combination order]. If by being punitive you mean keeping the offender out of regular circulation, you're tying up his time with a community service order more than perhaps with a combination order.

Sentencing policy

Most magistrates felt that their present powers were insufficient. Yet when asked about their use of their present maximum sentencing powers of 240 hours community service or six months in prison, or indeed any use of imprisonment, most of the participants paradoxically recorded little use of their powers as reported above.

The reason for their reluctance to use the legal powers to the full was explained by their deference to policy guidelines from others. As lay magistrates, many mentioned their deference to higher authorities, be these the local liaison judge, the justices' clerk, the Lord Chancellor's Department, or the Magistrates' Association. Reference was also made to the influence of the local bench culture.

Some magistrates recognise another contradiction: between a more flexible approach to sentencing and the problems of disparities in sentencing, and the difficulty of balancing the two very different approaches: one based on a tariff, reflecting the seriousness of the offence, and the second based on individual offender needs. If the magistrates individualise a sentence or adopt flexible strategies to suit offender needs they will be generating disparities in sentencing and the accusation of bias and inconsistency. The reforms of sentencing policy in recent years have attempted to reduce disparities by limiting discretion but have led to some frustration.

> We're hemmed in on all sides really because increasingly we've got the tariffs to operate. So although there is a range of options, a great deal of the time the options aren't really there.

> I think what we can literally do under the Act and what we're suggested we should do are often quite different things. The clerks say, 'let's not complicate things, let's keep this simple'.

Finally, there were some magistrates who took the view that to achieve a more credible form of tougher community sanction there was a need for a new agency to complement the Probation Service's social work role based on a surveillance and discipline approach.

> I suspect that the probation would be very much against wiping graffiti off walls because that has to be done in public and that would be degrading to their clients to have to be seen doing something in public.

> I don't think they need to be trained social workers. I think social workers are too soft.

> I would like a new role for the probation service around the concept of reparation...

Specific proposals for the reform of community sanctions

The discussion in the focus group panels generated a number of proposals as to how to solve the perceived gap in the system of sentencing between a tough (prison) sanction and a soft (community) sentence. The panel discussion suggested support for the ideas later quantified in a follow-up questionnaire, the collated results of which are in Appendix 1.

Weekend custody: Magistrates were overwhelmingly (96 per cent of respondents) in favour of some form of weekend custody. In their view only intermittent prison could realistically bridge the gap.

> It would be useful to have somewhere where people were deprived of their liberty for Saturday and Sunday, and if they could do some work into the bargain, I think that would be ideal.

> It's no use just sending someone away and sending them into a prison cell to read over the weekend. They've got to do something constructive whilst they're there.

> In a camp where you cannot go out, you can't make phone-calls and you can't watch television and you can't ...You're just there. You can't get pie-eyed down at the local.

Curfew and electronic monitoring: The responses indicated that of the 55 replies only 1 magistrate was opposed to the concept of home curfew and 7 to the idea of electronic monitoring. Most were in favour of both and some saw this as a possible way to overcome the perceived gap between community and custodial sentences. Magistrates did, however, indicate a concern about enforcing the curfew and the reliability of electronic monitoring.

> But the guy goes home, he says, 'sod the curfew, I'm going down to the pub'. You've got to have a closer monitoring and electronic tagging is something rather than nothing.

> If it works, then OK, I'm prepared to use anything that works.

> In other words you punish the person by saying, 'we're not going to put you in prison, but we're going to take away your liberty of movement so that you have to stay within your home and you have to record the fact that you're in your home' using this form of electronic tagging, say between 7 o'clock at night and 7 o'clock in the morning or something like that would, especially for a lot of young people, be a very severe kind of deprivation of liberty regardless of their lifestyle.

Discussions concerned the public profile of community sentences. In general the view was that public awareness about the nature and content of community service should be increased and more information made available to the public about the projects covered by community service, given the availability of appropriate tasks.

> I'm not necessarily saying it should be made to be done in public. I'm not looking for degradation of people etc. But it seems to me at the moment that the community work is being carried out in secret or in private and I don't see why it should happen in that way.

> If people are working in a public area, then I have quite a strong feeling for putting them into a uniform, even if it was just a jacket that said community worker on the back. I think that's pretty cruel in some ways but we do need something that's a deterrent as well.

> A program of public information, not necessarily education, public

> information as part of the raising of the profile of community sentences that are imposed and what happens to offenders ... public have the right to know what is being given to offenders who commit certain categories of crime and who keep re-offending.

While the replies in the follow-up questionnaire indicated a preference for more publicity to be given to community service projects, there was more ambivalence about using publicity to identify individual offenders doing community work. Sixty-nine per cent of magistrates thought it a good idea to publish a list of those given a community sentence, while 13 per cent were opposed. A question regarding the use of special clothing or uniforms for community service offenders found 46 per cent in favour and 42 per cent opposed to this idea. Discussions in the focus groups reflected these arguments.

Consideration of the proposals in the Green Paper (Ealing panels only)

The panellists in Ealing were asked to comment on proposals outlined in the green paper, *Strengthening Punishment in the Community*. It proposed the introduction of a single integrated community sentence (which might be designated the community sentence) replacing and incorporating all the current orders available in the adult courts, and increased discretion for courts to determine the content of community sentences in individual cases and to decide what restrictions and compulsions should apply to offenders in pursuance of the three principal purposes.

The main proposals were:

- the single flexible community sentence
- sentencers to have more input into the detail of order
- identifying the sentencing objectives
- feedback on progress of orders to magistrates
- introduction of curfew and electronic monitoring
- abolition of the need for the consent of the offender

The single prospect flexible community sentence incorporating all existing sentences was welcomed as removing some of the procedural difficulties and limitations inherent in the present system. The magistrates thus generally welcomed the opportunity to have more flexible orders to meet different circumstances. In the follow-up questionnaire respondents were asked whether they were in favour of more details in the pre-sentence report of the precise programme to be followed by those given a community sentence. Of the 29 replies, 26 were in favour and only one against.

Also welcomed was the suggestion that sentencers should have more input and control over the detail of community sentences, though concerns over the respective roles of probation and sentencer and implementation and training implications were expressed. However, some magistrates had reservations as to their role as regards their knowledge of suitable and available programmes and the resource implications of this proposal.

> I don't know at this stage whether I do want to have more power to determine sentences.
>
> Well, I'm not happy with what we have at the moment in so far as we don't get enough information and I'd like to have more direct control over sentences as a proposal.
>
> I think the principle is very good providing we are given the options of what is there for us to choose from.

The third proposal involved the matching of sentence elements to the three principal purposes of punishment in the community: restriction of liberty, reparation and prevention of re-offending.

Currently, magistrates felt loath to give reasons for sentences, and seem to be strongly advised not to by the clerks. Where they do give more than the statutory statement required by the Criminal Justice Act 1991 they do not tend to use the three categories suggested in the proposals. Some thought it would be useful but were inhibited by the fear of appeal. What is of interest is that a minority did feel that clearer explanation of an implicit denunciatory statement was appropriate.

> I will often say, 'well, have you thought about the old lady, or have you thought about the person who's come home and found their house in a mess?'
>
> If the clerks had their way, we wouldn't say anything at all [because it might] end up in the Court of Appeal.
>
> We'd have to be trained to give them appropriately and clearly.

> So...that sort of approach I'm sure would be more use for the public understanding and would be more use from the point of view of the criminal understanding, that you were actually saying that this is going to be unpleasant and you're going to jolly well have to put up with it because you've done what you have done.

Proposals for the introduction of curfew and electronic monitoring were generally welcomed if implementation fears could be allayed. There was a concern as to whether electronic monitoring equipment would work to provide adequate monitoring. Electronic monitoring found favour with fewer participants than curfew.

Another proposal involved more consistent access for courts to information on the progress and outcome of community sentences. In discussion, although some magistrates welcomed the idea, feeling that it would enable them to target sentences more accurately, others thought that feedback would be interesting but nothing more. Some magistrates felt the suggestion inappropriately imposed upon them a monitoring role. One magistrate thought that enhanced monitoring by the original sentencer would have a salutary effect on the offender. However, in the follow-up questionnaire 26 respondents out of 29 were in favour of more feedback.

The proposal for the removal of the present requirement that offenders consent to community orders received almost unanimous support, although a few saw an advantage in maintaining a system whereby the offender gave consent to a community sentence.

> It's either a punishment or it isn't. You don't have to ... give him a choice.

> If you're going to punish somebody you're going to impose upon them and to impose on them something that's in the open, I think that consent is important. I would like to keep it.

Conclusion

The receptiveness of magistrates to new ideas, whether they be the introduction of new penalties, such as the curfew, or of new ways of looking at existing penalties, such as the policy shifts examined in our research, is likely to be shaped by a number of influences and pressures.

Firstly, there is the difficulty inherent in trying to balance the multiple, and often competing, objectives of sentencing. Secondly, there are penological constraints such as policy decisions about the use or purpose of imprisonment. Thirdly, there are the legal and practical realities of procedures in the criminal process. Fourthly, there are the constraints of funding and administrative arrangements. Finally, there are the prejudices and customs that are carried in a culture. In the world of the magistrate as sentencer, this culture is influenced by magistrates' perceptions of their role in which they must balance their own personal views on sentencing with the views of the wider community which they are supposed to reflect.

All these matters contribute to the overall cultural context in which sentencing policy is formulated and implemented. The complexity of this process is one of the reasons why the ambitions of penal reformers are sometimes thwarted. The reformers, sharing a common agenda and aspirations, seem to speak a language of universal appeal, i.e. penological Esperanto. But those who interpret and implement the criminal justice system, when exposed to this international language spoken by the penal experts, will interpret it in the knowledge of the parochial concerns and the significance of these ideas for their own local situation, i.e. sentencing parochialism.

Following his tour of prisons in France, Switzerland, Belgium and Germany, John Howard the 18th Century penal reformer, was critical of the influence of culturally derived custom and prejudice on penal policy. In Howard's view the advantage of comparative inquiry is that it contrasts and challenges taken-for-granted assumptions. He cites in the extract below the apparent anomaly that in England during his time people were prepared to execute criminals but were reluctant to impose a sentence involving work.

> It was to counteract a notion, prevailing among us that compelling prisoners to work, especially in public, was inconsistent with the principles of English liberty; at the same time that taking away the lives of such numbers, either by executions, or the diseases of our prisons, seems to make little impression upon us. Of such force is custom and prejudice in silencing the voice of good sense and humanity. (John Howard, *The State of the Prison*, Bicentennial Edition, Professional Books, p. 146)

Howard's remarks about the advantage of foreign prison visits show that he regarded the exploration of other penal systems as desirable because they exposed people to new ideas and challenged their prejudices, leading onto, he no doubt hoped, a more humane and rational approach to penal policy. He was an early exponent of penological Esperanto.

It is our conclusion that the exposure to the penal ideas and sentencing practices of other countries can be useful in stimulating a fresh view of a familiar system. However, our research leads us to believe that the transplanting of ideas from one jurisdiction to another is much more complex than Howard and the penological Esperantists allow for. Vital in all this is the local culture of the criminal justice system and the tacit and explicit assumptions about its purpose and style.

Appendix: Results of the follow-up questionnaire to specific proposals for the reform of community penalties

The 58 magistrates who had participated in the focus group panels in Aylesbury and Ealing were asked to indicate their support, or not, for a number of proposals that emerged in the discussions. The magistrates who took part were sent a questionnaire and 55 replied. Their responses are summarised below.

To what extent would you like to see the following options introduced?

		very much in favour	in favour	neither in favour/nor opposed	opposed	very opposed
a)	Home curfew	*35%*	*40%*	*22%*	*2%*	*0%*
b)	Electronic monitoring of home curfew	*20%*	*44%*	*22%*	*11%*	*2%*
c)	Weekend custody	*69%*	*27%*	*4%*	*0%*	*0%*
d)	A published court list of those offenders given a community sentence	*36%*	*33%*	*16%*	*11%*	*2%*
e)	Special clothing to identify offenders on CSOs	*24%*	*22%*	*13%*	*31%*	*11%*
f)	More details in the Pre-Sentence Report of the precise programme to be followed by those given a community sentence	*82%*	*15%*	*2%*	*2%*	*0%*
g)	More feedback on the success/failure of individual offenders given community sentences	*75%*	*18%*	*5%*	*2%*	*0%*

[N=55]

4 Responses in Finland to Community Sanctions

JUKKA-PEKKA TAKALA

Introduction

This chapter reports on a focus group study on community sanctions involving Finnish judges, prosecutors and probation workers. The discussions within the focus groups focused on the community service order. This sanction was introduced on an experimental basis in 1991 and its future will be decided when it reappears on the parliamentary agenda, probably in 1996. Very few voices have been raised against its adoption as a permanent, regular part of the punishment repertoire, but its precise shape may be debated. The discussions for this research were, therefore, concerned with how a newly introduced system worked in practice, rather than, as in California and England, on policy documents and proposals for change.

Under the present temporary law, the Community Service Act of 1990, community service may be used in cases which otherwise would attract an unconditional prison sentence of eight months or less. Formally, the court first imposes an unconditional prison sentence of a specified length, and then commutes it into a community service order of a certain number of hours. The number of hours that can be ordered ranges from 20 to 200, and the suggested conversion rate (which also is the practical norm) is approximately one day of prison sentence for one hour of community service. To impose a community service order, the court must find it probable that the defendant is able to carry out the order. To help the court determine this, a semi-official organisation called the Probation and Aftercare Association assesses the defendant's suitability for community service on the request of the prosecutor or the court (or sometimes even at the defendant's request).

The focus group panellists were specifically asked to look at community service in the context of the whole punishment system. This involved taking a view, for instance, on the placement of community service in the penal tariff, relating it to other available punishments. These are quite few: either unconditional or conditional (suspended) prison sentences, and fines. Apart from fines and small-scale supervision affecting certain young offenders, there are no punishments in the regular repertoire that would prescribe the offenders to certain conduct while remaining at liberty, such as exists in many other countries, probation for example.

Immediately prior to this research, a government bill (Finnish Government Bill [FGB] 1994, no. 251) on 'youth punishment' was presented to the parliament. According to the bill, 'youth punishment' would consist of 10 to 60 hours of 'youth service' which was described as community service adjusted for 15-17-year-olds. In addition, the offender would be under supervision for three to 12 months. Although this proposal was not discussed with the panellists in any detail, it was mentioned, and the issue of suitable punishments for young people was discussed in all the focus group sessions as the new 'youth punishment' was a form of community sanction. Furthermore, at the time when the present 1990 legislation on community service proper was being prepared, many people hoped that it would be a new concrete and tangible punishment precisely for young offenders. They were, however, disappointed.

The 1990 community service order was not intended to be specifically a youth sentence, nor has it been used this way in practice. In 1991-92, only three per cent of those given this sanction were younger than 21 years; the mean age was 33.6 years (Takala, 1993a, p. 46). The bill on youth punishment can be seen as an attempt to respond to the demands for new types of sanctions for young offenders and to satisfy those who regret their virtual exclusion from the target population of the community service proper (Lappi-Seppälä, 1994b, p. 203). This proposal on youth punishment expired shortly after the focus group sessions were held, because it did not make the legislature's agenda before a parliamentary reelection in Spring 1995. A new bill is anticipated in the near future.

The purpose of the focus groups was to shed light on the practical use of community sanctions from the point of view of persons who impose them, and those who see that they are carried out. The opinions gleaned from the discussions could inform the planning of the new system after the present temporary legislation expires at the end of 1996. Although regular administrative records and earlier studies throw light on many aspects of the community service system – for instance, that it works approximately as planned – there are some unexplained parts of the machinery that focus group consultation may help solve.

First, there are practical details that run somewhat against published expectations. Why, for instance, is a suitability assessment requested only in a minority of the cases that seemed eligible? Is there something about the way prosecutors, courts or those involved with probation think and work that could shed light on this? While the legislation seemed to expect that virtually all defendants who were about to receive a commutable sentence would be sent for a suitability assessment for community service, this has been far from the case. During the first 18 months the suitability assessment requests covered only one quarter of such cases (Takala, 1993a, p. 52); their coverage seems to have increased since, but it is still far from complete. Another interesting detail that the *travaux préparatoires* did not clearly anticipate was the over-representation of drunk driving among the offences for which community service is imposed. Drunk driving is the offence in 75 per cent of the community service orders but in only about 42 per cent of the cases that were eligible on the severity of sentence criterion. Apart from maybe shedding light on the issues of suitability assessment coverage and offence type selection, the focus group sessions were expected to increase understanding of how the implementers went about their work in general and interpreted the different statutes regulating their role.

Second, it seemed worthwhile to get information on how the implementers thought about the sentencing principles that were at issue when community service was introduced. How do these officials feel about the relations between the new sanction and traditional aspects of the sentencing system? The community service order was introduced in a system that since the 1970s had emphasised neoclassical virtues. The ideal was a transparent and simple system with proportional, predictable, and uniform sentencing. (The label neoclassicism refers to the restoration, after being partly overshadowed by the rehabilitation or treatment school, of some aspects of an older penal justice ideology: the rule of law, legal safeguards, predictability in the application of law and proportionality in sentencing [Lappi-Seppälä 1993].) Community service brought in new elements, namely some individual tailoring of the sentence, based on an assessment of suitability that was independent of measurement of punishment and yet seemed related to it. These elements may cause friction. First, individual tailoring of sentences may run counter to the idea of a uniform and predictable system. Second, the new system seemed to contain this confusion about proportionality and equity. On the one hand, community service is supposed to be less detrimental but also less severe than the prison sentence that it replaces. On the other hand, the penal value of the two is declared to be equal. Both claims cannot be literally true simultaneously.

The first *travaux préparatoires* that supported the introduction of community service to the penal system were open about community service being less severe than imprisonment:

> If of two offenders who have committed a similar offence one were sent to prison while the other got away with a non-custodial sanction such as community service only because he appears better suited, this would not be fair. If the Finnish system should adopt community service, a point of departure should be that everyone who, based on the pettiness of his offence, could be an object of this sanction be assigned to work suitable for him. (Finnish Ministry of Justice, 1987, pp. 64-65)

However, the government bill that introduced the present system is more subdued on this issue. Rather than talk about alternatives of different *severity*, it just talks about different alternatives. A severity evaluation, nevertheless, comes through in some places. For instance, when the bill considers the problem that the sanction mode is partly selected based on an assessment of an individual's ability to carry out a community service order rather than on the standard sentencing criteria, it notes that the problem is alleviated by the fact that community service would imply 'a deviation to the *more lenient* direction from the present punishments' (FGB 1990, no. 62, pp. 8-9, emphasis added).

Of course, such equivocal positions are not unusual in the history of sentencing. There have been similar problems with other alternatives to prison, such as suspended or conditional sentences. They are introduced with a desire to retain the symbolic value of imprisonment and yet get rid of some of the trouble that it causes in practice. In the long run, this lack of trouble tends to erode much of the symbolic value.

Such then were some of the background issues that the focus groups were expected to analyse and discuss. As pointed out in the Introduction and Chapter One of this book, the criminal justice systems of different countries often use similar vocabularies that can have quite different meanings. Allowing translation between English and Finnish, many of the notions used in the Finnish system are similar to those in England or California, for instance: prison, sentence, community service, probation, proportionality. No doubt many of them also share much of their meaning. Nevertheless, in each jurisdiction they are used in the context of the specific local background. Prison is prison is prison, but Finnish prisons are small or mid-sized compared with the two other jurisdictions. Finnish legislation uses the term probation, but it bears little resemblance to its English or Californian namesakes, as will be explained below. The introduction of community service in Finland is a recent case that can be looked upon as borrowing a notion from fashionable international criminal justice vernacular. It relates to international currents of penal ideologies, such as the waning belief in the merits of imprisonment. But simultaneously, it is set in a specific Finnish context, and some background of the Finnish sentencing system is needed to grasp the meaning of community service in that country.

The Finnish penal system

Finland is a Scandinavian or Nordic country with a population of five million. The historical core of the Finnish legal system comes down from the time when the country was part of Sweden. When Sweden ceded it to Russia in 1809, Finland became an autonomous Grand Duchy with many of the Swedish laws kept in place, among them the Swedish criminal code of 1734. In 1889 a new criminal code was enacted. Heavily amended, it forms the skeleton of the present penal law. Finland declared independence from Russia in 1917. Apart from such exceptional times as the 1918 Civil War and wars with the Soviet Union (1939-40 and 1941-44), Finland has been a rather stable place. The first election to the Finnish parliament undr universal suffrage took place in 1907. Contrary to popular misconception, Finland was not occupied by any foreign army during the second world war, and its political and juridical structure stayed more or less intact.

On a fundamental level, the Finnish criminal justice system subscribes to the same principles as do other democratic countries. For instance, a legal punishment can only be meted out for an act defined as punishable in the law and the burden of proof in a criminal trial is wholly on the prosecutor.

The Finnish system differs, however, in several respects from the common law jurisdictions. The system is much more centralised, top-down, and much less dependent on the local community than it is in the USA or England. This is evident in all branches of the system. The source of law is almost exclusively the written, enacted law, there being no case law as such, apart from cases that indicate how some laws have been interpreted. The police is a national force, there are no community-based police departments. There is no jury of peers in a trial. There are lay members in the body that decides on guilt and sentencing, but they are not appointed for just one case but take part in many. Lay judges are appointed by the municipal council for the term of the council (four years), but the most influential members of the lower courts, the legally trained professional judges, are tenured and they are appointed by the President of the Republic, based on a graded short list made by the court of appeal of the area. Professional judges do not need to seek reelection by means of populist campaigns or impressive punishments, and the perks for lay judges are too small for them to bother either.

The public prosecutor has a duty to prosecute all crimes that come to his or her knowledge, with some exceptions. The prosecutor does not seek (officially) a specific punishment, but gives a description of the act and gives an opinion as to which definition of crime in the Penal Code it satisfies. The rubric of the offence sets certain lower and upper limits for the punishment, but prosecutors are advised not to battle about minor changes of rubrics. The prosecutor also has to present all the aggravating as well as mitigating circumstances pertinent to the case. Depending on the presiding judge, the prosecutor may be asked to give his or her opinion on the sentence. The prosecutor is expected not to be concerned with the fine tuning of the sentence, meaning that only evident deviations by the court from the approved sentencing principles should be challenged, for instance through an appeal to a court of appeal (Chancellor of Justice 1986; Kalske, Nissinen, and Tohkanen 1990).

The victim of a crime is independently entitled to prosecute. The victim presents his or her compensation claims in the criminal proceedings, and it is therefore not necessary to initiate another process to get compensation, since compensation is a routine matter of the standard proceedings.

There is no plea-bargaining, nor any room for it. The strong role of the judges, combined with the limited discretion of the prosecutor, and the right of the victim to indict make it unfeasible. Furthermore, the process-economical need for plea-bargaining is not that great, since with no jury even a full trial can be a relatively slim machinery.

The role of the judge in a trial is somewhat more independent than it is in a common law jurisdiction. The judges have a duty to find out the relevant facts; they are not restricted to the information offered. Rules of evidence are also flexible. There is no exclusionary rule that would require the court to disregard certain types of evidence. The court is simply required to weigh everything that has been revealed in the case in order to 'decide what is to be deemed the truth in the matter' as the Code of Judicial Procedure states it (Joutsen, 1995, p. 15).

Sentencing is also probably more predictable in Finland. For one, the court can only choose from a rather limited number of sanction types. The court has no licence to invent new punishments, or give special conditions for using those of the existing repertoire. The court, for instance, has no say on whether a person sent to prison will go to a traditional closed prison or an open work institution: both count as 'prison'. Neither can the court determine what sort of a work someone ordered to community service must do. For another, uniformity in sentencing is a specific objective that the court is required to observe. Judges are made aware of the current punishment levels through means such as public statistics on typical punishments, handouts in professional conferences, and suggestions or guidelines by individual judges or courts that circulate informally. The leading principle in sentencing is proportionality between the seriousness of the offence and the severity of the sanction. Thus the sentence is to be based on 'blameworthiness of the offence and guilt manifest in the act', as the 1976 sentencing rules put it.

The composition of the court: The local court normally consists of one legally trained judge and three lay judges. In a complex case, the composition may be supplemented by a second legally trained judge and a fourth lay judge. Petty crimes can be dealt with in a court consisting of just one judge; he or she can impose at most a fine, but can also decide on conversion to imprisonment of unpaid fines (Joutsen, 1995).

In practice, the greatest number of fines for petty crimes, such as traffic violations or breaches of municipal ordinances, are imposed by the police, in the form of summary penal judgments, or 'penal orders'. This penal order is then affirmed by a prosecutor. The alleged offender can bring the matter to court to be dealt with in the regular procedure.

The sanctions available

The Finnish Penal Code (Chapter 2, article 1) lists three types of 'general punishments'. They are imprisonment, fine, and petty fine. Imprisonment comes in two forms that have a significant practical difference, either as unconditional or conditional (practically: suspended) imprisonment. And as mentioned above, the new community service order is also treated as a subordinate form of unconditional imprisonment, which brings about a third expression to that basic sanction form. In addition to these general punishments, the Penal Code article designates 'special punishments' for public office-holders (dismissal and caution) and 'disciplinary punishments' for military personnel, but these are very rarely used. Furthermore, the court can make use of a few other measures that are not treated as regular punishments in legal doctrine (or reported in court statistics) but are no doubt taken as such by a good many of their beneficiaries. Practically, the most important is suspension of the driving licence; a sample study of lower courts indicates that at least some 93 per cent of all drunk driving convictions are accompanied by a driving prohibition of some duration (Lappi-Seppälä, 1994a).

Waiving of sanctions: Criminal law textbooks also list waiving of measures at some stage (forbearing measures by the police, waiving of prosecution by the prosecutor, or of sentencing by the court) as a form of sanction, or consequence, of crime. This sanction requires that the guilt of the defendant has been established, and is thus different from acquittal based on innocence or lack of evidence. Although the term, waiving of prosecution or punishment, does not convey terribly energetic punitiveness, it is hoped that the process will serve as a warning. Recent legislation has explicit reference to oral cautions made by a police officer or prosecutor.

Petty fines: Of the general punishments mentioned, the petty fine is the most recent in the punishment catalogue. It was adopted in 1983. There are now five levels of petty fines, 40 through 300 markkaa (£6 to £43 or $9 to $69 at August 1995 exchange rates: £1=FIM6.9, $1=FIM4.35). The level depends on the gravity of the infraction, but the amount is fixed in the sense that it is independent of the means of the offender. So far the petty fine is used only for minor traffic offences, such as failure to use a seat-belt or non-serious speeding. Petty fine orders are usually given by the police. The alleged offender may bring the case to the court, but only 2-3 out of every thousand petty fines are actually contested, one-third successfully.

Day-fines: Regular fines are (since 1921) imposed as so-called day-fines, i.e., as a certain number of days (1 through 120) at a certain sum each day. The number of days is based on the blameworthiness of the offence, the daily sum depends on the resources of the offender and is about one third of his or her daily gross income. If the offender does not pay, the day-fine may be eventually converted into imprisonment at the rate of one day of imprisonment for two day-fines. In 1993, nearly 3,000 fine defaulters were imprisoned. This is nearly three times the mid-1980s figures, a change probably related to the economic recession. In 1993, fine-defaulters made up about seven per cent of the daily prison population, but one-third of the yearly inflow.

Day-fines are the most widely used sanctions. They outnumber petty fines more than five-fold. In 1990, 395,000 fines were imposed, 83,000 of them at trial and the other 312,000 through penalty orders. The huge majority of all offences punished with fines were traffic violations; about 82,000 or one-fifth were crimes against the Penal Code. The median number of day-fines imposed for Penal Code offences was 25 and the median amount was 20 markkaa; the latter figure is equal to the minimum amount allowed by the law, which implies that more than half of the persons fined for Penal Code offences had a very low or no income.

Prison: Imprisonment is the most severe punishment form known to the Finnish Penal Code. Imprisonment is imposed for a fixed term, whose general minimum is 14 days and maximum twelve years, or fifteen years when several prison sentences are combined. Murder is punishable by life imprisonment.

Prisoners are normally paroled after having served a certain part of their sentence. This is one-half for first-timers (one-third in the special youth prison), and two-thirds for others. Prisoners serving a life sentence may be released only by a pardon granted by the President of the Republic. The average time served in prison by lifers has been 10-12 years.

Community service: As mentioned in the introduction to this chapter, community service order is, in the current temporary law, officially only available as a commuted unconditional prison sentence. Serious breach of a community service order leads to enforcement of the original prison sentence.

Conditional sentence: Prison sentences of up to two years can be made conditional. The court may do so 'if the maintenance of general obedience to the law does not demand an unconditional sentence' (Conditional Sentence Act, 1976). In official doctrine the conditional sentence is, then, a form of imprisonment. This conception is enhanced, among other things, by the fact that the court specifies a prison term of a certain length, before declaring it to be conditional with a specified probation time (one to three years). Hence, the sentence looks different from those suspended sentences in some jurisdictions which indicate no punishment form or amount. In practical terms, however, one would call it rather an authoritative warning than a prison sentence, since the term conditional has now little meaning that would link it to the everyday use of the word. The condition is activated only if the offender, during the probation period, commits a new offence which merits a prison sentence; in this case, the court may order that also the earlier conditional sentence is to be enforced in full or in part. So there is probation in the Finnish sentencing system, but, for adult offenders, it does not imply any supervision or any other special obligation; it only marks a period of time during which new crimes worthy of imprisonment are likely to be sanctioned more severely than otherwise.

Deciding on conditionality: In practice the choice between conditional and unconditional imprisonment depends on the offender's past criminality. First-timers are hardly ever actually imprisoned, unless, of course, the sentence exceeds the upper limit of conditionality, two years. According to a 1990 court sample studied by Lappi-Seppälä (1991, 1994a), in cases of 'aggravated drunk driving' with no serious concomitant offences, only two per cent of the first-timers were imprisoned unconditionally. ('Aggravated drunk driving' in 1990 required a blood alcohol content of 0.15 per cent or higher; since 1994 the limit is 0.12 per cent.) One earlier recent conviction for a similar crime raised the proportion of unconditional imprisonments to 60 per cent of the disposals. Where repeat offending is flagrant the court may cite a special clause of the 1976 sentencing rules to the effect that 'previous criminality ...shows that the offender is apparently heedless of the prohibitions and commands of law'. If this was done, then 38 out of 39 decisions came out as unconditional prison sentences. Lappi-Seppälä obtained comparable results also from analyses of theft, fraud, unauthorised use of motor vehicle, and other crimes, although the proportion of unconditional sentences at each recidivism level varied depending on crime category.

Combination punishments: Regular punishments cannot be freely combined. One valid combination, introduced by the 1976 recast of the conditional sentence, is that a subsidiary fine can be attached to conditional imprisonment. This is done in five-sixths of conditional sentences for drunken driving (Lappi-Seppälä 1994a), but it is not as pervasive in other crime types.

Special rules for young offenders: There is no special juvenile justice so labelled in Finland. The age of criminal responsibility is fifteen years. Crimes by persons younger than that are not dealt with by any court, but the cases can be handed over to the social authorities. However, even persons below the age of criminal responsibility have an obligation to compensate for damages caused by their offences. Compensation plans are sometimes settled in voluntary offender-victim reconciliation schemes. Offenders who are 15 or older are dealt with in the normal courts, but there are some special rules for them. Offenders below the age of eighteen (at offending) stand a greater chance of having sanctions waived and they are subject to a mitigated scale of punishment. Furthermore, since 1989, an offender under 18 years cannot be sentenced to unconditional imprisonment 'unless there are weighty reasons' for doing so. This provision influences the composition of the target group of community service. As community service is considered a mode of unconditional imprisonment, it inherits all the rules regulating it. Hence, an offender under 18 can be sentenced to community service only in exceptional cases. And if offenders below the age of 21 are sentenced to actual prison, they are likely to be sent to a special juvenile prison. This prison can grant parole sooner than other prisons, after one-third of the sentence for first-timers.

A young offender (15-20 years) who is given a conditional sentence is automatically put under supervision for the probation period, unless the court explicitly decides against it, 'considering that the young person sentenced will mend his ways even without supervision'. A person under supervision must inform the supervisor of his place of residence and of work, and report to the supervisor on request of the supervisor. However, there are no real sanctions that can be inflicted on a youth who fails to meet his or her conditions for supervision, although not all young offenders are aware of this.

Crime and sentencing trends

International victimisation surveys indicate that Finns are victimised by crime more rarely than the European average. This is true for most crimes, for instance victimisation to burglary is considerably lower than the average, but victimisation to violence is somewhat higher than the average (van Dijk and Mayhew, 1993). The two rounds of the international survey are too close in time (1989, 1992) to allow reliable assessment of longer trends (there was, however, a slight increase in victimisation in Finland). Finnish national victimisation surveys go a little further back – and have larger samples. They suggest that property offences kept about constant between the first two rounds of the survey, 1980 and 1988, but then increased by forty per cent by the time of the third survey, conducted in 1993. Victimisation to violence decreased slightly between 1980 and 1988 and rose since, but was in 1993 still below the 1980 level. (Heiskanen *et al*, 1991, pp. 119-123; Heiskanen, 1991; Aromaa and Heiskanen, 1994)

As in comparable countries, crime recorded by the police has considerably increased in Finland during the past decades (Table 4.1). Recorded theft has increased almost eightfold since 1950, and assaults are two or three times as common. The victimisation surveys, which asked also whether crimes were reported to the police, suggest that at least part of the recent increase is attributable to higher reporting. And at some points, such as between 1980 and 1988, higher reporting may even account for nearly all of the increase in recorded crime. But simultaneously it is highly probable that property crime has actually risen during the past decades.

Table 4.1 Crimes known to the police, 1950-1993

Per 100,000 population

	1950	1960	1970	1980	1990	1993
Larceny offences	504	675	1,251	2,113	3,274	3,886
Assaults	147	125	243	292	413	367
Drunk driving	401	96	202	427	95	435

Table compiled from: NRILP (1980), *Criminality in Finland: Annual Report for 1979*; NRILP (1991), *Criminality in Finland: Annual Report for 1990*; NRILP (1994), *Criminality in Finland: Annual Report for 1993*; Statistics Finland (1952), *Criminality known to the police, 1951-1952*; Törnudd, P. (1978), *Crime Trends in Finland 1950-1977.*

The number of sentences has also increased (Table 4.2), but not as much as recorded crime. This is partly due to falling clearance rates and the fact that convictions for multiple offences have become more common.

Another clear pattern is that the proportion of the more serious disposals has decreased. In 1950, unconditional imprisonments accounted for five per cent of all sentences, in 1990, for less than three per cent. A more striking fact is that, despite a considerable absolute increase in unconditional imprisonments, the daily prison population has fallen by almost two-thirds since 1950 (Table 4.3). The same table also reveals the main key to this seeming inconsistency: shorter sentences. Decreased enforcement of conditional imprisonments and more consistent release on parole probably explain the rest.

Table 4.2 Sentences in Finland, 1950-1990

	1950	**1960**	**1970**	**1980**	**1990**
Sentenced offences	129,189	199,315	208,441	321,476	393,605
Unconditional imprisonment	6,471	6,900	10,212	10,326	11,657
Conditional imprisonment	2,812	3,686	5,215	14,556	17,428
Day fine by the court	39,027	40,818	42,248	47,401	52,542
Day fine by penalty order	80,525	147,650	150,542	249,006	311,889
- of these traffic violations	-	-	129,140	189,752	252,239
-petty fine (traffic violations)	-	-	-	-	69,291

Source: Lappi-Seppälä T. (1994b), *Alternative Penal Sanctions*, p. 204.

Table 4.3 Sentences imposed by lower courts, 1950-1990

				Per 100,000 population	
	1950	**1960**	**1970**	**1980**	**1990**
Unconditional imprisonment	161	155	220	212	233
Conditional imprisonment	70	83	111	298	349
Day fines	2,967	4,239	4,188	6,191	7,291

Table compiled from: Aho, T. (1982) *Nordic Journal of Criminology*, pp.169-76; NRILP (1993), *Criminality in Finland: Annual Report for 1992*; Statistics Finland (1994), *Yearbook of Justice Statistics.*

Table 4.4 Prison population and lengths of prison sentences, 1950-1990

	1950	**1960**	**1970**	**1980**	**1990**
Population on 1 January	8,000	7,000	5,000	5,000	3,000
Mean daily prison population per 100,000 population	194	153	112	106	69
Median length of sentences of imprisonment (in months)					
- all offences	7.6	5.9	5.0	3.7	3.0
- theft offences	9.8	7.7	6.6	4.6	2.9
- assault offences	8.6	6.4	5.7	4.9	4.3

Table compiled from: Department of Prison Administration (1971), *Annual Report for 1970*: Joutsen, M. (1985), *The Criminal Justice System of Finland*, p. 31: NRILP (1992), *Criminality in Finland: Annual Report for 1991:* NRILP (1994), Criminality in Finland: Annual Report for 1993, p. 129.

High incarceration rates as a social problem

The recent trends in Finland's prison population are a stark contrast to other industrial countries, where numbers in prison have risen considerably during the past one or two decades. However, there are no clear differences in either the crime level in international comparisons or trends in crime rates that would offer an easy solution to the Finnish prisoner rates. At least part of the explanation is even easier. To a great extent, Finland's path is a result of a deliberate policy that, starting in the 1960s, defined the (then) high prison population as a social problem. In the decades following the second world war, Finland's prison population was larger than that of the other Scandinavian countries. Criminologists showed that the common sense explanation, 'Finns are more criminal than their neighbours', did not hold true. With the exception of homicide and serious violence, the level of crime was lower in Finland than the Nordic average. The Finnish crime clear-up rates were, however, very high and a large proportion of the convicted offenders were sentenced to imprisonment. Prison sentences tended to be systematically longer in Finland (Anttila and Törnudd, 1973, p. 83).

As elsewhere, the belief in the salutary effects of prisons on their inmates was waning in Finland. A 1972 Government Bill (FGB 1972, no. 239, p. 3) for new legislation on enforcement of sentencing said this:

> Research has been unable to show that a prison sentence would have a 'rehabilitative' influence on an individual offender. Instead, it has been found that antisocial attitudes become stronger in institutions for punishment. Their former inmates commit a new crime considerably more often than persons sentenced to other sanctions.

Even though the bill admitted that the finding may be caused by a selection bias (persons with poorer prognosis are selected for prison in the first place), it is the former lesson that stands out: prison is detrimental.

The definition of high prisoner rates as a social problem was accepted quite broadly. It was meshed with a philosophy of crime control saying, approximately, that the criminal justice system primarily operates through mechanisms of general moral prevention, not deterrence through fear. This penal doctrine seeks general prevention but this is a notion different from general deterrence, as it is commonly understood. It is thought important to catch offenders and to denounce their offences, but it is not believed that making punishment more severe makes a great difference in crime prevention; the system as a whole is thought to work as a moral force that supports (and sometimes creates) norms that people abide by, not out of great fear but because they think they are legitimate and because they do want to avoid censure.

Elements of this philosophy can be found in different government documents. A central founding document of the continuing reform of the Penal Code is the 1976 *Criminal Law Committee Report*. When the report discusses ways in which the criminal justice system influences people's behaviour, deterrence is mentioned, but the system's educative and moral-creating and moral-maintaining aspects get more space. This comprehensive view is emphasised and topped with a specific warning against over-reliance on deterrence, or prevention through fear, 'behavioural regulation that is based mainly on the deterrent effect can only have a passing success during a crisis' (Finnish Ministry of Justice, 1976, p. 40). Similarly a 1988 bill introducing the first stage of the ongoing total reform of the penal code can be interpreted as supporting the view that, while it is important that there is a criminal justice system in place, generally tough penalties are not necessary for its operation:

> Available criminological research does not ... warrant the expectation that minor and gradual lowering of the level of punishment would affect the general preventive efficacy of punishments. (FGB 1988, no. 66, pp. 17-18)

This is quite different from the ideas of the 1940s and 1950s school of general deterrence. That old school held it very important that punishments were punitive. A striking example of this stance can be found in one statement in a late 1940s exchange on the appropriateness of labour colonies for serving prison sentences:

> The morale in the labour colonies is ... spirited and supportive of society. Regarding the general preventive effect of the labour colony, this state of affairs is not desirable... Staying in a labour colony does not amount to serving a sentence in the customary sense but rather to a sort of caution; it is not appropriate to liken it to staying in a penal institution. (The Law Drafting Company of the Ministry of Justice, cited in Uusitalo, 1968, p. 21)

The new 'soft' general preventionism was different from tough deterrence thought, but it was also different from the rehabilitation school that opposed the harsh retributivists. The new approach does not challenge the need for retribution or denunciation but only questions the need for harsh or severe punishments. Earlier retributivists also hardly saw the levels of conviction and imprisonment as something that could be made objects of a policy deliberation. They were conceived of as inevitable consequences of the laws that had been enacted and the organisations for detecting and solving crimes that were in place.

Modern criminology, however, had learned to look at crime and punishment as relative and variable concepts. Criminalisation, prosecution and sentencing were seen as something that could be debated, even taking into consideration the effects on the prison population of different decisions regarding those questions. Hence, the retributive core of sentencing was put in the framework of a larger criminal control perspective. This means that the goals of the criminal justice system as a whole and those of sentencing are seen to be of a different order. The utilitarian functions of the system come about best when utilitarian reasoning is abandoned for a mildly retributive one at the stage of sentencing. Or so one could interpret the philosophy behind much of the recent reforms in the Finnish criminal justice system. The idea of selecting specific goals for any given sentence (Morris and Tonry 1990) is somewhat remote to this ideology.

The ideology of general prevention through the moral influence of a consistently functioning criminal justice system is accepted or tolerated by a great majority of those who teach and speak publicly on crime control in Finland. This includes law professors and prison administrators, and often the police. As Törnudd puts it:

> The small group of experts who were in charge of reform planning or who worked as crime control experts in research institutes and universities shared an almost unanimous conviction that Finland's internationally high prisoner rate was a disgrace and that it would be possible to significantly reduce the amount and length of prison sentences without serious repercussions on the crime situation. (Törnudd, 1993, p. 5)

'Getting tough on crime' has not emerged as a significant political slogan in Finland. For instance, during the parliamentary elections in Spring 1995, campaigns which emphasised crime or law and order issues were few, and the candidates who did raise it as an issue were largely unsuccessful.

There are few systematic polls that would gauge how well these views have sunk into the population at large. Anecdotal evidence is available to show that they are not totally foreign. For instance, in a report on youngsters' views on justice, based on interviews with 50 young people, Grönfors and Hirvonen report that they viewed 'the level of punishment more as symbolic, moral, as something expressing denunciation rather than as a means of retribution or crime reduction' (Grönfors and Hirvonen, 1990, p. 65).

From tough treatment towards soft moral retribution

In Finland there has been a movement towards more lenient sentences, at least since World War II. There are exceptions, but as a gradual, overall development this seems true for Finland. During this century the pendulum has swung between the ideas of individual rehabilitation and general prevention. Individual prevention and rehabilitation gained currency towards the middle of the century. After that, there was a long swing towards moral retribution and a dismantling of many rehabilitative designs. Now, for a decade or so, there have been some signs of a reversal, as some ideas of individual treatment are gaining support (c.f. Lahti, 1993).

One area that experienced some movement first towards and then away from an individual prevention and rehabilitation ideology is the treatment of young offenders. The Young Offenders Act, enacted in 1940 and much of which is still in operation, indicated an optimism about rehabilitation and treatment. It provides a framework for considering the causes of crimes committed by young offenders. The court might take these causes as grounds for not making the offender 'pay the full price' for the crime, and they might also be helpful when devising appropriate correctional treatment. The law emphasises that the courts well acquaint themselves, not only with the offence committed and its motives, but also with the personality of the young offender, and the previous circumstances in which he has lived. This is done based on a pre-sentence report on the defendant, which is prepared by probation or social workers. Regulations on the pre-sentence reports state:

> When investigating the subject's earlier periods of life, particular attention must be paid also on whether there has occurred criminality or misbehaving or mental illness in the subject's family.

Though the rule is still technically part of the law, today's investigators usually do not seriously try to find out about family history of mental illness. Overall, the importance and numbers of these pre-sentence reports have declined over the years. In the late 1980s, there were about 8-9,000 of them yearly, whereas in 1994 there were only 3,500. (Probation and Aftercare Association 1995).

The language of the Young Offenders Act is not exactly in tune with the post-1970 legislation - it is one of the most clearly rehabilitation-orientated penal laws still surviving. However, a 1950 proposal went even further. It suggested that young offenders who merited a prison sentence be sent to special youth institutions. The length of their stay would be largely dependent on how the authorities thought they progressed, how well they were rehabilitated. The proposal was, however, not accepted. The critics seemed to shun responses both too generous and too harsh. They did not like indeterminate institutionalisation, or wide options for dropping all sanctions, or renaming youth *prison* as something nicer while keeping the contents practically identical. (The proposal and an influential Supreme Court critique are published in [Anttila 1952].) The critics' ideas were not unlike those of the more radical 1960s critique of the treatment ideology, except that they wanted to be tough on criminals; this is consistent with traditional notions of deterrence through fear of pain.

Nevertheless, the advocates of retribution and deterrence may have helped prevent Finland from adopting indeterminate sentencing or prison terms based on evaluations of rehabilitation.

> While neighbouring Sweden wholeheartedly accepted the rehabilitation ideology in the 1940s and 1950s, the Finns did not seriously begin to reform the criminal justice system before the 1960s. But then it was too late for the rehabilitation ideology to become dominant. (Törnudd, 1993, p. 3)

Indeterminate institutionalisation under the criminal law never gained much of a foothold when based on a treatment or rehabilitation rationale. It was somewhat more successful on incapacitation grounds. The law on dangerous repeat offenders, first enacted in 1931, said that a repeat offender 'dangerous to private or public safety' could be kept in an institution even after his sentence had expired.

In the 1960s, six per cent of the prison population on a given day, or four-hundred persons, were in indeterminate incarceration under this law (Anttila 1985). Amendments in 1971 and later, radically tightened the criteria for preventive detention and now the daily number of these prisoners is around ten (Department of Prison Administration, 1993). And though the law still allows them to be kept in prison longer than their original sentence, this is hardly ever done now: usually all prisoners classified under this act are still in fact serving the original sentence (Ritva Turunen, Prison administration, personal communication, September 1995). They are, however, usually not paroled while their sentence is running, as are other prisoners.

Fitting the conditional sentence into a neoclassical system

Cutting down on ideas of individual prevention and rehabilitation as central pillars of penal policy has put the conditional sentence into a new context that has inevitably changed its content. Historically, the criteria for the conditional sentence were closer to what one would expect by just looking at its label. Originally, a precondition for a conditional sentence was that the offender can be 'expected to mend his ways even if the sentence is not implemented' (article 3 of the 1918 Conditional Sentence Act). A 1939 amendment also authorised enforcement of the conditional sentence because of the 'offender's inebriety, or immoral or otherwise ill-behaved life' during probation, a possibility that was seldom used at the time when the 1976 Act on conditional sentence dropped it. Since then, only a new crime punishable with imprisonment could bring about implementation of the original sentence.

As indicated above, these changes can be seen partly as expressions of a general move against legislation and crime control policies that rely too much on individual prevention and rehabilitation ideology. Simultaneously, the changes brought the conditional sentence into the dimension of proportional sentencing. The conditional sentence started to look as a punishment in its own right, not as exceptional clemency befalling some of those who had merited and incurred a prison sentence. It started to appear as a form of punishment clearly lesser in severity than actual imprisonment. This implied new contradictions in the system. Earlier imprisonment was suspended (supposedly) because the offender seemed willing and capable of mending his ways without being actually sent to prison. Now it is suspended because the offence was less evil than those meriting imprisonment. If a suspended sentence is less severe and imposed for lesser crimes, it is hard to hold that it is equal to an enforced one. However, this is just what the prevailing criminal law doctrine tried to do for a long time.

An authoritative 1976 handbook on sentencing still claimed that the choice between actual and conditional imprisonment was a question that went beyond the issue of proportionality between crime and punishment. Matching punishment severity with the blameworthiness of crime, it said, only has to do with the nominal length of imprisonment, not with whether the offender actually goes to prison or not:

> '[T]he issue of conditionality ... is a question of crime control policy that falls outside the measurement of punishment' (Nousiainen, 1976, p. 99)

When this handbook appeared, there still was partial support for its argument of equal penal worth of conditional and unconditional imprisonment. The declared length of a conditional imprisonment could turn out to be anything but fiction. When a new offence was serious enough the court had no choice but to enforce the earlier conditional sentence in full. Recent law amendments have given the court discretion on this issue, breaking the one inflexible link to real imprisonment. With it, the conditional imprisonment and its stated length are bound to be perceived as more and more purely symbolic. There is also a lot of evidence that judges as well as other people have long perceived the conditionality choice as affecting the severity of the punishment (Lappi-Seppälä, 1987, pp. 604-6 and 1993, p. 31; Blom, 1979, pp. 54-57).

Introduction of the community service order

The trial of community service in Finland under a temporary law began in January 1991, in a number of jurisdictions and covering one tenth of the population. In October 1992 the area was extended to about one third of the population, and, since April 1994, the whole country.

In Finland, the community service order and an 'equivalent' prison term are officially similar as far as punishment worth or preventive goals are concerned. Though the goal of using community service to replace imprisonment is shared with the other Nordic countries, Finland does not officially attach individual preventive goals to community service or state that it has a lower general-preventive effect than prison. As mentioned above, the conversion rate between imprisonment and community service in Finnish courts equates one day of prison sentence with one hour of community service. Since there is no equivalent to parole for community service, in practical terms this implies that one community service hour equals one half-day to two-thirds of a day of real prison time. The conversion rate was suggested in the government bill introducing community service, and is not unlike those used in many other jurisdictions, including the other Nordic countries, though it is, of course, starkly different from, say, the '1 day = 8 hours' formula used in some other places.

The Finnish community service order procedure is to attract normal societal organisations as hosts for service tasks. No artificial arrangement set up just for the purpose of carrying out community service is considered as useful. Hence, the offenders who are thought likely to fail to comply must be excluded. This brings about a selection, and a test for that. In Finland, the Probation and Aftercare Association makes a suitability assessment of offenders for the purposes of sentencing. The same organisation also engages service hosts and supervises the carrying out of the order as well as trying to organise different support measures, such as alcoholism treatment.

However, selection should not violate the principle of proportional and fair punishment. Every offender whose crime fits the penal range (14 days through 8 months of unconditional imprisonment can be commuted to community service) is in principle eligible.

There is a problem in that the suitability assessment virtually decides between prison and community service, two alternatives of different severity. But the criteria for suitability for community service are not criteria that are usually thought relevant for lowering punishment in a system that emphasises proportionality between offence and punishment. The system can also be expected to lead to social bias in selection. And those given a community service order have turned out to be socially somewhat better off than those sentenced to an 'equivalent' prison term. Drunk drivers also receive a community service order more often than other offenders — a bias that on present data cannot be explained away by other variables (Takala 1993a).

The research in Finland

This study was sponsored by the National Research Institute of Legal Policy, which is an independent research agency in the ministry of justice. The Institute has a mandate to independently study issues of criminality, crime control policy and the criminal justice system. Experts on sentencing and community service in the ministry of justice were consulted about the themes of the meetings, as was the national office of the

Probation and Aftercare Association, but they were not directly involved in the study.

An earlier study conducted at the Research Institute of Legal Policy on the first 18 months of the Finnish community service experiment (Takala 1993a) indicated that there were problems in determining the place of this sanction in the penal system. A focus group study, such as that conducted in California (Davies 1993), seemed a good way to tap into the moods and opinions of the people who were implementing the new sanction. Earlier, I had conducted individual interviews, but the focus group method offered a more economic and potentially more inspiring way of doing it.

In some ways, however, focus groups did not seem so terribly different from those administrative and training routines that were in place in the Finnish criminal justice community. For instance, law proposals by different committees and task forces are often circulated among the courts and other relevant agencies and organisations, including universities and research bodies, for preview, comments, and critique. Similarly, the Ministry of Justice organises regular training for and consultation with the judges; these conferences deal much with problems of new legislation.

It seemed possible, nevertheless, that a focus study might bring about some information that would not be obtained by other means. Solicitations for comments on law drafts are not very frequent, and training is a notion different from specifically asking for the advice and opinion of the local experts implementing the law.

Methodology

Six focus group sessions were held in six different areas of Finland between October and December 1994. At the time of the meetings, four areas (Turku, Mikkeli, Vaasa, Rovaniemi) had community service available for just under four years, the other two (Lahti, Tampere), for a little over two years.

Each session had at least one representative of each of these three: court judges, prosecutors, Probation and Aftercare Association workers. In addition, there were police officers in some sessions, social workers from other agencies dealing with offenders, and people from organisations providing service placement for offenders sentenced to community service. There were 38 panellists in total. All the twelve participating judges were legally trained, full-time professional judges, i.e. no lay judges were present in the sessions. Nine judges were from the lower courts and three from courts of appeal.

The meetings were held in different locales: two were hosted by lower courts, one by a district court of appeal, two by the local offices of the Probation and Aftercare Association, and one by a city prosecutor. Hosting was deliberately solicited from these various agencies to give it a more balanced feel, although we did not see it necessary to find completely neutral meeting locales. All the panels were held early in the afternoon, about an hour or so after the regular lunch break.

The sessions lasted between 90 minutes and two hours. With just one exception, all participants were present throughout the whole session.

Feedback on the sessions: There was no systematic retrieval of opinions of the participants on the usefulness or otherwise of the sessions. A number of spontaneous expressions of satisfaction were, however, presented. Some persons were satisfied with the meeting as a method of finding out about issues: 'This is a nice method. Could be used in other contexts, as well'. Others were pleased because they had learned about things and ways of thinking that they found useful. Some judges and prosecutors said they had learned about the practice of community service orders. Some Probation and Aftercare Association workers were glad they had learned about the way judges and prosecutors think.

Selection of panellists: Two methods were used to select the appropriate people to invite to the sessions. The preferred method was to contact the local head of each of the three main agencies (court, prosecutors, probation) and ask her or him to suggest one or two persons from the agency to participate. For reasons of expediency, in some cases, selection was based on the suggestion of one or two local key informants. We then contacted the suggested persons directly. There were a few last-minute replacements and some whose identity was not known prior to the meeting.

When soliciting suggestions for participants, we emphasised that we were interested in divergent opinions. Nevertheless, it seems probable that there may have been over-representation of persons favourable to community sanctions as opposed to those who are critical of them. This follows from general considerations of the methodology (see Chapter 1). There are also some anecdotal data that are consistent with this assumption. For instance, one agency had initially designated a person who was known to be very critical of community service; at the last minute, this person, however, had withdrawn from the task and someone else was sent as replacement. Also at least in two sessions, there were references to absent members of the local criminal justice community who were said to be extremely critical of the community service idea (and no allusions to absent persons who would be overly enthusiastic about it).

One might also note that the Probation and Aftercare Association office-holders may have a professional interest at stake that is different from that of the judges and prosecutors. Running the community service system is a major part of the probation association's work while it does not make a great difference in the judges' or prosecutors' professional life. Compared to the other focus group studies reported in this book, the inclusion of probation workers in the panels may be significant for the treatment of some issues. On the one hand, one might expect that if the other panellists are suspicious or critical of community service in general, or of the way that it is dealt with at the stage of preparing suitability assessments or enforcing the order, they might air their criticism more politely or cautiously when probation workers are present. On the other hand, their presence allows real exchange on such issues, something that indeed took place in the sessions.

While most of the panellists were full-time workers in the criminal justice system, some of the people from organisations serving as hosts for offenders doing their community service were not. Some of them had little knowledge of the official placement of community service (or any other punishment) in the severity scale relative to common crimes. For instance, one such person did not appreciate that community service was not meant for the first-time offender. They were typically unaware of the fact that courts very seldom imposed a conviction of imprisonment, let alone of unconditional imprisonment, to first-time offenders. Such an innocent view surfaced in two or three meetings, but they did not lead to much discussion, probably since the rest of the panellists knew better, and knew that most of the other professionals knew too.

The participants were asked to state their own views, not to try to represent their respective agencies. Of course, one cannot be sure that they did this. Apart from the fact that many of them may genuinely identify with the views of their agencies (whenever one exists), prudence sets some limits to what can be said in a session where people from other agencies are present with whom one must cooperate in the future. We also said that we sought opinions on the merits of the legislation, not just on how best to implement it, but, again, some people may have felt they could not be very critical.

A moderator with a view: Resource constraints meant that only two people worked on the research, the present author and a research secretary. This forced some compromises to the ideal focus group script (see Chapter 1). Potentially the most serious compromise was that the moderator had known views on the subject, having published a report on the community service experiment covering some of the issues being presented to the panels for discussion (Takala 1993a; some of the pertinent issues are discussed in 1993b). The report criticised the risks to sentencing equality and proportionality brought by having only voluntary service hosts and suitability assessments geared to that system. It suggested relaxing the suitability selection or, alternatively, giving up the definite conversion rate between community service hours and prison days. The first alternative, the report admitted, might require that there be available other kinds of service hosts besides the present ones which are completely voluntary.

The presence of a moderator with a view presented a number of methodological problems to overcome. Some of the questions posed derived in part from the report. Most of the probation workers were aware of the report and the report was mentioned a number of times. To reduce the impact of these problems, I suggested to the panellists a number of possible angles to the argument, rather than speaking in defence of the report. Fortunately, the panellists were themselves skilled in bringing out diverse opinions in the debates.

An issue originally thought to be factual disagreement was satisfactorily clarified by the panel and instead was deemed to be a political question of preferences and frameworks of reference. Participants were unhappy with the suggestion made in the background paper that 'offenders selected to community service are somewhat better-off socially than those sentenced to comparable regular imprisonment', and went on to contend that many of these people were in fact quite unfortunate. I admitted that this was true, if compared to the population in general, but maintained that in the comparison mentioned, they were indeed better-off, although it might have been better to say, 'less badly-off'.

Background paper: A background paper was sent to the participants a few days before the sessions along with a letter that stated the purpose and form of the study in more general terms, as well as specifying the time and venue of the meeting. The paper summarised recent developments in the criminal justice system, particularly the new modes of punishment, and posed the following questions for consideration.

Was there any need for new forms of sanctions in the first place? By which criteria should one choose the form of punishment or determine the amount of punishment? How important is the blameworthiness of the offence and the culpability of the offender? To what extent may the individual characteristics of the offender influence the choice and grading of the sanction?

Following these questions, discussion themes were suggested. They dealt with goals of punishment, the placement of community service (and youth punishment) on the penal scale, selection of offenders for community service with respect to their social characteristics, offence type or other factors. The panellists were invited to include anything else about the penal system they would like to discuss. The themes presented were somewhat different from the Californian and English studies and this was due partly to the different political agendas. For instance, there was little perceived need for 'making community sentences more credible', at least in those terms. In Finland there is very limited experience of community sentences, and the existing community service order was credible in respects of the toughness with which the compliance of the offender was monitored and the swiftness with which breaches of the order lead to imprisonment.

Criminal justice officials' views of community sentences

The goals of community sentences

The first item in the background paper asked about the panellists' views on the goals of community sentences. The paper listed eleven sentencing goals. The panellists were asked to indicate whether or not they agreed or disagreed with any of the item as a possible goal and their responses are listed below.

Goals of community sentences

Items mentioned in the background paper	**Mentions Yes/no**
satisfaction of justice	7/0
reducing the detrimental effects of punishment	14/0
public censure of forbidden conduct	10/0
deterring potential offenders	1/4
warning and correcting an offender	3/1
atonement	10/2

a concrete restitution to society	4/1
controlling and reducing opportunities and temptations for crime	2/1
rehabilitation	12/1
providing sound and sensible experience for the offender	9/1
saving money	15/0

Items introduced by the panellists

educational influence	4/0
increasing the safety of society	2/0

It must be emphasised that these figures are a crude measure of opinions, because the response form was not standardised but depended on the vagaries of the flow of discussion in each session and because the classification of many items is open to differing interpretations. Nevertheless, it seems a reasonable starting point for an analysis of the discussion on the goals of community sanctions.

Many panellists defined the question more accurately for their own answer. There were also subtle differences regarding to whom they attributed the ownership of opinions given. Some opinions were given as if simply and uncomplicatedly their own views, or their views and those of the criminal justice community. Some others, in turn, were attributed to society at large, the legislature, or the law-drafters.

Some made a distinction between reasons for punishing in general and reasons for using community service or something like the proposed youth punishment in particular. It is noteworthy that the two items with the highest number of citations, i.e. saving money and reducing the detrimental effects of punishment, were often mentioned as reasons for just these new types of punishment. These were also important items in the public discussion on community service when it was introduced. Of these two reasons, reducing the detrimental effects of punishment was virtually always given as genuinely important, saving money sometimes just as an incidental gain. Some panellists also mentioned saving money as an important reason for the decision-makers, but made it clear that they did not share this view nor did they think it should be an important factor:

> If it is economic saving that controls some decisions, then there is no point talking about some issues; surely, issues should be decided regardless of that, and then there may be economic saving in them.

Several panellists made it clear that while community service was cheaper than imprisonment in principle, real savings would accrue only if it enabled closing down prison departments or saved building new ones. It might be worth remembering in this context, that prison overcrowding has not been an acute problem in Finland where prisoner rates have been falling since 1950.

Also frequently mentioned was the public censure of forbidden conduct or satisfaction of justice, which were spoken of as goals for any punishments, not particularly for community service or other community sanctions.

Atonement was another frequent item, and it requires a short comment. The word 'atonement' stands here for the Finnish 'sovitus', which, again, was used in the background paper for lack of a better term for 'retribution' (it is frequently so used in Finnish criminal justice textbooks, for instance, Nuutila, 1995). The comments on this item, however, were such that it seems best to render it in English with 'atonement' or 'reconciliation' rather than 'retribution'. Most of those panellists who went on to explain what aspects of atonement they thought important referred to the subjective feelings of the offender:

> Atonement is definitely present, but more so from the point of view of the offender.

> There is atonement. The offender feels he is doing meaningful work.

Some speakers saw atonement as a two-way interaction, or linked it to practical mediation or reconciliation, something that the Finnish word easily lends itself to.

> After a completed community service, we have a ceremony with coffee and cake. In the closing discussion I remind why this sentence was imposed and how society expresses its disapproval through the sentence and that one must not act like that, but that through this service you have expiated your offence for society. I think a human being must be given a chance to work for a clear balance sheet.

> Maybe atonement is involved in a way. One can hide inside a prison, but a community servant goes publicly even to a big work

> place, it is almost as though sitting in the stocks on the church hill.
>
> The biggest advantage is atonement, repairing for the offence in a different way. This will then be reflected as a reduction of the detrimental effects of punishments and as a concrete compensation to society, although it would be better if the victim got the compensation directly.

One person thought that atonement and punishment were contradictory terms:

> Atonement means reconciliation while with a punishment you really want to punish.

The relatively high number of panellists agreeing with the goal of rehabilitation is noteworthy, because the government bill introducing community service was rather cautious about possibilities of positive rehabilitation by means of community service and expressed rather more confident hopes about the indirect benefits of the avoidance of prison. It is, however, difficult to tell how many of the participants endorse the idea of positive rehabilitation through community service, instead of just the relative one compared to imprisonment. Although there definitely was some optimism:

> If one has problems with intoxicants and is tied to community service for four months and carries it out properly, it is bound to come out that his use of alcohol has diminished.

Another panellist pointed out that hopes of rehabilitation or offering constructive experience for the offender are not reasons for punishing in the first place, but it is easier to link such goals to community service and other proposed community sanctions than to other punishments. And then some panellists were quite self-consciously supporters of the rehabilitation idea:

> Most crimes are linked to social problems. A sanction should be individually preventive... I, for one, announce myself as an adherent of treatment ideas. The substance of punishment ought to be such that these problems could be sorted out... What is positive about community service is that one can attach supportive services

to it and incorporate a period of alcoholism treatment as part of the punishment, even if only cautiously.

Although this particular opinion was not directly challenged in the session, there were explicit critiques of treatment ideology in other meetings. 'It is not any business of the court to order someone to treatment', said one panellist.

In a context such as this, many panellists remarked that there had been some movement in the prevailing penal philosophy from exclusive concentration on the offence to a view that paid more attention to the individual characteristics of the offender. This development was usually cited approvingly although some added that it should be properly related to the principles of proportionality and equality in sentencing.

The only item receiving more negative than positive mentions was 'deterring potential offenders'. A police officer quipped that it had been included as an undeclared test for the panellists: find the item that does not belong in this collection.

Controlling and reducing opportunities and temptations for crime was mentioned explicitly only by three panellists. Two held that this was a possible outcome:

> Doing something sensible can reduce temptations of crime, one may even get a job through community service.

> If you are booked up in the evenings or weekends even the time available for lawbreaking becomes less.

The third panellist who did not think community sanctions had much of this effect compared it explicitly with prison, which more radically cuts down on one's chances for offending. However, there was some additional discussion and disagreement about the incapacitative effect of community service in the sessions. A few panellists suspected that offenders would go on offending while under community service order, and certainly there are cases when this has happened. Suspicions also arise that there are cases where an offender doing his service may have provided information to others about goods worth stealing. On the other hand, there was some agreement that the structure that community service brings into one's weekly schedule may help some offenders to better keep to the straight and narrow.

A number of panellists mentioned 'education' as a goal and they emphasised the moral aspects of education, such as learning a work ethic, or elementary self-discipline:

> While in prison, one does not have to take any responsibility. When one has to go twice a week in the evening [to do one's community service], one must really discipline oneself.

Another panellist, however, saw a certain irony here:

> It is ridiculous to put a country farmer to work as he is working all the time anyway. There is no need to readjust him to society... It is most urgent to do it with a youngster who has never learned to work or take responsibility... Community service has been a punishment for drunk drivers because there are so many of them. If one is not allowed to put young people to this, there are few alternatives.

Two participants, both probation workers, formulated another goal that was not included in the background paper (although similar ideas were expressed in California and England with regard to community sentences). Community service, when used instead of imprisonment, was seen as something that made society safer by preventing defiance, or at least by not helping defiance grow:

> There will be less people who come out of the prison bitter, frustrated and dangerous.

Community sentences and the severity scale

The current experimental legislation stipulates that community service be used only in cases which otherwise would attract an unconditional prison sentence. The questions dealing with this placement aroused much discussion. Most panellists believe that community service is quite a bit easier than unconditional imprisonment. Some judges and prosecutors pleaded ignorance on this matter saying as they did not know in detail how community service orders were carried out, they did not really know about the severity scale. Several panellists brought to the fore that some people they knew think that community service is too lenient compared to the imprisonment it allegedly replaces.

> I've heard the police say that the defendant gets off too easy; I do not completely agree myself.

> When I present to the lay members of the court that this implies forty hours of community service in lieu of forty days of prison, they say, 'So little! That's only one week of eight-hour days and that's it.' I do not know enough to be able to tell them how it is actually carried out.

This prompted the probation workers to explain about the practical running of community service orders.

> Usually it is twice a week, 3-4 hours each time. We need the approval of the central office (of Probation and Aftercare Association) if we were to suggest that someone would do more than four hours at a time, there is no intention that the hours would be cleared fast, say within two weeks, and then a pause kept. We have a worker standing-by at any one time someone has a service hour scheduled, even at nights and during weekends. We have a mobile telephone to which the host organisation calls if the person does not appear as scheduled. If such a call comes in, our worker goes right then to the person's home address to see what the problem might be. Although they don't stay home, if they have gone on a binge, as one person stated in a literary treatise: 'you don't think I would be as crazy as that, that's the first place the probation worker turns up to'.

Absence due to drinking leads to a written warning the first time. The second time, it usually leads to a revocation of the community service order and to an enforcement of the original prison sentence (subtracted by the equivalence of the completed community service hours). The organisation of the community sentence in Finland, and the way in which the probation workers supervise it, seems to avoid some of the potential credibility problems that its English counterpart currently faces.

There were arguments saying that 'in some cases' defendants had felt that they would rather take imprisonment than community service:

> This person who had a positive suitability report said he prefers going to prison.

Similarly, it was portrayed how the schedule imposed by the community service order would be tough for many offenders.

> There is this boy whose order is the maximum, 200 hours. He must be there in the service location twice every week for eight months. Seems easy to us, we use a diary anyway. These people don't have diaries. Some of them say, it's a pity it isn't every day, one could be sober. A 30 day prison sentence, it means only two weeks in practice. Community service is not much easier.

One person from a disabled persons' home that served as a host to community service offenders said that her colleagues had thought community service had first considered community service as easy. However, on meeting people doing community service, they came to appreciate that it was not always easy for them.

> It can be a terrible punishment. They cannot hang around the city with their buddies, they cannot go for a cider, they cannot do most anything, they have to refashion their whole life because of those two days.

There were, however, also mentions of community service being easier for those without a work than for the employed:

> For persons without work or work history it makes no difference where you spend your day, community service affects people in different ways.

Also there were several persons who were satisfied with referring to what the current law stated: community service and imprisonment are set on a par, treating them otherwise would imply changing the law. Others seemed prepared to do just that.

The panellists were also asked whether it is necessary that the legislature fix the conversion rates between community service and imprisonment, or could one allow these things to be settled with time in the court practice. Most speakers seemed to be happy with the fact that there is a common conversion table. Otherwise 'uniformity of sentencing would be jeopardised'. Others, however, suggested mixed systems, in which the conversion rates were partly set nationally and partly by any given court.

Overall, while most agreed that community service was a more lenient sanction it was not as lenient as one would think just by looking at the conversion rates, especially if the details of implementation are taken into account. Probation officials, in particular, emphasised that community service restricted the freedom of the offender for a longer period of time than an actual imprisonment, which is shortened by routine parole. This observation lead to an idea in an early focus group session which was then tested in later ones: what if a 60 hour community service order was labelled as a 60 *day* community service sentence, since this is what it meant, doing work twice a week, 3-4 hours a time, for the duration of two months. This suggestion was usually met with moderate approval, although some problems were observed with such an arrangement.
Overall, although they had different ideas about what it meant, most panellists tended to think that community service 'really' is somewhere between unconditional imprisonment and a conditional sentence, in terms of punitiveness. In assessing this they were not different from the general public, whose opinions on sentencing happened to be gauged before and after the introduction of community service. Support for community service as a suitable punishment for a repeat burglar increased considerably during this time, but the increase derived mainly from fines and conditional punishment, not unconditional imprisonment as the official placement would have it (see Table 4.5 in the conclusion of Chapter 4).

Community sentences as alternatives to unconditional sentences?

I have argued elsewhere that it seems likely that a great majority of Finnish community service orders replace unconditional prison sentences, as was intended by the legislation (Takala, 1993a, pp. 115-128). Nevertheless, the result is somewhat speculative and the issue is a complicated one, and it is interesting to learn what the focus groups thought.

Is community service in reality ordered only instead of unconditional imprisonment? The participants were of the opinion that it is used as the law says, i.e. instead of the unconditional sentence. Particularly they said that they themselves, if they were judges or prosecutors, worked with this in mind. However, several of them were able to tell of cases in which someone else had intended to use community service as an alternative to a conditional sentence.

For instance, a prosecutor told of a case in which the court asked her to acquire a suitability assessment. She argued that the case only merited a conditional sentence and said she would go to the court of appeal if an unconditional sentence was given (even if that be in the form of a community service order). The court handed down a conditional prison sentence.

> They had not internalised that community service is a punishment to be used instead of an unconditional sentence, not of a conditional one.

Most probably there are many similar cases in which nobody intervened and community service was imposed when it otherwise would have resulted in a conditional sentence. Another close call:

> There was this case that almost certainly would have been a community service if the offender had been willing and suitable, but now it turned into a conditional sentence.

Hence, one can surmise that in this case the real choice was made directly between a community service order and a conditional (suspended) sentence. This is materially in conflict with the official rules that require - as mentioned above - that a choice be made between conditional and unconditional imprisonment as if the community service option did not exist. Only at a later stage, provided that the outcome of the earlier deliberation was an 'unconditional prison sentence', would the court consider commuting it into community service. When the result of cases like this is community service, one can say that community service is in fact given as an alternative to a conditional (suspended) sentence, not unconditional imprisonment. The written verdict would, of course, still claim that an unconditional prison sentence was handed down and the community service order was then given in its lieu. One could say that this would be a 'pre-adjustment' of the initial sentence. However, not all 'pre-adjustments' of the background sentence (anticipating a community service order) need go in the direction of more severity. For instance, a case was mentioned in which 'in all probability' the initial sentence was made slightly shorter in order to fit it within the eight month limit for community service.

The difficulty of spontaneously seeing community service as an alternative to imprisonment was a theme in many contributions by the panellists:

When this started you had to consciously suppress your idea...Very easily you might slip into thinking like this. If this system were not available, it would be a conditional, but as it is such a fine treatment mode, you would want to give a service sentence, you wouldn't dream of giving an unconditional one.

Also, most participants who thought it important that the present community service replaces unconditional sentences said that they considered the unconditional sentence to be more severe. In practice, this issue became critical when sentencing repeat offenders, particularly persons who had been sentenced to community service earlier. This issue caused some debate in at least two sessions, as the following illustrates:

A: I've once sentenced a person to community service for a second time...There was nothing in the government bill that would have precluded this.

B: Can it be considered suitable for you if it does not stop you leading a criminal life?

A: How about prison, if that does not help either?

B: It does for the duration, and it is clearly a punishment.

A: Well, if you commit a crime during a community service, there are specific articles applicable to that...Anyway, the bill said nothing about precluding repeated sentencing to community service.

B: Yes, but one must make use of the general reasoning principles.

There was one type of opinion that was satisfied with citing the present legislation and its motivation to the effect that community service was set at an equal penal value with unconditional imprisonment and that hence there was no problem in sentencing an offender repeatedly to community service, particularly if that person had managed it well. Others harked back to how they felt the true penal value of community service was and did not think it 'morally right', as one put it, to give community service orders time and time again. Some persons presented arguments in favour of both views, saying, for instance, that in principle repeat sentencing to community service is fine although they do have second thoughts with some offenders, particularly if they seem to have too good a time doing their service.

> It sometimes occurs to me that I give a 'hardened' community service, meaning that I discuss the issue firmly with the person and explain that all prison sentences will not automatically be commuted to community service.

It seems then that the criminal law officials have learned to live with the present community service system. Although most of them spontaneously feel that community service and its official prison equivalent are not really equal, they usually seem to have little problem with going by that formula in their work. Problems emerge in cases of repeat offending, and only a few judges or prosecutors embraced the view that commuting imprisonment to community service time and time again was a good idea.

Decision process with community service sentencing

In reaching a decision to give a community service sentence, the first step, theoretically, is the choice between a prison sentence or non-prison sentence. Secondly, if imprisonment, then to decide between unconditional and conditional (suspended imprisonment), and only then, if an unconditional sentence was chosen, between community service and regular imprisonment.

One judge said that this is at least the public manner of consideration when he deliberates the sentence together with the lay members of the court:

> Community service is not talked about; one looks at what the punishment would be, what the criminal record shows and others. And only when the length of the prison sentence is being estimated, this option is laid on the table, by the way, there is this community service option, you know, perhaps we will look up the conversion table and see how it comes out.

Some participants, however, strongly insisted that community service should be an independent punishment:

> I feel community service should be recognised as an independent punishment, not an alternative to another. It is somewhat strange to

> think that an unconditional prison sentence can be exchanged to another punishment more agreeable to the offender, such as community service or some treatment. Community service is an independent punishment that can be handed down under certain conditions.

Not suitable for community service or prison: Offenders selected to do community service are socially somewhat less 'badly off' than those sentenced to comparable regular imprisonment. The agency conducting the suitability assessments (the Probation and Aftercare Association) is expected to pay attention to circumstances that could obstruct the carrying out of a community service order but are preventable by social welfare measures. These can range from alcoholism treatment (in Finland mostly under the social welfare authorities) to providing a city council day-care placement for a child whose mother needs to do her community service. Even allowing some success to these measures, the problem is likely to remain, as many panellists said. An equality problem exists with the present community service system, as those found unsuitable for community service often ended up with a tougher punishment. New ways to alleviate the problem were sought in the sessions.

> We ought to think of ways of compensating to those offenders who cannot be sentenced to community service.

This problem might be visible at every actual short imprisonment, independent of why this particular sentence was not commuted into community service, but many speakers seemed to think of certain particularly pitiable types of offenders. For instance, good workmen that every now and then happened to drink for a period of a few days, and who could surely deliver the number of hours required but not necessarily as scheduled. Or they would be persons who had mental problems that made them unsuitable for community service 'but who were not suitable for prison either'.

One line of thought that was explored was other forms of community service that could accommodate persons that voluntary hosts were reluctant to take.

> Maybe the government could create work for these, such as cleaning up woods, or other closely supervised menial tasks.

Another idea was just relaxing the schedules so that persons who had trouble keeping timetables on a sustained basis could manage. These ideas were, however, not supported by everyone. Many panellists thought that one ought not to risk the relatively tough reputation that the present system has among those familiar with it, as revealed in these three comments.

> You could develop it along those lines, but we don't want to create too much burden on the contact persons of the service host organisations. I don't believe we can keep those hosts if they're asked, 'It's OK if I turn up next week, isn't it?'

> Community Service is a clear sanction, one ought to develop others for persons who cannot manage it. If drinking precludes use of community service, then we should provide options that include treatment.

> Too casual enforcement would not be a good idea, it would make it even more lenient. I don't think you could sell this idea, 'come as you please', revoking community service must be clear-cut, there is a warning and then, after another violation, you are off to a prison.

In particular, several probation workers clearly supported the adoption of a sanction that would include some treatment, such as counselling for drinking problems. (Even now, since a 1994 amendment of the Community Service Act, five hours of a community service order can be spent using alcoholism treatment services.) At least two panellists also opined that sentencing to treatment would be an appropriate alternative for many offenders with 'diminished responsibility' by reason of mental disorder. These treatment ideas did not usually meet any specific opposition in the meetings, although there were a few persons who said they did not think the court should involve itself with treatment or therapy.

Many panellists then felt uneasiness about the equation between imprisonment and community service in two particular situations: when coming across with the question of repeat community service orders and when seeing persons who had to be sent to prison because some sad eventuality tended to designate them as unsuitable for community service. Some ways to deal with these problems were explored, the most general ones being 'learning to live with it' and 'compensating it for those who cannot go to community service'. The latter option elicits this follow-up idea (which did not come up in the sessions). It is conceivable that if community service becomes the normal punishment for certain offences, the remaining actual imprisonments will be gauged through the service alternative and be made shorter. If this happens, community service would have helped reduce imprisonment in two ways, by replacing some prison sentences and by reducing the length of others.

Conditional prison sentence

The conditional sentence was discussed at every session, and always it drew only criticism.

> You give routinely a conditional sentence in these cases, the person goes home pleased, says 'I got nothing', tears to pieces the fine ticket and goes on offending.

> Young persons don't consider repeated conditional sentences at all as punishments. They say 'well it is only a period of time, it does not hurt you'.

However, since the conditional sentence was not presented as an independent theme for discussion, its condemnation may not be as cut and dried as that. It emerged most often in the context of sentences available for young people, and compounded with discussions of the youth sentence. The most unanimous message, probably, was that compared to the conditional sentence, the proposed youth sentence was a good step forward. Simultaneously, however, the panellists were worried about the plans (included in the bill on youth punishment) to drop the supervision of young offenders who are given a conditional sentence. As the youth punishment was meant only for offenders under 18 years of age, this would have implied that for the age bracket 18-20 there would in fact be a smaller selection of concrete community sanctions available.

The target population for community service

The panellists did not usually complain about the fact that the Community Service Act treated this punishment as neutral towards different offence types and offenders (other than requiring that they be capable of carrying it out). A few cited this fact with approval and none suggested that it be changed.

> A: My opinion is that community service is appropriate for drunk drivers and property offenders, but in an assault case, if it is even slightly more aggravated, I find community service unfair.

However, this might have been a case dealing more with a need to mark punitiveness more generally than just in cases of violent offences. This opinion was immediately challenged:

> B: I would say, based on experience, that very seldom a sober man hits another...In principle, one could impose community service even ten times in a row, if it is carried out every time.
>
> A: but if you take a moral point of view...
>
> C: and think of public opinion
>
> A: Is it sufficient as a punishment?
>
> B: when the law on community service was written, it was, after all, an alternative to imprisonment, in no way is it more lenient.

The probation workers asserted that, in preparing suitability reports or assigning persons to carry out their service, they did not pay undue attention to the specific needs and wishes of the available community service hosts. A general ability to manage was what they were testing. Once this threshold was passed, they would usually rather easily find a host for the service. Some hosts, they admitted, were wary of offenders other than drunk drivers, but with time even these could be coaxed into taking property offenders.

The probation workers also strongly supported that a suitability assessment be made. They usually also thought it is placed in the right place in the process. When it takes place before trial, as the system now normally has it, the offender is more motivated to do the service than he would be if it were presented to him only after the trial.

The panellists who addressed this issue were rather unanimous that drunk drivers more often than other offenders truly met the suitability criteria for community service. This, combined with their great numbers, was the explanation for their major representation in community service. This in itself was not considered a problem, the problem was too few offenders from other crime categories. Several persons spoke of conscious efforts to see that for instance more property offenders are adequately considered for community service.

> Like many other judges, I started with drunk drivers. Later on, we've made attempts with property offenders as well.

The use of community service in Finnish law is bound only to the blameworthiness of the offence, and it is not meant to be preferred or avoided based on offence category. Nevertheless, a great majority (75 per cent) of those ordered to community service have been drunk drivers.

In 1991, a community service order was handed down in about 15 per cent of the cases which were eligible, based on the severity of the parent sentence, i.e. unconditional prison sentences of eight months or less. There are big differences between districts. Two meetings were held in the areas Rovaniemi and Mikkeli where the utilisation is over 50 per cent. The panellists from these districts did not believe that there could have been eligible cases that would not have been properly considered for community service. Overall, the sessions could not bring up any simple solution to why community service numbers were lower than seemed technically possible. Its novelty as well as the experimental status of community service were cited as possible reasons that discouraged some prosecutors and judges from using it. Some prosecutors claimed they routinely sent every conceivable case to suitability assessment, and this may indeed apply to those prosecutors who were present in the focus group sessions.

Conclusion

The views of the panellists in the focus groups in Finland indicate a strong commitment to community service, in contrast to the more ambivalent situation in California and England. There is less concern about community service being regarded as a soft option in Finland, in contrast to the other two jurisdictions. And in fact, conditional sentences drew significantly more criticism on the grounds of softness. The standing of community service is due in part to its relative toughness in comparison with the imposition and enforcement of conditional sentences in Finland.

An international crime survey were carried out in 15 countries in 1989 and 13 in 1992 (Europe, including England and Finland, and some other countries, Australia, Canada, Japan, New Zealand and the USA). The survey asked respondents about their experiences of crime in the year prior to the survey. Samples of about 2,000 respondents were taken in each country. Between the two rounds of the international crime survey (van Dijk, Mayhew, 1993), the Finnish respondents grew more supportive of the community service order as a punishment when asked what type of sentence they would regard as suitable for a 21-year-old male repeat burglar who steals a television set.

Table 4.5 Popularity of sentences in Finland

	1989 %	1992 %
Fine	18.9	12.7
Prison	15.0	13.5
Community service	36.8	55.9
Suspended (conditional) service	21.6	11.2
Other punishment	4.7	3.1
Don't know	3.1	3.6

Table compiled from: Aromaa, K. (1993), *Understanding Crime: Experiences of Crime and Crime Control*, p. 529: Aromaa, K. and Kinnunen, A. (1995), *Two Country Reports from the 1989 International Crime Survey: Finland and Norway*, p. 139.

The increase in the proportion of those who regarded community service as the most suitable sentence, 36.8 per cent to 55.9 per cent, shows a strengthening of support for community service between 1989 and 1992. The same question elicited a fall in those who thought the fine was appropriate, 18.9 per cent to 12.7 per cent and, most significantly, shows a fall from, 21.6 per cent to 11.2 per cent, of those who thought the conditional sentence was most appropriate. The shift in approval for community sentences suggests that many people who previously would have agreed with the imposition of a conditional sentence or fine would agree now to the imposition of a community sentence.

This trend in part reflects the anxiety shown in focus group discussions that in the case of a conditional sentence, in effect, nothing happens to the offender, they 'get off'. This might have played a part in explaining the increased public support for community service and suggests a role for community service as an intermediate sanction, a sanction between imprisonment and effectively the fine in Finland. Of course this role for community service will conflict with its role as an alternative to custody in which it is considered equivalent to prison for those sentenced up to eight months in prison. It will be difficult to reconcile the two in a jurisdiction with a long history of commitment to proportionality in sentencing.

Even if the place of community service in the severity ladder may remain unstable, the available evidence would point to the conclusion that community sentences as such in Finland have the support of, and credibility with, criminal justice officials and the general public.

5 Penological Esperanto and Sentencing Parochialism: Convergence and Divergence in Sentencing Policy

MALCOLM DAVIES

This book has looked at the response of officials in the criminal justice system to the idea of community sentences in three jurisdictions. Our research points to some common themes in the intellectual development of the reforms and some major departures between them. This final chapter will examine the themes of universalism, convergence and divergence in sentencing policy.

New ideas in sentencing and penal policy spread rapidly between jurisdictions. When discussing matters of sentencing reforms, experts from different countries across the western world seem to speak in the same language at the same time - a penological version of Esperanto. However, this convergence in penal thinking does not extend into the implementation stage. Sentencing policies and practices take a more diverse course as they respond to the parochial influences of local systems of criminal justice and different cultural, political and economic contexts.

Of course it must be understood that within each jurisdiction there is never a complete harmony of view or consensus of opinion about sentencing issues. Nonetheless, it is possible to present a version of the dominant penal paradigms that exist in the different jurisdictions without resorting to the impression that there is a single or coherent view of sentencing philosophy. It is apparent to anyone engaged in the field of sentencing policy that there are differences in interpretation and disagreements as to the objectives of penal policy within a jurisdiction. We need also to take account of the fluidity of sentencing policies and philosophies which are not static but, rather, constantly being re-appraised and reformulated.

The continuous re-examination and reconstruction of sentencing principles seems to be an inevitable feature of sentencing discourse in democratic societies. This dynamic feature of sentencing needs to be understood before the policy concerns about certainty and fairness in sentencing can be dealt with. The advantages of a culturally sensitive approach to this issue has been the methodological theme of this book. This aspect will be included in the factors examined in this chapter which endeavours to isolate the convergent and divergent influences on matters of sentencing policy and practice.

Comparing the similarities and differences between criminal justice systems, Knut Sveri suggests that the apparent differences between the continental traditions of Europe and Scandinavia and the common-law countries such as England and North American states are not so easy to detect when we look at the type of behaviour criminalised. He says, 'if a person does something which is considered to be a crime in Sweden, it will practically always be considered to be a crime in New York'. Secondly, he points out that the types of sanctions imposed on offenders are very similar, except for the use of the death penalty in some states of the USA. He recognises that when we look at the role of the criminal justice agencies and criminal procedure that greater diversity becomes apparent. However, it is when we start comparing sentencing practice and how the sentences are executed that we find real differences between the systems. (Sveri, 1990, p. 12)

This chapter begins with the assumption that there is some validity in the thesis that cross-jurisdictional and universal influences do result in a remarkably similar but not identical range of penal sanctions, i.e. a convergence on *the modes of punishment*. However, more parochial factors are at work when we look at the way officials and sentencers in different jurisdictions use these penal sanctions in practice, i.e. a divergence in *the distribution of punishment*.

Universalism and convergence

Over the last hundred years, common orientations across jurisdictions have been apparent in the response to crime across a number of western jurisdictions with respect to sentencing and penal policy, most notably: offender-instrumental sentencing, the revival of offence-focused sentencing, the growth of community sanctions, the prison reductionist movement, and a systems approach to sentencing policy.

Offender-instrumental sentencing: At the end of the 19th century and the first half of the 20th century, offender-instrumental theories of sentencing became fashionable. Patrik Törnudd comments, 'During the first half of this century many European countries experienced an ideological shift from a classical ideology based on retribution and deterrence towards penal philosophies based on treatment and rehabilitation' (Törnudd, 1993, p. 3).

Similarities and parallels with developments across other jurisdictions are very apparent in this comment on sentencing reforms in Sweden:

> A hundred years ago, the general penalties of the Swedish Penal Code (1864) were restricted to capital punishment, fines, and two forms of determinate incarceration, one for longer sentences (penal labour) and one for shorter sentences (imprisonment)....The first decade of the twentieth century witnessed the reluctant and cautious introduction of legal measures based on preventive considerations: compulsory education for criminals aged 15-17 years (1902), the suspended sentence (1906), and parole (1906). The so-called day-fine system was adopted in 1931....indeterminate incarceration for young offenders in 1935. The English borstal system served as a model for the latter sanction. (Jareborg, 1995, p. 95)

The move towards offender-instrumental theories of sentencing found in the first half of the 20th century in California, England, and the rest of Scandinavia was to reach Finland too late to become established in the way that it had in other countries. The influence of cross-jurisdictional ideas on sentencing is apparent in this extract from Patrik Törnudd:

> This reorientation reached Finland in the 1930s and 1940s but the war years and the opposition by influential old-school experts slowed down the process. While neighbouring Sweden wholeheartedly accepted the rehabilitation ideology in the 1940s and 1950s, the Finns did not seriously begin to reform the criminal justice system before the 1960s. But then it was too late for the rehabilitation ideology to become dominant. The wave of criticism against the ideology of coercive treatment of offenders had at that time already reached Finland. We had learned that treatment institutions are not necessarily more humane than prisons and that sophisticated, controlled experimental studies did not usually demonstrate any dramatic crime-reducing effect of coercive treatment. As the new generation of criminologists and reform-oriented lawyers were the first to adopt this critical stance against the idea of coercive

treatment, the slow move towards a Swedish style correctional philosophy stopped altogether. (Törnudd, 1993, p. 3)

In more recent years we have seen the cross-jurisdictional consequences as countries adapted to new post-1960 orthodoxies in response to the failure of rehabilitative sentencing strategies in general, and the particularly noticeable failure of prisons to correct criminal conduct. The concern with sentencing disparities and the subsequent introduction of a variety of sentencing reforms to achieve greater uniformity indicated a shift in penal rationales from offender-instrumental theories, such as deterrence and rehabilitation, to just deserts. It was an approach which incorporated, for the first time, a higher profile for the civil rights of prisoners and also generate a greater concern for the rights of the victim. But most of all it was an approach which shifted the focal concern of sentencing away from the idea that the offender was of primary concern, to a view in which it was the offence that was paramount and its ranking was measured in terms of seriousness (just deserts) or reprehensibility (denunciation).

Revival of offence-focused sentencing: The dominant penal paradigm in many jurisdictions in recent decades has shifted to reflect a disillusionment with rehabilitative strategies and a greater emphasis given to just deserts. Tony Bottoms comments, 'In many jurisdictions, ranging from Scandinavia to the United Kingdom to the United States, the theory of just deserts has had substantial influence, and that influence is seen especially when one compares present philosophies and practices with those adopted by many countries in the early post-war year period.' (Bottoms, 1995, p. 22).

The spread of cross-jurisdictional penal ideas was commented upon in the British Government's publication, *Crime, Justice and Protecting the Public*, 1990. With respect to just deserts, the Home Office publication noted the universal trend of common law countries to move towards sentencing policies based on just deserts. 'Other common law jurisdictions, for example, in the United States, Canada and Australia are moving in this direction or are thinking of doing so' (Home Office, 1990, p. 5).

Cross-jurisdictional similarities can also be recognised in this list compiled by Raimo Lahti of trends in Finnish criminal policy since the 1960s:

> Criticism of so-called treatment ideology (c. the 1960s); emphasis on cost-benefit thinking (c. the beginning of the 1970s); the so-called neo-classicalism in criminal law (c. the end of the 1970s and the beginning of the 1980s); pragmatic reform work by utilising modified ideas of the above-mentioned movements (the 1980s). (Lahti, 1989, p. 65)

Trends in the 1980s and 1990s have reflected the growing concern with the cost of imprisonment and the undesirable consequences that prisons have on inmates in terms of making them more, rather than less, likely to re-offend: a message that has been successfully repeated in Europe, if not in the USA. A number of policy experts such as Andrew Rutherford and UK pressure groups, such as NACRO and the Howard League, argued for a reduction in the penal population. The prison reductionist movement was influential in the UK and Scandinavia and gave rise to the search for community sanctions as either alternatives to prison or as intermediate sanctions.

Community sanctions: Since the 1970s we have seen a number of jurisdictions, most noticeably in the USA and Europe, moving towards a policy of greater use of community sentences. In the United States the spread of community corrections legislation across the state-based penal codes of the US was commented upon in a National Institute of Justice publication. 'Eighteen states currently operate under Community Corrections Legislation - significant growth since 1973 when Minnesota adopted the first Community Corrections Act' (National Institute of Justice, 1993, p. 68).

The extracts quoted in the introduction to this book, taken from the reports published in 1990 in California and England, illustrate the universalism and convergence in thinking with regard to the case for community sentences as intermediate sanctions. These two reports (published within ten days of each other), share several common penological themes and conclusions, despite coming from jurisdictions 6,000 miles apart. Both these official publications showed that the hunt was on for a secondary sanction which would not replace imprisonment but would provide a step in the hierarchy of penalties available to the courts, and which would function as an intermediate punishment. Both reports targeted prison-bound inmate populations, focusing on property offenders, and effectively highlighted the issue of what to do with persistent thieves and burglars if we did not send them to prison. These reports stressed the need for new sentencing options which could be regarded as punishment, while recognising the failure of imprisonment in deterrent and rehabilitative terms. Commenting on developments in Europe, Inkeri Anttila writes:

> Community service, which is a fashionable matter in some European countries, is being experimented with at the moment in Denmark and Norway. In both Finland and Sweden the problems that are seen to be involved in community service include not only the practical difficulties in arranging for the necessary organisation and in finding suitable jobs, but the theory of the matter. (Anttila, 1986, p. 45)

The need for a theory to locate community sentences within a framework which relates them in a plausible way is important for their credibility. This absence of a sentencing logic, other than to avoid net widening might help to understand the comments we heard in the focus groups in Finland. The problem in England relates to the confusion that emerges from the conflicting perspectives as to whether community sanctions are primarily a form of rehabilitation or a punishment.

Prison reductionists: The prison reductionist arguments have been heard repeatedly, and clearly, in many jurisdictions. Ulla Bondeson's comment, on the Scandinavian policy experts' commitment to the prison reductionist viewpoint, is a good example of penological Esperanto:

> In the Scandinavian countries there has been a political awareness that prisons are not working according to the legal doctrines of prevention. Many official committees have declared that correctional institutions are not correcting. During the last 20 years declarations have accordingly been made that since prisons are not effective the use of imprisonment should be reduced...The trend, however, has not been towards a decreased use of imprisonment but rather the contrary. In the Scandinavian countries, as in most other western countries, we have seen a tendency to an increase in incarceration. Finland has been the only exception. (Bondeson, 1990, p. 19)

The above extract is not only a good example of penological Esperanto, as the policy experts agree on a common view, but also reveals the influence of other, more divergent influences, as Sweden's prison population goes up at a time when Finland's is going down. However, the reductionist message is well established, if amended to: if prisons work at all, it is not to rehabilitate or deter those who are sent to them.

The prison reductionist message of the failure of imprisonment, in offender-instrumental terms, has given a fillip to the search for non-custodial sentences and more use of community corrections that can widen the range of sentences available to the courts. The emphasis in Scandinavia in general, and Finland in particular, as shown by our research, is that whereas the policy makers accepted that imprisonment was unlikely to deter or rehabilitate offenders, they did not seek an intermediate sanction: between prison and other sentences, but an alternative to custody, so as to avoid net widening. Community sanctions were sought in Finland to increase sentencing choice, but only in lieu of imprisonment.

In the UK there has been a number of changes in the declared role of community sentences. Initially the community service order was presented as an alternative to custody, but later policy documents identify it as an intermediate sanction. A struggle still exists in the UK as to whether community sentences should be used for rehabilitative purpose or as a punishment. Changes in official policy statements have also varied as to the role of imprisonment. Home Secretaries from Roy Jenkins' days in the 1960s had repeated the prison reductionist message. This was true of Home Secretaries from both political parties. In the early 1980s the message was the same, despite coming from a Conservative Government, elected in 1979 on a strong law and order manifesto. William Whitelaw, the Home Secretary, commented in a speech to Leicester magistrates in 1981:

> Hopes for a sustained reduction in the prison population must, in my view, rest primarily on a renewed commitment to avoiding custody wherever possible and, in cases where imprisonment is thought essential, a move towards shorter sentences for all except the violent offender. I must emphasise that the case for change in these directions does not rest solely on the crisis in the prison system, grave though it is. There are also important considerations of

> principle which reflect a significant shift in penological thinking over the last decade or so. (Quoted in A. Rutherford, 1988, p. 98)

However, a swing in opinion became apparent in the UK when Michael Howard, the Home Secretary, told the Conservative Party Conference in October 1993, 'Let us be clear. Prison works. It ensures that we are protected from murderers, muggers and rapists - and it makes many who are tempted to commit crime think twice'.

Systems approach to sentencing: It was almost certainly the cost and the numbers going through the courts and the prisons that turned policy makers' attention in the 1980s to the concern to better understand the decision-making process that led to incarceration. The growth in managerialism became more obvious in official documents with the mandatory initial aim of mission statements to making maximum and efficient use of the resources spent by public agencies. The taxpayers' revolt in California and a similar development in the UK made public-bodies more cost conscious than was apparent in previous decades. In the UK and in California the private sector was brought in to run prisons and accountants became more influential in the administration of criminal justice agencies.

The awareness that prisons were costly and, if the prison reductionist claim is correct, largely ineffective institutions, forced planners and budgetary experts to analyse the ways of controlling this expensive aspect of public policy. In an early example of the influence of resources on sentencing policy, the Minnesota Sentencing Commission set up in 1980, which pioneered the idea of the sentencing grid to reduce sentencing disparities, included a constraint on sentence lengths in that overall prison terms had to be compatible with the existing state prison population.

Most jurisdictions were unwilling to take such a direct approach to the resource implications of the activities of sentencers, sensitive to the criticism of interfering with the independence of the judiciary. Both in California and the UK , as shown in Chapters 2 and 3, the development of systems awareness came to be a new direction in sentencing statements. In fact a recognition that the judges were part of a wider criminal justice system, and that the agencies in that system were interdependent as the suspect became the accused, then defendant, then inmate or client of the system. In the same speech to the Leicester magistrates in 1981, William

Whitelaw illustrated this new appreciation of the systems nature of justice with regard to the problems of managing overcrowded prisons:

> There is no easy way of funding a solution through more prison spaces. We must look to the criminal justice system as a whole, of which the prison system is an integral part. And in so doing, we must look at the sentencing practice which, directly and indirectly, produces the prison population. (Quoted in A. Rutherford, 1988, p. 101)

Some scholars see this concern with planning, resource management and systems analysis as reflecting a new penology (Feeley and Simon, 1992) that moves away from the concern of classical criminal law and the desire to punish and the offender-instrumental desire to change the offender. The task is managerial, not transformative. A central feature of the 'new discourse' is the replacement of a moral or clinical description of the individual with an actuarial language of probability (p. 452). 'It is concerned with the rationality not of individual behaviour or even community organisation but of managerial processes. Its goal is not to eliminate crime but to make it tolerable through systemic coordination' (Feeley and Simon, 1992, p. 455). Within this perspective Feeley and simon discuss community sanctions:

> From the perspective of the new penology, the growth of community corrections in the shadow of imprisonment is not surprising. The new penology does not regard prison as a special institution capable of making a difference in the individuals who pass through it. Rather it functions as but one of several custodial options. Thus, community-based sanctions can be understood in terms of risk management rather than rehabilitative or correctional aspirations. Rather than instruments of reintegrating offenders into the community, they function as mechanisms to maintain control (often through frequent drug testing) over low-risk offenders for whom the more secure forms of custody are judged too expensive or unnecessary. (Feeley and Simon, 1992, pp. 460-461)

Whether these resource and management concerns represent a 'new penology', or they are an extension of the inevitable concern with fiscal constraint that has become highlighted by the growth in cost of prisons and the doubts about its efficacy. Certainly true, however, is the cross-jurisdictional evidence that many official agencies are no longer bound by the taboo that sentencing is a matter solely for the judges and that there is a willingness to analyse sentencing and penal policy within the context of a system of criminal justice.

Universalism

How might we explain the spread of ideas about sentencing policy and the cross-jurisdictional convergence of policy debates?

A number of factors are at work encouraging penal policy makers to keep a look out for innovations in sentencing policy from other jurisdictions. These factors could include: similar problems with public concerns about rising crime; a frustration with the effectiveness of the present system; electoral and political pressure to appear to be doing something about crime; the rising costs and fiscal implications of the system; the optimism of those who search for the latest way to curb, cure, or eradicate crime; and not forgetting the cadre of policy thinkers in academic and government circles whose job it is to be first with the forecast of the shifts in the penal breeze.

International contacts: Carrying penological knowledge beyond jurisdictional boundaries into international settings is more evident in the 20th century. The age of modernity is defined by some in terms of the globalisation of knowledge. There is a growth of international conferences, symposiums, sabbaticals and international journals amongst academics and greater contact between officials, policy makers, politicians and journalists. The modern world is a smaller one in the sense of meeting people and exchanging information. The reference in the Annual Report of the Prison Commission (1927, p. xiii) to a resolution passed in support of the idea of the 'uselessness of the short [prison] sentence' at the International Penitentiary Congress in 1925 suggests that international conferences have played their part in the diffusion of new ideas and in strengthening the resolve of policy makers to move in new directions.

Lucy Zedner comments that the conference circuit has shrunk the academic world, thus enhancing the tendency of criminological knowledge toward even greater homogeneity:

> Certainly there is evidence of what Heidensohn terms the 'diffusion of new discovery' (Heidensohn, 1991, p. 8), so that new concerns or new knowledge enter our national consciousness with a rapidity second only to the latest Hollywood blockbuster. A good example is the entry of the victim into the criminological scene. Universally, the 'forgotten actor' of criminal justice a few decades ago, the victim sprang to the front of the criminological agenda thanks largely to the collaborative effort of an international network of academics who hosted conferences, set up journals, and carried out cross-national victim surveys. So it is that we can talk of the common outlook and shared agenda of the international 'victims' movement'. (Zedner, 1995, p. 20)

In 1986 an international conference was held in Amsterdam to mark the centenary of the Dutch Criminal Code. Inkeri Anttila in the published papers from that conference commented on the nature of cross-national influences. She identifies how this starts from a common cultural basis and sometimes result in the establishment of a new organisation to promote greater harmonisation, as was the case with the Nordic Council with representatives from Denmark, Finland, Iceland, Norway and Sweden.

> Finnish legal culture is part of the general Scandinavian legal culture. All of the Scandinavian countries share a legal heritage, the broad outlines of which can still be seen. Furthermore, for several decades there has been a deliberate effort to harmonise Scandinavian legislation. In 1962, a special agreement on cooperation was prepared, and in 1960, a permanent body called the Nordic Criminal Law Committee was established. Efforts along these lines have been justified not only by tradition but above all by the argument that these countries have grown closer to one another also in their economic and cultural relations. (Anttila, 1986, p. 37)

Convergence in cultural and other respects is easier if there is a shared language. The influence of a common language should not be underestimated. It is not a coincidence that the USA, Commonwealth countries such as Australia and Canada, and those northern-European countries such as Scandinavia and Holland where much scholarship is conducted in the English language should be influenced by more readily accessible ideas. Reforms in jurisdictions with a common cultural link will also have most significance and will act as a point of comparative reference. Thus, for policy makers in Finland, the activities in other Scandinavian countries are of most importance, as to a lesser extent are developments in parts of Europe.

Ways of seeing the penal enterprise: Some of the developments in sentencing policy reflect a shift in the penal paradigm; in effect, a new insight or collection of insights are brought together to offer a new way of dealing with the universal problem of social deviance. These shifts have been represented by the commentators in terms of the dominance at any point in time of particular ways of seeing the world and responding to it. This does not mean that everyone subscribes equally to one view, but that official and professional discourse maintain shared assumptions and approaches to issues or fields of professional activities, which are reflected in the organisations established at the time, the agencies allowed to participate and a common orientation of many who take part.

The need to allow for the orientation of participants to be included in an analysis of penal policy is made clear by Feeley and Simon who comment on the attempt by Zimring and Hawkins to explain the rise in the prison population across the USA.

> The conventional understanding of this rise links it to demographic changes, social changes (like increased drug use), improvement in the efficiency of law enforcement, and increases in the punitiveness of sentencing systems. More can be accomplished with models that allow for the contingent interaction of all these factors (Zimring and Hawkins, 1991, p. 157). A shortfall of this approach, however, is that it in effect holds constant the nature of the penal enterprise while varying the external pressures and internal policy shifts. (Feeley and Simon, 1992, pp. 450-51)

Another commentator who thinks it is important to take seriously the 'penal enterprise' is Antoine Peters. He sees a shift in the penal enterprise over the last hundred years from the classical, to the modern, to the social control model of sentencing. These dominant paradigms or ways of seeing the penal enterprise are another reflection of the theme of universalism as they capture the movement of ideas and institutions across jurisdictions.

> The criminal law of the Classical School was animated by a spirit of restraint. The idea was that since the criminal law imposed limitations on people's liberty and inflicted hardship on them in the form of punishment there ought to be as little of it as possible... Restraint was also the leading notion in the three most important principles of classical criminal law: legality, *mens rea*, and proportionality of punishment. Legality meant that the law should clearly state what behaviour was punishable, and how it was to be punished. Punishable offences, punishments, and the conditions for their imposition were to be clearly specified. The principle of *mens rea*, or individual guilt, held that no person could be punished for things he had not willed or for which he could not otherwise be blamed. Proportionality of punishment meant that penal sanctions should be proportionate to, and should not exceed, the seriousness of the offence. By protecting individual citizens in their rights and providing them with security from arbitary prosecution and punishment, classical criminal law directed and regulated the very considerable judicial and police powers of the State and formed thereby an important element in modern constitutionalism. (Peters, 1986, p. 23)

The classical school was to give way in some jurisdictions to the modernist agenda based on a belief in progress through the application of rationality and scientific method. The emergence of the offender-instrumental orientation in sentencing in the later part of the 19th century was very much a product of the growing confidence in the abilities of science to effect progress and the emerging power of professional groups as they expanded their spheres of influence and colonised problem areas (Paulus 1974). The modernist agenda promised progress, the aspiration of the modernist era being that the achievements of science in medicine, engineering and the physical sciences, could be applied to the problems of society. Cesare Lombroso was one of the first to employ, literally, the tools of the scientists. Antoine Peters writes, 'It was no longer the primary function of punishment to maintain and clarify the legal definition of moral wrong, but to serve as a technique of resocialisation' (Peters, 1986, p. 30).

The modernist era of correctionalism saw the application of science to the problems of crime. Peters quotes Von Liszt and his programmatic statement of 1882, which states that we should, 'study crime as a social phenomena and punishment as a social function, in order to be able to determine with scientific certainty the efficacy of punishment for the protection of legal interests and for the prevention of crime' (Peters, 1986, p. 26). 'Its function had to be correction of those criminals who could be corrected, deterrence of those who were not in need of correction, and incapacitation through incarceration for life or for an indefinite period of those who were deemed "incorrigible".' (Peters, 1986, p. 26).

Harry Barnes, at the height of the confidence in the modernist methods in the 1930s, dismissed the classical law concerns as anachronistic: 'It is futile to punish a criminal as it is to punish a person suffering from a physical or mental disease...it is not the crime that needs to be dealt with but the criminal' (Barnes, 1930, p. 265). The emphasis on the individual offender was to find willing accomplices with the professionals able to colonise activities with clients, be they the criminal lawyer in court or the probation officer. It also allowed space for the judiciary to claim the need to individualise each case because of the unique nature of each case and each individual. The criminal courts were already offender focused because of the adversarial process, with the responsibility of the prosecution to establish guilt beyond all reasonable doubt. The correctionalist theme of the modernist social engineers was to move the sentencing stage as well as the adjudication process in the courts into the individualistic focus. Feeley and Simon wrote:

> Modern American law, whose concepts still form the core of law school education, concentrates on individuals; the individual is the unit of analysis. This concern is especially emphasised in the criminal process. Criminal law focuses on intention in order to assign guilt. Criminal procedure has erected barriers to conviction to test evidence and protect the accused individual in the face of the powerful state. Criminal sanctioning has been aimed at individual-based theories of punishment. (Feeley and Simon, 1992, p. 451)

It was therefore likely, with the shift in the focus of the penal enterprise, that the concerns of equity, parity and certainty in sentencing were to take a secondary role, except in those jurisdictions that did not go down the modernist path, such as Finland. Equally likely was that community concerns about crime were to be ignored for several generations in the absence of professionals to speak on behalf of the neighbourhood or community. A later generation of politicians were to finally break the silence on behalf of the wider community. Again, this was not the case in Finland. They had never abandoned a concern with just deserts or the denunciatory role of sentencing as an expression of morality. Therefore, although we can see aspects of a common universal penal enterprise, a penological Esperanto, it was also clear that not all jurisdictions were to commit themselves to the project in the same way, or to the same degree, and some even were never to board the 'promise of progress train' offered by the modernist era.

Divergence: Multiple and conflicting objectives

It is not realistic to assume that there is only one view on which all policy makers agree, or a single goal to which all sentencers must aspire. On the contrary, the ebb and flow of debate about the balance between the six objectives of sentencing is an inevitable consequence of the search for a sentencing strategy that can simultaneously, 'denounce the wrongful, deter the calculating, incapacitate the incorrigible, rehabilitate the wayward, recompense the victim and punish only the culpable' (Davies, 1988, p. 6).

People hold different views as to the nature of the causes of crime and the role of sentencing. Different penal paradigms line up for inclusion in sentencing policy. There is never just one view. Conflict exists within jurisdictions over the ranking of sentencing objectives. This is often apparent in the commitment to a welfare and individualist sentencing approach amongst probation professionals, in contrast to a crime control concern of police and prosecutors, and a denunciatory role of the sentencers. There are several goals of sentencing policy and they are not all necessarily approved of to the same degree by the participants in the system, even when a clear lead is given by legislation. Internal opposition, and sometimes confusion, is very apparent, especially in California and England.

In addition to the problems of identifying penal policy shifts between the multiple goals of sentencing, there is another source of confusion caused by political rhetoric in democracies and their various constituencies. Some claim that there has been a change of direction in policy regarding the use of imprisonment in the UK in the aftermath of the Criminal Justice Act 1991 and its reforms based on just deserts sentencing principles. To an extent this is true in that most reforms are likely to stimulate some form of backlash as the implications of the reforms become apparent. In the UK, the resistance of some professionals, including judges and magistrates, did lead to reversals. The 1993 Criminal Justice Act repealed the unit fine system introduced in the 1991 Act, and amended the sections of the Act that referred to the role of previous convictions and multiple incidents in sentencing an offender. Political rhetoric would also suggest a change of direction. Michael Howard's 1993 declaration, 'Let us be clear. Prison works', appears to contradict the comment of the 1990 white paper in respect of the usefulness of deterrence as an objective of sentencing policy. However, the Home Office has continued its search for credible and more demanding community sentences and expressed its policy commitment in the 1995 publication, *Strengthening Punishment in the Community*.

Sentencing policy is not achieved merely by the publication of an official document. The subsequent developments following the publication are important stages in policy evolution. The development of community sanctions was to be less rigorously pursued in subsequent years in California. In part this was to do with the difference in status between the reports in London and Sacramento. In the UK a white paper indicates a Government commitment, unlike the Blue Ribbon Commission report in California. A white paper is a prelude to legislation, and so clarifies the details of the Government's legislative proposals. This white paper was followed by a Criminal Justice Bill which was enacted in 1991. The California Blue Ribbon Commission was jointly sponsored by the legislature and Governor's office. Such a partnership has ramifications for the usefulness of the final report. As the legislature had a majority of Democratic representatives and senators whereas the governor was a Republican, and the commission represented nominees of both the legislature and the Governor's office, the final report represented a number of compromises and bound no one to subsequent action. This contrasts with the policy process in Britain which can proceed from green paper to white paper, to a bill from the sponsoring government department.

Having translated penal thinking into legislation is not the end of the matter. Several factors intervene before an idea is translated into policy and then practice. In the UK the Criminal Justice Act 1991 was a major piece of sentencing reform and as such generated much controversy with respect to the unit fine, the limitations of the court's power to take into consideration the previous offences for which an offender had been sentenced, and the use of electronic monitoring with a curfew order. The curfew order was enacted as a new provision. The curfew order would last for a maximum of six months and could order offenders over 16 to remain at a specified place for periods of between two and 12 hours per day. The 1990 White Paper, which preceded the Act, explains that it was not intended to keep people at home for all of the day.

> The aim is to enable them to go to work, to attend training courses or probation centres, to carry out community service or to receive treatment for drug abuse. Curfews could be helpful in reducing some forms of crime, thefts of, or from cars, pub brawls and other types of disorder. A curfew order could be used to keep people away from particular places, such as shopping centres or pubs, or to keep them at home in the evenings or at weekends. (Home Office, 1990, p. 22)

The legislation did not make it clear how the curfew order and the electronic monitoring component were to be implemented. This was a significant oversight, for there was hostility to the idea of curfews and electronic monitoring. Opposition came from the Probation Service, penal pressure groups such as the National Association for the Care and Resettlement of Offenders (NACRO), and the Labour Party, who said that if it was elected to Government it would not implement curfew orders or electronic monitoring.

Electronic monitoring and home curfew were included in the 1991 Criminal Justice Act but their implementation is still in doubt because of the opposition to it and also because of the funding problems associated with central government expenditure. In the Criminal Justice and Public Order Act 1994 a provision for four experimental electronic monitoring schemes was included, starting in 1995. Sveri's thesis quoted at the beginning of this chapter, 'the penal sanctions with which the states threaten those who transgress the law are almost identical in all countries' needs amending, as Sveri recognised with respect to capital punishment in the USA, to include, for the present anyway, electronic monitoring and home curfew, which is well established across the USA but has yet to get a toehold in Europe.

The fate of electronic monitoring in England and Wales is one example of the effect of professional cultures. Legislative success is necessary but not always sufficient to bring about change. The details of operational implementation must also be carefully thought through. The role of the existing agencies within the criminal justice system becomes vital for the successful implementation of a new idea.

While a convergence of universally appealing ideas met with approval amongst penal policy experts, the subsequent attempts to translate this penological Esperanto into policy and practice were to be influenced by the particular characteristics of the respective criminal justice systems, and external or contextual factors which are unique to each jurisdiction. And although there may be shared political and ideological assumptions about crime, and a similar policy orientation on punishment, the cultural, political, professional and administrative decision-making processes are very different, and each process will subsequently influence the evolution of policy recommendations.

Divergence: Culture and structure of the criminal justice agencies

The local criminal justice system is a key variable in understanding what happens to a proposal for sentencing reform. The internal factors within a criminal justice system that will act on impending reform will include: the professional interests and ideologies of the key participants in the system; the role of the key participants in the criminal law process; the agencies' priorities; the conflicts and discorrespondence between the agencies; and not least the nature and extent of crime and the subsequent caseloads that the agencies have to deal with and the public's perception of responsibilities for crime control. All jurisdictions do not face the same problems - nor do all envisage the same solutions.

A good illustration of contrasts in sentencing is provided by a comparison of the use of the fine in California and Europe. 'Traditionally, fines have been very commonly used in the Scandinavian countries, and today they account for some 80-90 per cent of all punishments' (Anttila, 1986, p. 45). In England they were given to 77 per cent of offenders sentenced in 1993 by the criminal courts, i.e. 1,091,500 of the 1,425,000 (Table 3.4). In California, by contrast, the fine is used in less than two per cent of sentences given by the Lower Court and less than that in the Superior Court (Tables 2.3 and 2.4). These variations in use will not just be a matter of making a type of sentence available for the courts to use but, as examined in our studies, the confidence in them. This will be influenced by the perceptions of usefulness and appropriateness by a number of identifiable participants in the criminal justice system, prosecutor, victim and judge, and also the general cultural context that reflects public attitudes.

The criminal justice system is not simply a series of distinctive agencies with separate budgets and bureaucracies but also reflects differing working ideologies and professional commitments, i.e distinctive cultures. To achieve reforms, and to have policy changes successfully implemented, an awareness of the criminal justice culture is essential so as to avoid the utopianism of naive sentencing reformers. Culture exists because it provides 'a guide to living' both in terms of daily routines but also at the level of legitimating the everyday practical activities of professionals and officials. This is as true of the criminal justice system as any other area of life. Understanding the local criminal justice culture will provide an insight into how the practitioners define their world-taken-for-granted and helps to make sense of the traditions associated with specific agencies in criminal justice systems.

Sveri points out that these agency traditions can vary between systems which otherwise appear very similar. He wrote that the man from the moon on a tour of Scandinavia may, on:

> Meeting a Norwegian police officer, would probably find this unarmed constable to be much more like an English bobby than a Swedish police officer, who openly carries a long, vicious looking stick and a heavy gun. And on entering the court in Copenhagen where suspects are remanded in custody he would find himself at home if he had been visiting the night court in New York, but he would find it strangely different to the City Court of Stockholm. If he proceeds to a Finnish prison, he would find that it does not differ very much from an English one, but that it is quite different from what he saw in Sweden. (Sveri, 1990, p. 13)

In the USA, Michael Tonry in his analysis of the effects of sentencing commissions on sentencing practice, argues that an understanding of the constraints imposed by the local legal and political culture will help to explain the different impact that sentencing commissions have had in the states that have introduced them.

> Perhaps the only generalisation that can be offered concerning political and legal culture is that the potential and the effectiveness of a sentencing commission will depend on how it addresses and accommodates constraints imposed by the local culture. (Tonry, 1987, p. 59)

John Patten, the junior minister at the Home Office in 1991, identified the significance of the traditions of the criminal justice system as a reason why he thought the idea of a sentencing council would not work in Britain. He wrote, 'Those who ponder sentencing councils must not ignore that which is already in place, potentially providing so much of what they want to see, but in a way that works with the grain of the criminal justice traditions in this country. For there is a fast developing framework for judges and magistrates' (*The Times*, 5 February, 1991).

The criminal justice traditions, or the culture of different jurisdictions, provides an insight into the world-taken-for-granted of practitioners. It is one crucial factor which will help to explain the success or not of a penal reform, in terms of getting it through into a statutory form, and in determining whether it will be made to work by the practitioners.

In England the professional culture of judges is strongly committed to the principle of the independence of the judiciary. This would seem to be a justifiable position with regard to the judges' autonomy in handling individual trials and in sentencing individual offenders but is less convincing when the focus is the administration of justice and the very aims of sentencing. It has been the resistance from the judges to the standardising of sentencing strategies that has contributed to the lack of success for initiatives seeking greater uniformity of sentencing policy in the UK.

In England and Wales it is not only the judges who operate with a professional culture as is shown by the magistrates' response to unit fines, introduced in the Criminal Justice Act, 1991. Unit fines were part of the package of reforms to attempt to avoid disparities in sentencing practices, particularly between different magistrates' courts. Resistance by some magistrates and some well publicised horror stories in the media helped to undermine this policy. Their opposition encompassed a variety of different objections. Some magistrates objected to the absence of discretion with respect to unit fines. Others found the impact on offenders unfair. For instance, for the same ten unit offence one offender calculated as having the maximum weekly disposable income of £100 would pay a £1000 fine while someone on the minimum weekly disposable income of £4 would pay only £40. The Magistrates' Association sought modification of the scheme. However, by Easter 1993, only six months after its implementation in October 1992, the Home Secretary Kenneth Clarke announced his intention to abolish the unit fine system.

Another example of the way professional cultures influence policy developments also relates to the Criminal Justice Act of 1991 and the legislation that introduced electronic monitoring and home curfews. The Probation Service in England and Wales made their hostility to this idea clear and they generally resist any attempt to shift their role from rehabilitation to surveillance. They saw the attempt to introduce the idea of home curfew and electronic monitoring as an aspect of this. In California many of these experiments are now in place with the cooperation of probation and parole officers. In England, Bill Beaumont the general secretary of the National Association of Probation Officers commented in April 1988: 'Proposals about operating a curfew and pinning people to their homes amount to a shift in the probation officers' role to a policing role or being "screws" (prison officers) on wheels'.

Professional cultures are not always so rigid and static. In California, the shifting fads of rehabilitative treatment strategies during the 1950s and 1960s are revealed by Bob Grove who was psychiatrically trained and was associate superintendent of the California Institution for Men at Chino. In an interview in 1983 he said:

> In the 1960s we were going to cure everybody. My basic orientation in school in the 1950s was classical Freudian. In the late 1950s we started to get fairly heavily into client-centred approaches, such as Rogerian and some of the more phenomenological approaches to psychology. By the time I hit California, California was heavy into transactional analysis with Eric Bernes, the hierarchy

> stuff and self-actualisation. And beginning to get into the more radical stuff of touch, feel, let your feelings out, guys like Perls and Rolf got into the prisons particularly with the different attempts to utilise Maxwell Jones's stuff on the therapeutic community.

In Britain the professionals seem to be an effective block on technology reforms. The importance of professionalism has meant that criminal justice officials and judges do not regard themselves as directly accountable to the public. British judges and prosecutors are not elected in contrast to the US, and British judges are a very influential group.

The significant role that culture plays in shaping responses to sanctions means that despite universal movements in ideas, justice is local as Michael Tonry explains:

> Notions of community abound in relation to sentencing - the movement for community-based sanctions, interest in devolving power to local levels, concern in an avowedly pluralist world that communities vary widely in their composition and in their predominant values and traditions. All these are important ideas and together they reveal a powerful constraint on national, provincial, or state sentencing policies - justice is local. (Tonry, 1995, p. 277)

Where the public mandate or political leadership is less than clear, the role of the professionals in the criminal justice system can play a vital role. Long evolved professional ideologies define areas of expertise. They also justify monopoly positions which are jealously guarded. Regarding themselves as having a degree of autonomy, and meaning they are not answerable to client, public, nor politicians, the resistance to change can be formidable. They define alternative definitions of the 'public good' in opposition to that presented by the politicians.

Another consideration shows that the absence of a professional group or the lack of a specialist agency to take on a new role can impede a development otherwise taking off. The example of electronic monitoring in the UK is a case in point. The lack of a treatment orientated psychopathic institution in Finland, although common in other Scandinavian countries was explained by Inkeri Anttila, 'The difference between Finland and other Scandinavian countries can be explained partly on ideological grounds, partly on the lack of resources. Finland was less willing to give up the principles of classical criminal law, and to replace punishment with other measures. Also there was no specialised group of criminal psychiatrists that could be found after the Second World War' (Anttila, 1986, p. 46).

The culture of the criminal justice agencies and professionals is one major filter that any reform must pass through. The structure, or organisation, of the criminal justice system is a second. These two factors are related. The structure and goals of the system in part justifies the professional thinking of the separate agencies. In part, professional ideologies are a consequence of the principle of the 'separation of powers'. The division of labour between the agencies and stages in the criminal justice system may generate some tensions between the professional groups. Some inter-agency tension is intended as with the roles associated in the courtroom with the adversarial system. Others come about through bureaucratic and professional rivalry over status and resources, and others through the differential commitment of the agencies to the competing multiple goals of the criminal justice system.

Criminal justice and penal agencies are not autonomous, they operate within an administrative and social framework. Prisons cannot be successfully reformed in isolation from the criminal justice system, any more than they can be analysed in isolation from the contextual realities of the system of which they are part. Reform requires an understanding of how prisons interact with other agencies in the criminal justice system.

Sentencing policy, for instance, is not something that can be left solely to the judges, as other participants affect the distribution of sentences in reality. In her comparative study of the prosecutor's role in England and Wales, Holland, Germany and Scotland, Julia Fionda points out their influence on sentencing decisions:

> The public prosecutor is inherently involved in the process of sentencing defendants in the criminal justice system. This involvement may simply take the form of an indirect influence over judicial sentencing through pre-trial decision-making. The mainland European systems considered here have shown how the prosecutor's involvement in sentencing can be more proactive, actually penalising offenders at this early stage. (Fionda, 1995, p. 235)

Within the agencies, the professionals and managers who run them keep keen boundaries of responsibilities and jurisdiction. The police are the front-line definers of crime and are therefore the gatekeepers of the numbers of offenders that enter the system. To what extent should each agency have autonomy regardless of the consequences for the next agency in the criminal justice system? Should autonomy be retained regardless of the resource implications. In California the counties are squeezed between the policy-makers in Sacramento and the police who define in operational terms how the laws should be interpreted in terms of deployment of resources and manpower. Sixty-one per cent of police manpower is under the administrative control of the cities, whereas 80 per cent of the prosecution costs and court costs are borne by the counties.

In economic terms there is considerable interdependency as one agency's output, e.g. the courts, will be another agency's input. This resource interdependency has some implications. In 1985-86 superior court disposition in criminal cases rose by 18 per cent. Fortunately in terms of the flow and cost of cases only seven per cent of criminal cases resulted in trial. 'Guilty pleas' make the process organisationally and financially tenable. Yet if the courts saw a return to the 17 per cent disposition by trial that existed before the 1976 Determinate Sentencing Law was introduced, the delay and cost would be unthinkable. This is just one part of the wider problem of the fragmentation or 'Balkanisation' of the justice and punishment process in California.

In contrasting the development of intermediate sanctions in Britain and California, the shape of sentencing reforms in Britain was heavily influenced by factors within the criminal justice system, most notably through the pressure of the professions and officials, though not in isolation from political and fiscal factors. In California the external political climate seemed to be the overwhelming factor to shape sentencing policy, most obviously through the elected officials, and representatives, desire not to be seen as going soft on crime. Such a climate has an impact both on the California state legislature, and the Governor and the administration. Electoral sensitivity to sentencing policy is apparent in a state where a referendum can be used to determine, for example, whether a conviction for burglary of a domestic property should result in an automatic prison sentence, and where judges, district attorneys and sheriffs have to face the electoral process.

Divergence: External context

The spread of ideas proposed in the penological Esperanto thesis is illustrated in the influence of the classical school of criminal law from the end of the 18th till the end of the 19th century. In that period, described by Foucault as a time when the target of penal repression shifted from the body to the mind, we find the emergence of the ideas that were to provide the rationale for the penitentiary. Antoine Peters sees the construction of criminal codes that were adopted in this era as being, 'typically products of the early modern nation state and they embodied its authority. Law has always been intimately tied up with political power' (Peters, 1986, p. 20).

The relationship between penological ideas and political power is not something that can be understood by simple reductionist notions of the cultural superstructure reflecting the economic base of society. However, understanding the interdependency between material and cultural relations is as important in the penological world as any other in that the influence of power and economic relations acts to delimit choices of those who are involved. What crude conflict theorists ignore is that these constraints, be they material or cultural, constrain the powerful as well as the powerless. However, to understand the development of penal ideas and their spread across jurisdictions it is vital to appreciate the external constraints that are perceived by the opinion formers, be they officials, scholars, journalists, professionals or dominant elites or classes. In contemporary society it is the professionals and officials who have the front line role in defining and redefining the agenda of action and in shaping the dominant penal paradigm.

The different roles played by the professional bodies in shaping sentencing policy is in part a feature of the cultural and political differences between the countries. To understand the way these external factors play a role, it is first necessary to identify the elements that make up the administrative and political environment. This will include: lobbying by interest and pressure groups, the mobilisation of bias around the issue of crime, and an understanding of the role played by constitutional factors, the political parties, government mandates, public opinion and the fiscal constraints of public taxation and expenditure.

Of the many contextual factors that shape the development of sentencing policy, two are of paramount importance in all criminal justice systems: firstly, the politico-cultural influences that determine the representation of crime issues; and secondly, the governmental process and its influence on constitutional, administrative and fiscal factors.

The crime rate will be one factor that will stimulate public and political interest in the role and effectiveness of the criminal justice system. The public's concern about crime will explain part of the differences in crime policies in different jurisdictions. A sensitivity to public attitudes was apparent in Britain and California. An awareness of the importance of public confidence was apparent in this statement in the 1990 White Paper, 'Effective supervision...which has the confidence of the courts and the public', is the key to the success of punishment in the community.

Sveri does not think the differences between systems is as a result of the response to the amount of crime, but the effect of different administrative and policy traditions;

> When we start looking at how the criminal justice systems actually work, the differences predominate. The reason for this seems to be not so much any big differences in crime, but rather the effect of different administrative and policy traditions. However, such traditions do not develop in a vacuum, but must have their roots in differences which have existed (and perhaps still exist) in how violence is looked upon by the public and what kind of philosophy of punishment those in power believe in. (Sveri, 1990, p. 27)

Governmental Process

Who makes policy? Patrik Törnudd comments:

> In some countries the direction of reforms is largely dominated by the public debate, by the relative strength of the different political parties and their reform agendas and also by the personal convictions and preferences of the Minister in charge of crime control issues. Other countries have a more bureaucratic power structure, where the convictions of the senior civil servants decide the shape and direction of the reforms. If countries are ranked according to this dimension - which depending on your point of view may be called the dimension of eliticism or the dimension of populism - the Nordic countries can generally be characterised as fairly expert-orientated and Finland has been said to be the most expert-orientated among the Scandinavian

> countries. Certainly it is true that crime control never has been a central political issue in election campaigns in Finland. (Törnudd, 1993, p. 4)

Nils Jareborg's account of the reform process in Sweden suggests, 'there is a political culture in Sweden in which practitioners and academic experts are deferred to by politicians to a degree inconceivable in England' (Jareborg, 1995, p. 13). A very similar point is made by Patrick Törnudd to explain the influence of the prison reductionist's viewpoint in Finland;

> But the fact that it became possible to carry out a large number of reforms aimed at reducing the level of punishment was ultimately dependent on the fact that the small group of experts who were in charge of reform planning or who work as crime control experts in research institutes and universities shared an almost unanimous conviction that Finland's internationally high prisoner rate was a disgrace and that it would be possible to significantly reduce the amount and length of prison sentences without serious repercussions on the crime situation. (Törnudd, 1993, p. 5)

How centralised is the system of government? The extent to which a system of government is centralised, coordinated or fragmented will have a considerable impact on the pace of reform. The constitutional, political and administrative arrangements are vital factors in the process of policy making and implementation. The governments of Finland and the UK have much more control over the direction and implementation of reforms than their Californian counterparts. This is a consequence of three factors. Firstly, the constitutional influence on decision making, and in particular the significance of the separation of powers. Secondly, the impact of the political culture, especially as regards the unity and coherence of political parties and their role in forming governments. Thirdly, the relationship between the central administration and the local government and the division of responsibilities and the control over funding.

In the UK, parliamentary government and cohesive political parties means that single-issue and constituency specific issues are not as crucial to the elected representatives at Westminster, as they are to their counterparts in Sacramento. Furthermore, there is no regular use of the referendum in the UK as no voter or public initiative system exists. Public initiatives in California make it difficult to develop and implement long-term policy plans for sentencing and corrections as the law might be altered annually by voter referendum.

The British politician is not so directly exposed to the views of the electorate, because of the nature of parliamentary government. This difference is vividly illustrated by the British Parliament's refusal to re-introduce the death penalty despite support for such a law amongst 70 per cent of the voters, as public opinion polls in the UK have consistently shown since its abolition in 1965.

Parliamentary government also means that, in normal circumstances during its period of office, the Government controls the legislative agenda for the parliamentary year. So once policy deliberation has taken place, (and this is the purpose of issuing a green paper), the formulation of proposals in a white paper will have considerable credibility as they will form the basis of future legislation. Thus the Criminal Justice Act enacted in 1991 was based on the recommendations of the 1990 White Paper. In contrast the Blue Ribbon Commission could describe a problem and offer a cure but without the authority of knowing whether its proposals would gain sufficient support in the executive and legislative circles.

In Finland and the UK, the centralisation of administrative power facilitates planning and the coordination of the criminal justice and penal systems in term of its operation and budgetary needs. In California, the executive branch of government is fragmented, with the administrative division of responsibilities for penal and criminal policy being shared between the 58 counties and the state administration in Sacramento. State government is further fragmented by the separate election of the governor and attorney general. The governor is responsible for the overall budget, the prisons and parole system and the appointment of judges. The attorney general is elected separately and can be a member of a different political party from the governor and not regard him or herself as part of the state administration. From 1982-1990 California had a Republican Governor, George Deukmejian, and a Democrat Attorney General, John Van de Kamp. Needless to say, there are far more opportunities for fragmented and uncoordinated decision-making and policy implementation in California than in Finland or the UK.

The Penal Code in California was enacted in 1872, at a time when the counties were the natural unit of administration in a state where the people were scattered across wide distances, living in predominantly rural areas or small towns, with poor transportation and slow communications. A decentralised system was needed for an essentially localised criminal justice system. Today the majority of Californians no longer have a rural, small-town lifestyle; three quarters of them live in the four sprawling conurbations of Los Angeles, San Diego, Sacramento and the Bay area. They are less likely to see the advantages of local autonomy when services are unevenly delivered and impeded by a fragmented administrative system. There are 58 counties that vary in size of population. The biggest is Los Angeles with 8 million people. The smallest is Alpine County which has a population of just over 1,000.

> They vary in style. They vary in size of organisation. A telephone call to one sheriff's office led to the following dialogue with the receptionist: 'Are you the sheriff's secretary?' 'I'm the nearest thing he's got to a secretary'. (Davies, 1988, p. 2)

The California political culture also makes a difference as seen with the frequency of new legislation on crime and the unique role that the referendum plays in California as regards the initiation of legislation with direct policy consequences. The frequency by which legislative bills are introduced in Sacramento is startling when compared with the more disciplined approach to the introduction of new legislation in London and Helsinki.

> In 1987, 150 bills were introduced. Only one sought shorter prison terms. One quarter of all bills introduced annually concern criminal justice topics. From 1976-86, of 18 bills offering sentence lengths which became laws, only two resulted in reduced time for offenders. Between 1980-1986, 187 bills were passed by the legislature which increased sentence lengths. This annual lottery makes for uncertainty and difficulty for planning for the future. (Davies, 1993, pp. 86-87)

Key sentencing policy decisions were made on the basis of legislative bills introduced by individual legislators; Rains Senate Bill 200 (1982) resulted in residential burglary being punished as a first degree burglary and the Beverly Burglary Bill (1981) denied probation to those convicted of burglary. In May 1988 the California legislature had one rambling late-night session, reminiscent of the all-night sittings of the House of Commons but unusual in California, to decide the authorship of the bill permitting wire tapping in major drug investigations. The get-tough-on-crime approach of the politicians continues with very little resistance within the legislature. On 1st June 1988 the Assembly voted for legislation which would allow a sentence of life imprisonment without the possibility of parole for murderers convicted of first-degree murder. It was passed by 63 votes to 4 'after a minimum of debate' according to the *Los Angeles Times*.

The Blue Ribbon Commission commented on the unsystematic approach of the criminal justice system in California in relation to the main concern of its report which was to make recommendations as to how to manage the rapidly expanding state prison population. It also made the following point about the *ad hoc* nature of changes in sentencing law:

> The proliferation of sentencing and enhancement laws as developed by the legislature has resulted in a 'piecemeal' approach to sentencing, without attention to any precise sentencing structure. The result has been the development of an extremely complex system which now has become increasingly difficult for defense attorneys, prosecutors and the judiciary to administer. This proliferation of sentencing laws is also responsible for a portion of the State's jail and prison population increases. (Blue Ribbon Commission, 1990, p. 97)

They recommend the establishment, in such circumstances, of a Sentencing Law Review Commission for California. The establishment of a sentencing forum or commission might have an added advantage of providing a buffer between the public demands on sentencing policy and the creation of new policy. In California, the political culture is a crucial variable for understanding the direction of penal change and the response to the types of reforms recommended in the Blue Ribbon Commission.

Political culture of law and order : In the state legislature in California the impact of new criminal justice policy is less important than appearing 'tough on crime'. The cultural agenda is set by a media which sensationalises and simplifies crime issues. The sheriffs, prosecutors and judges are elected directly by the county voters. In such a context you have a recipe for short-term, unplanned, and uncoordinated response to the next panic about crime. Despite the recent expansion of the system the crime problem has not been solved and the public's anxiety about crime continues.

It is in the nature of things that politics takes precedence over government in California. Politics and government in California takes place in a state dominated by the Hollywood style of media coverage of events and was described by Judge Anthony Kennedy, at the time of his nomination to the US Supreme Court as, 'a land of the 30-second news clip and the three-minute interview' (*Sacramento Bee,* 21 May 1988).

Therefore, it was no surprise that when the Blue Ribbon report was published there was very little media coverage compared with the coverage of the white paper in Britain. On the morning of its release in Britain, the serious newspapers had front page coverage as well as extensive detailed summaries of the white paper. In contrast the coverage of the Blue Ribbon report in the Californian press was very limited.

If there is little enthusiasm for coverage of prison issues in the Californian press there is equal reluctance among the politicians to engage in the reform of the prison system. The Republican Governor Deukmejian for the period 1982-90, as indeed his successor in 1990, Pete Wilson, resolved to stick with imprisonment as his major penal strategy. Deukmejian's stance on alternatives to imprisonment was made clear in his 'State of the State Address' in January 1988:

> Currently 35% of convicted felons are sent to state prisons. The remaining 65% receive alternative sentences. We should not consider further alternatives to incarceration, so long as there are hardened criminals who will not consider alternatives to crime. (Davies, 1993, p. 49)

Mrs. Thatcher, a conservative ideologue from the same mould as Governor Deukmejian used the same words at the Conservative Party Conference in Blackpool in 1988, 'We should not consider further alternatives to incarceration, so long as there are hardened criminals who will not consider alternatives to crime'. But her Government was at that time considering not alternatives but the possibility of community-based intermediate sanctions and a recognition of the limitations of imprisonment. John Patten, Home Office minister announced: 'We are on the threshold of a major and lasting change in the criminal justice system' (*Observer*, 24 April, 1988). The prison system's manifest failure to make an impact on crime rates was given as the reason for this radical departure. The promise is to limit the use of imprisonment to violent and serious non-violent offences with punishment in the community for other offenders.

Constraints: fiscal and legal: With the largest legal profession in the world, and with more lawyers per head of population than anywhere else, it is not surprising that prisoners act just like other Californians and turn to litigation to pursue their interests. Overcrowded jails and prisons lead to conditions which are claimed to be unhygienic, cramped, and dangerous to inmates. The courts have put population limits on prisons and jails.

The cost of employing a sufficient number of lawyers in the Department of Justice to handle the litigation by inmates against the CDC was $5.25 million in 1987. This expense does not include the lawyers employed directly by the CDC, or the para-legals employed in its Compliance Division. In 1988, 18 counties had court-ordered population caps on their jails.

Prison growth has required an increased fiscal budget for the Department of Corrections. This generates a problem for although Californians desire to see more criminals incarcerated they do not want to pay higher taxes. Thus budgetary considerations become another factor on the development of public policy as regards sentencing. In the preamble to Senate Bill 279 in 1987, which established the Blue Ribbon Commission, the dramatic growth in public expenditure on prisons was mentioned, 'In the past 10 years, the Department of Corrections' operating budget has doubled and by 1991, the state will spend about one-tenth of its General Fund budget to maintain its correctional system if current correctional policies continue'. In March 1988 Governor Deukmejian announced his intention of making the prisons pay for themselves, a recognition of the economic balancing act that the state administration had to achieve between the reluctant taxpayers in California and the wide number of localities, employees and businesses that have financial interests in maintaining a large correctional industry.

The economic advantages of a large prison population has been quickly spotted by the construction company lobbyists. 'The Prison Construction and Operations Committee, a joint legislative committee chaired by Senator Robert Presley, holds public meetings to discuss the issue of prison planning and site location. Prison construction is the latest form of unofficial regional economic aid and results in "planning hearings" taking the form of a series of marketing talks from town representatives' (Davies, 1993, p. 85). In October 1987 in the Los Angeles Harbor Commission Board Room the Presley Committee met to hear representation about 'The Concept of Prison Ships'. Spokesmen from the USA and from the UK declared their expertise as prison ship builders. A money lender from Chase Securities of Marina del Rey announced his willingness to lend money for the project.

Equally, enthusiasm is found amongst representatives of business and labour from the rural small towns that suffer from localised economic recession.

> It used to be that towns prayed for a railroad station or airport. Today in California the Chamber of Commerce representatives beat a path to the Department of Corrections to sell their town as the ideal location for a new prison. Most of the new prisons are being located in or near small and rural communities, in part because they want them and the larger urban areas do not. If these towns become economically dependent on the prison payroll then this could be another rivet in the California penal system which locks it into a reliance on the use of high incarceration rates. When the Director of the Department of Correction, Ray Procunier, tried to shut down Susanville prison in the early 1970s at a time of prison population decline, the populace of this small, rural and remote community in Lassen County successfully lobbied, on the grounds of the town's dependence on the prison payroll, to overturn his decision. (Davies, 1993, p. 85)

The 28,379 California Correctional and Peace Officers Association (CCPOA) and the Department of Corrections 31,578 employees in 1993 have become another group with a vested interest in maintaining a policy of high-rate incarceration. With its political contacts and lobbying skills it is bound to become another powerful entrenched group that could restrict future policy options.

> The CCPOA has been noticeably generous with its campaign donations to politicians. Between $40,000-$80,000 was spent to

> defeat a ballot-initiative concerned with campaign reforms. 'They are now the leading contributor to political campaign among public-employee unions' according to the Sacramento Bee, which continues: 'This year, the guards have already given $316,374 to candidates and initiative campaigns'. In 1987 their level of political contributions made them the fifth largest spender after the California Trial Lawyers Association, the Insurers Political Action Committee, the California Medical Association, and the corporation G. Tech. They are vying with the professional associations and private corporations to buy political influence. (Davies, 1993, p. 84)

In California, the prison officers union in California has encouraged and supported the growth of the system and uses in its negotiations public, inmate and staff safety as a bargaining issue. On 15th June, 1988 at the State Capitol the 'Joint Legislative Committee on Prison Construction and Operations' (Presley Committee) scheduled a hearing (later cancelled) to discuss: 'Safety of Control Booth Design'. Of concern was the safety aspect of the control booth in place in the newly completed state prisons. The prototypical prison housing unit has a control booth in which one guard monitors one hundred cells (most of them with double occupancy) in the manner envisaged in Jeremy Bentham's panopticon. The main difference being that instead of a 360-degree area of vision to survey, the Californian guards have a 270-degree angle, which gives the system the name (The 270 Design). In this three-quarter panopticon: 'The booth was designed to cut department costs by reducing the number of officers needed in each unit'. It explains in the agenda notes for the hearing: 'However, corrections officers from the CCPOA have voiced concerns for their safety and believe the booth should be manned by two officers'.

Similar concern about manning levels and safety have been raised by the trade union in the UK representing the prison officers. Following a riot and mass breakout of more than 100 inmates at Haverigg Prison in June 1988, the incident was used to highlight the need for more staff and to blame cost-cutting efforts involving the re-classification of offenders. The vice-chairman of the Prison Officers Association, Mr. George Elliot, blamed the government's policy of recategorising prisoners as the cause of the riot and escape. He said: 'In an attempt to save money the security status of serious offenders was being downgraded, resulting in potentially violent criminals being sent to low-category jails'. Haverigg Prison is a low-security institution for Category C inmates. In Parliament, on 14th June 1988, the same point was raised and used to embarrass the government by Dr. John Cunningham, Labour Member of Parliament, who said it was the 'cosmetic categorisation of prisoners as being of low-security risk in order to ease the severe strain on high-security prisons, that had led directly to the appalling consequences of the riot and mass breakout from the prison'.

Why are parochialism and divergence most pronounced in sentencing policy?

Sentencing is more than a technical, academic, administrative or even legal issue. It is an aspect of the criminal justice system which focuses and stimulates the public imagination on matters of justice and morality. News of sentencing decisions reaches the public via the media or through encounters with friends, neighbours or family involved as employees, witnesses, jury members or as victims of a crime. The response to news about sentencing and the punishment of local offenders, filters into everyday discourse in a way that is not easily regulated or censored by public officials. Most crime and, the sentences given if a conviction follows, will go unreported but even these will have a victim with a view about the appropriateness of the sentence for the crime. There are occasions when a particularly high profile case will act as a catalyst to moral debate and this will provide an opportunity for people to express their emotional responses and outrage at such behaviour and in so doing to collectively engage in an act of denunciation and condemnation of behaviour that is regarded as unacceptable. The distinctiveness of a community is partially defined in this way. It is because community values vary more than penological ideas that sentencing policy, if an input from the public is allowed, will show the greatest variations between criminal justice systems. Sentencing will reflect variations in communities. Sentencing provides the occasion, in a concrete, personalised form, for the community to define itself. How we punish is a mark of our civilisation. What we punish defines our civilisation.

The denunciatory-retributive aspect of sentencing has become more apparent since the relative demise of rehabilitation and the resurgence of just deserts policies. Modernity in sentencing policy meant moving towards an expert-led system of indeterminate sentencing; a system portrayed as more scientific, humane and effective. Since the emergence of the back-to-justice movement in the 1970s, a greater deference to voters' concerns is apparent in sentencing policy.

In the era of rehabilitation and indeterminate sentences the treatment and corrections experts played a key role. The mystique of expertise was to provide an ideological barrier to public participation. Technical and professional barriers to lay participation were justified by medical and psychiatric ideologies. In short, the experts knew best. Public contribution could be portrayed as uninformed, unscientific and lacking in knowledge. The public, denied a say in the development of sentencing policy by the legitimating rhetoric of the expert and the professionals in the era of correctionalism, was to make its views very clear in California once the opportunity became available. Their chance came in the post-1970s shift in emphasis away from the individual-offender theories of behaviour-modification to the more community concerned theories of denunciation and retribution. In California the barrier to public participation was unwittingly dissolved by the 1976 Uniform and Determinate Sentencing Act:

> The theoretical nature of the two models of punishment - rehabilitation and 'Justice' - differ not only in terms of their ontological assumptions, sentencing distribution and operation, but also in the way sentencing issues correspond to views in the wider community, particularly in the way they encourage or debar public contribution. It seems that rehabilitation provides a barrier to political debate on sentencing, while a 'Justice' approach invites it. (Davies, 1985, p. 18)

With the shift to punishment and just deserts in California the question of appropriate penalties opened up into a public auction of bids. After all 'deserved' punishment is not a matter of science, nor is it based on absolute or natural criteria but a matter of social judgment. More punitive judgments about deserved sentence lengths, and false expectations about the protection provided by incarceration coalesced into campaigns for more mandatory and tougher sentences.

> The new system...introduced into the Penal Code a notion of 'proportionate' punishment related to 'the seriousness of the

> offence'. But what is deserved? In the absence of a fundamentalist and absolutist moral code, how were legislators and sentencers to decide, first, on the hierarchy of seriousness necessary for proportionality and, secondly, what were these punishments which were proportionate to the crime's seriousness? Hence a crucial consequence of the 'Justice' approach is its de-reification of the decisions about punishment in terms of who makes them, on what basis, and with what degree of legitimacy and acceptance. (Davies, 1985, p. 19)

The revival of just deserts philosophy raises the question, 'who should set the tariff in a democracy?'. The removal of the barrier to public intervention by the de-reification associated with the decline of the role of the professional expert, stimulated debates about how far sentencing should reflect public opinion. The liberals who tend to dominate the ranks of penal experts mistrust the public and their opinions, and perceive them as the villains or the dupes of other villains, the judges, politicians and press barons who through law and order issues manipulate the public. The public seemed to collude in their manipulation.

The public and their view of crime were not the only factors to influence the sentencing tariffs that were emerging under just deserts approaches. Tony Bottoms identifies three sources of diversity:

> While the broad concept of 'just deserts' had indeed been very influential in a general sense in many jurisdictions in recent years, what actually counted as 'just deserts' seemed to vary a good deal from one jurisdiction to another. That is indeed the case, and the variation seems to have three main sources. First, as von Hirsch himself concedes, because there are no positive absolute scales, judgments about the 'seriousness' of given offences may vary culturally from one country to another. Secondly, there is a continuing and unresolved debate as to what role previous convictions should play in desert theory; hence, different jurisdictions might well take different stances on this matter. Thirdly, no modern version of desert theory completely excludes instrumental considerations in sentencing. (Bottoms, 1995, p. 22)

In the UK the denunciatory aspect of sentencing was not noticeable as a declared aim of sentencing policy until the 1990 White Paper which stated, 'Punishment can effectively denounce criminal behaviour and exact retribution for it. The sentence of the court expresses public repugnance of criminal behaviour and determines the punishment for it' (Home Office, 1990, p. 5). In Finland this function of sentencing has long been incorporated into policy goals.

> Both the official ideology and the reform ideology manifested in text-books and committee reports thus came to be based on the idea that the criminal justice system primarily operates through mechanisms of general prevention (not deterrence!). The aim of punishment is to demonstrate society's disapproval of the act and to teach the public the limits of acceptable behaviour. As the new generation of criminologists were sociologists, this thesis is usually supplemented with the observation that while every society needs a criminal justice system, the immediate impact of penalties is very small, as the general preventative effect mainly operates through indirect mechanisms. From a general prevention point of view it is important that thieves are caught and that society demonstrates its disapproval of the theft through some punitive action, but the length of a prison sentence is in comparison a minor issue. A prison sentence of a few weeks may be almost as effective in demonstrating society's condemnation as a prison sentence of a few months. (Törnudd, 1993, p. 3)

The use of sentencing decisions to condemn and denounce is not merely a matter of personal outrage: it is also concerned with the nature of the community as it defines an expectation of behaviour and censures unacceptable behaviour. This is achieved in a concrete way through the exposure to real crimes and criminals in the courts, which tests our assessment of reprehensibilty. The acceptance of the denunciatory tradition is found in the recent 1990 document in the UK, but is absent in the California literature. However, it is long established in Scandinavia where it is clearly demarcated as a theory distinct from general deterrence, which is how it tends to be misleadingly presented in the UK. Inkeri Anttila explains this point:

> In Scandinavia, it is generally felt that punishments have, and should have, a general preventive effect. This may be the suitable approach for small, homogenous societies with only a small amount of organised crime. But in Scandinavia, the term general prevention does not seem to be the same as another term often used as a synonym, general deterrence. One component of general prevention, of course, is the deterrent effect: this, in turn, depends on both the severity and the certainty of punishment, and of these two the certainty of punishment is probably the more important. But another, and perhaps more important component of general prevention is the maintenance of standards of morality by publicly denouncing undesirable behaviour as morally wrong. (Anttila, 1986, p. 43)

The denunciatory element of sentencing brings together a number of relatively abstract notions: the morality of the offence; the control of the citizenry; the definitions of normality in the community; the role of the state and its representatives in the criminal justice system; and in a democracy, the level of public confidence in their decisions. Knut Sveri wrote:

> If, after all, there is some fundamental difference between Continental legal systems and common-law systems, we shall not find it if we restrict ourselves to looking at 'the law in books', but only by looking at the legal systems as parts of the general culture of the nation to which they belong. The pertinent problem is: What place does the criminal law and the criminal justice system have in structuring the relationship between the state and the citizens? (Sveri, 1990, p. 13)

To understand the relationship between the state and the citizen, in the context of criminal justice policy, we first need to understand the relationship between sentencing policy and public confidence.

Sentencing has six basic aims: denunciation, deterrence, incapacitation, rehabilitation, restitution and retribution. The balance between these six aims shifts over time in response to changing pressures and perceptions of the problems facing the criminal justice system. It is a system with a dynamic equilibrium, with tensions that encourage constant re-evaluation. Despite penological trends being evident across jurisdictions, the balance between these goals at any specific moment is bound to reflect the shifting pressures from internal and external factors within a criminal justice system in a particular community, and is one reason why sentencing is the most volatile and differentiated of the characteristics of criminal justice systems.

Conclusion

Universal shifts in the penal enterprise were apparent in western jurisdictions at the end of the 18th and 19th centuries. In the 1780s and 1880s we saw the origins of new penal modes of intervention, respectively, prisons and probation. In the 1980s and 1990s we have seen an equally active search in the UK and the USA for new modes of sanctions in response to the rising costs of imprisonment and the failure of both prison and probation to achieve the ambitious correctional goal of resocialising criminals. The search was a matter of some urgency in California where prison populations have risen sharply. It was in this context that we set out to see what confidence criminal justice officials in California, England and Finland had in community sentences.

What did we discover from our examination of community sanctions in these three jurisdictions? We discovered shared concerns and a common vocabulary but with different significance and implications as the California and Finnish officials and judges and the English magistrates saw very different potential for, and problems with, the introduction and use of community sanctions.

It was very apparent when comparing the policy debates and shifts in penal thinking that there were many similarities in the official thinking on policy developments in California and England, echoed in other jurisdictions, especially in many of the states across the USA. However, the focus groups revealed that the penological Esperanto of the policy draftsmen took on different meanings and significance. The same terminology was used, but often a different meaning was evident in the responses of the criminal justice officials in our three jurisdictions.

The meanings became apparent when the specific histories and focal concerns of the local criminal justice systems were articulated. In California, for instance, the anxiety over the role of the state government in terms of funding and encroachment on local jurisdictions was apparent in a way that was of little concern in Finland but had some resonance in England with questions about whether the Home Office would listen and whether the Treasury would be prepared to meet the cost of sentencing initiatives. In the UK the first initiatives with community sentences, such as probation and community service orders, were introduced as an alternatives to a prison sentence. By the late 1980s and 1990s in California and England the arguments were more about whether they could be credible intermediate sanctions rather than as alternatives to custody. Our studies examined the credibility of community sentences. In Finland officials were not unhappy to see them used as alternatives to custody. This is a country where the aims of retribution and denunciation have traditionally been paramount and where the prison population has been falling steadily with little public anxiety.

In California, the state administration and the local counties have, in response to the cost of incarceration, promoted a number of developments and experiments: electronic monitoring, home curfews, community correctional centres and rehabilitation centres. Despite these innovations the research in California did not suggest that community sanctions were received with much enthusiasm by the officials in the focus groups. Most could appreciate the economic factors behind their promotion and most could envisage a limited role for them as an intermediate sanction. But there was not the faintest chance, in the officials' opinion, of community sanctions being used to replace imprisonment or jail to any large degree.

However, in Finland, a country whose prison population has declined over several decades, there seemed very little concern shown about the use of community sanctions for those who would otherwise be sentenced to serve up to eight months in prison. Nor were they regarded as a soft option. In Finland they were regarded as more demanding than the conditional (suspended) prison sentence where effectively nothing happened by way of a punishment. Thus the Finnish officials foresaw no major problem in using community sanctions as alternatives to custody. The Finnish experience contrasts starkly with that of the Californian officials or the English magistrates. In both countries the rehabilitative focus of previous community sentences has left a history of distrust in which community sanctions were represented as a soft option. This was particularly noticed amongst the English magistrates, many of whom were keen on the concept of community service but were disheartened by the lack of rigour in its implementation.

Why was there more confidence in community sanctions in Finland? It is my view that the answer to this question is related to our observation that in Finland there is relatively less political struggle over crime and sentencing policy in terms of who should set the tariff. In Finland there is less suspicion of the role of central government in penal policy and more trust of experts.

The reason for this is found in the specific histories of the criminal justice systems and the relationship between the policy makers and the public. California adopted individualised and indeterminate sentencing on a grand scale. In England the commitment to offender-instrumental sentencing strategies was apparent if not as pronounced as in California. The failure to deliver the promise of rehabilitation left its mark in these two jurisdictions, with a reluctance to move towards anything resembling the soft approaches of the previous era. The modernist approach was perceived as not working and adding new problems of inequities and unfairness to the sentencing situation. The disillusionment with the rehabilitative approach to sentencing goes very deep in California.

It was the professional and experts who successfully convinced governments to introduce and adopt the offender-instrumental strategies and which finally resulted in suspicion of, and the weakening of, the liberal agenda on penal issues. The liberal and modernist agenda has left a mark in terms of public disillusionment with community sentencing in the English speaking countries.

Usually the liberal penal reformers want simultaneously to take the politics out of penal debate but want to introduce reforms with little public support, as happened with the repeal of capital punishment. The parliamentary debates in the UK on the abolition of capital punishment encouraged the politicisation of crime issues in that country. Before then, politicians had regarded crime as a nonpartisan issue and the press, particularly the Sunday newspapers, had regarded court room crime as a source of salacious details with court room revelations about the deeds committed by the murderer and his mistress. This was to change as the public continuously refused on this issue to be persuaded that the death penalty, depite the insistence of the experts that capital punishment did not work, should be abolished. The alienation of the public from the experts and the arrival of sentencing policy on the political agenda was a response to the build up of mistrust of experts and officials who had held out the modernist agenda of progress on crime matters through the reform, rather than the punishment, of criminals.

Public alienation increased in response to the modernist agenda that sought to deny the significance of morality; the idea being to cure rather than blame. Antoine Peters comments, 'The classical codes were based on a view of man as being associated with his fellow men in a common moral community for which he carried joint responsibility' (Peters, 1986, p. 31). Peters thinks that recent developments have increased the moral alienation:

> In more recent times the criminal law has increasingly acquired an aspect of politically concocted rules that are administered according to criteria of administrative rationality from which ordinary citizens in their everyday life have become quite alienated but to which they nonetheless have to submit. The moral alienation affecting the criminal law has become even more salient under the influence of the third, and last main current of criminal law theory to be discussed [Social Control]. (Peters, 1986, p. 31)

Finland never relinquished a just deserts and denunciatory approach and so the links between morality, behaviour and proportionate sentences were maintained, and so was the confidence of the officials and the public. In contrast in California, denunciation seemed to be non-existent. In the UK it made an appearance in the 1990 White Paper from the Home Office, but one of the findings of the focus groups was that it meant little and most magistrates still think primarily in offender-instrumental terms.

Public confidence is an essential quality for sentencing reform. Persuading the legislature to reform the law is one step. Persuading the officials and judges who must implement the law is another. Also the public must be reassured that the link between morality and public expectation of behaviour can be reinforced, even if only symbolically, through the enforcement of the criminal law.

Winning public confidence though, is only partly reliant on a rational, 'what works' approach to sentencing. Sentencing policy in a democratic society must also appeal to the public and to achieve this the emotional, irrational and symbolic aspects of the collective consciousness cannot be ignored if public alienation is to be avoided. The failure to retain public confidence is likely to result in the politicisation of sentencing policy in the way witnessed in California.

Sentencing is an issue that captures the irrational and emotive side of the human mind. It is, as the denouncers understand, about irrational communal forces that define communities and the people in them. The belief that there is a strictly rational approach to sentencing policy based on the impact of sentencing decisions on offenders' future behaviour fails to recognise the need for an opportunity to allow the community to express retributive and denunciatory concerns. Incorporating the denunciatory-retributive element of sentencing requires a sensitivity to local perceptions of morally unacceptable behaviour and is unlikely to be achieved by postulating universal solutions of a global nature.

Global, universal solutions are patently not the answer no matter how impressive they may appear at international conferences. The Finnish example is testament to this. What is accepted in Finland in terms of community sentences clearly has not been anywhere as readily accepted elsewhere. The expression of opinion in the focus groups in California and in England illustrates the point.

Lucia Zedner (1995) asks whether we in this postmodern era are 'more sensitised to the fragmentary and kaleidoscopic qualities of social life and less prepared to accept the grand visions of modernism. If we recognise that criminality is contingent on local political, social, and economic structure (Lacey 1994), then we must expect criminology (or rather criminologies) also to be local and heterogeneous' (Zedner, 1995, p.20).

Where does this leave us? The argument in the penological world, that something more advanced and more sophisticated is happening elsewhere should no longer cause the policy makers to automatically think that they are being left behind. What is happening elsewhere from our experience will inevitably be different from the rhetoric about it. 'While "one size fits all" may work with bathrobes and synthetic socks, it will not work for sentencing policy. Different jurisdictions have different problems' (Tonry, 1995, p.268). The commonalities of the penological enterprise across jurisdictions do reveal elements of a penological Esperanto, but the fate of sentencing reform is very dependent on the culture of the local criminal justice system which is informed by the specific cultural and political histories and experiences of the public and officials.

The search for non-prison forms of punishment will undoubtedly continue. The success of this search will depend on whether the ideas of the policy makers have credibility in the eyes of the public and legitimacy with officials in the criminal justice system. The lesson from our research is that success is more likely when sentencing policy is undertaken within a framework that is sensitive to denunciatory and retributive principles, as has been the case until recently in Finland. The intellectual heritage left by the offender-instrumental perspective that has dominated sentencing policy for much of the 20th century in Britain and California will continue to act as a barrier to reform proposals in the search for non-prison punishments.

Bibliography

Aho, T. (1982), Faktorer som inverkat på valet av straffart och fångtalet under åren 1950-1982 i Finland. (Factors that have Influenced the Choice of Punishment Type and the Number of Prisoners in the years 1950-1982 in Finland), *Nordisk Tidsskrift for Kriminalvidenskap*, (Nordic Journal of Criminology) vol. 71, pp. 169-76.

Anttila, I. (1952), *Nuori lainrikkoja* (The Young Offender), Suomalaisen lakimiesyhdistyksen julkaisuja, B-sarja No 53. WSOY, Porvoo, and Helsinki.

Anttila, I. and Törnudd, P. (1973), *Kriminologi i kriminalpolitisk perspektiv*, (Criminology in a Crime Control Policy Perspective), Norstedts, Stockholm.

Anttila, I. (1985), 'Criminal Justice and Trends in Criminal Policy', in Jaakko Uotila (ed) *The Finnish legal system*, (Second edition), Finnish Lawyers' Publishing Company, Helsinki.

Anttila, I. (1986), 'Trends in Criminal Law' in van Dijk, J. *et al* (eds.), *Criminal Law in Action*, Kluwer Law and Taxation Publishing, Gouda Quint, Arnhem.

Aromaa, K. (1993), 'Finland' in Anna Alvazzi del Frate, Ugljesa Zvekic, and Jan J. M. van Dijk (eds.), *Understanding crime: Experiences of Crime and Crime Control*, Publication No. 49, United Nations Inter-Regional Crime and Justice Research Institute, Rome.

Aromaa, K. and Kinnunen, A. (1995), *Rikoksen uhrit Suomessa ja Norjassa. Vuoden 1989 kansainvälisen uhritutkimuksen tuloksia.* (Two Country Reports from the 1989 International Crime Survey: Finland and Norway), National Research Institute of Legal Policy, Publication No. 127, Helsinki.

Axelrod, M.D. (1975), 'Ten Essentials for Good Qualitative Research', *Marketing News*, 8, pp. 10-11.

Barnes, H.E. (1930), *The Story of Punishment: The Story of Man's Inhumanity to Man*, 2nd edition, 1972, Patterson Smith, Montclair, New Jersey.

Berk, R. A. (1990), *Thinking About Program Evaluation*, Sage, California.

Bishop, N. (1990), *Scandinavian Criminal Policy and Criminology*, Scandinavian Research Council for Criminology, Stockholm.

Blom, R. (1979), *Rikostuomiot ja Suomen tuomioistuinlakimiehet*, (Sentences and Finnish Court Laywers), Acta Universitatis Tamperensis ser. A, vol. 99, University of Tampere, Finland.

Blue Ribbon Commission (1990), *Report on Inmate Population Management*, Department of Corrections, Sacramento.

Blue Ribbon Commission (1990), *Inmate Population Management*, Department of Corrections, Sacramento.

Blumstein, A., Cohen, J. and Gooding, W. (1973), 'The Influence of Capacity on Prison Population: A Critical Review of Some Recent Evidence', *Crime and Delinquency*, vol. 29, pp. 1-51.

Bondeson, U.V. (1990), 'Innovative Non-Custodial Sanctions' in *Scandinavian Criminal Policy and Criminology*, Scandinavian Research Council for Criminology, Stockholm.

Bottoms, A. (1986), 'Limiting Prison Use: Experience in England and Wales', in van Dijk J. *et al*, (eds.), *Criminal Law in Action*, Kluwer Law and Taxation Publishing, Gouda Quint, Arnhem.

Bottoms, A. (1985), 'The Philosophy and Politics of Punishment and Sentencing', in Clarkson, C. and Morgan, R. (eds.), *The Politics of Sentencing Reform*, Clarendon Press, Oxford.

Brittan, A. (1981), 'The Symbolic Dimension of Law and Social Control', in Podgorecki, A. and Whelan, C. (eds.), *Sociological Approaches to Law*, Croom Helm, London.

Bulmer, M. (1982), *The Uses of Social Research: Social Investigation in Public Policy-Making*, Unwin, London.

California Department of Corrections (1992), *CDC Facts*, July 1, 1992, Sacramento.

California Department of Corrections (1995a), *California Prisoner and Parolees 1992*, Sacramento.

California Department of Corrections (1995b), *CDC Weekly Population Report*, November 1, 1995, Sacramento.

California Department of Justice (1994), *Crime and Delinquency in California, 1993*, Sacramento.

California Department of Justice (1994), *Californian Criminal Justice Profile, 1993*, Sacramento.

Chancellor of Justice (1986), *Recommendations to Prosecutors from the Chancellor of Justice*, Office of the Chancellor of Justice, Helsinki.

Clarkson, C. and Morgan, R. (eds.) (1995), *The Politics of Sentencing Reform*, Clarendon Press, Oxford.

Cross, R. (1971), *Punishment, Prison and the Public*, Stevens & Sons, London.

Davies, M. (1985), 'Determinate Sentencing Reform in California and its Impact on the Penal System', *British Journal of Criminology* vol. 25, no. 1, January 1985.

Davies, M. (1988a), *Coordinating Justice in California: There ought to be a law about it*, Forum Series, Department of Justice, Sacramento, California.

Davies, M. (1988b), *Survey Report: The Expansion of the Criminal Justice and Penal System in California. Is greater cooperation required?* California Department of Justice, BCS monograph series, Sacramento, California.

Davies, M. (1991), *A Policy Role for Focus Groups: Community Corrections*, Forum Series, California Department of Justice, Sacramento.

Davies, M. (1993), *Punishing Criminals: Developing Community-Based Intermediate Sanctions*, Greenwood Press, Westport, Connecticut.

Davies, M. Croall, H. and Tyrer, J. (1995), *Criminal Justice: An Introduction to the Criminal Justice System in England and Wales*, Longmans, London.

Department of Prison Administration (1971), *Annual Report for 1970*, Ministry of Justice, Helsinki.

Department of Prison Administration, [Finland], (1993), *Annual Report for 1992*, Ministry of Justice, Helsinki.

Doble, J. (1987), *Crime and Punishment: The Public's View*, Public Agenda Foundation, New York.

Feeley, M. and Simon, J. (1992), 'The New Penology: Notes on the Emerging Strategy of Corrections and its Implications', *Criminology*, vol. 30, pp. 449-74.

Finnish Criminal Law Committee (1976), *Criminal Law Committee Report*, Helsinki.

Fionda, J. (1995), *Public Prosecutors and Discretion: A Comparative Study*, Oxford University Press, Oxford.

Glaser, B. and Strauss, A. (1967), *The Discovery of Grounded Theory*, Aldine Publishing Company, Chicago.

Grönfors, M. and Hirvonen, A. (1990), *Nuorten oikeuskäsityksiä*, (Young Persons' Views on Justice), Kansalaiskasvatuksen Keskus Ry, Helsinki.

Halsey, A. (ed.) (1972), *Trends in British Society Since 1900*, Macmillan, London.

Heidensohn, F. (1991), 'Introduction: Convergence, Diversity and Change', in Heidensohn, F. and Farrell, M. (eds.), *Crime in Europe*, Routledge, London.

Heiskanen, M. (1991), *Omaisuusrikokset 1988, Haastattelututkimus henkilöön kohdistuneista omaisuusrikoksista*, (Property Crime 1988, A Survey on Personal Victimization to Property Crimes), Oikeus 1991 no. 3, Statistics Finland, Helsinki.

Heiskanen, M., Aromaa, K., Niemi, H., Ruusinen, A. and Sirén, R. (1991), *Accidents and Violence 1988*, National Research Institute of Legal Policy, Central Statistical Office of Finland, Helsinki.

Hedges, A. (1985), 'Group Interviewing', in Walker, R. (ed.), *Applied Qualitative Research*, Gower, Aldershot.

HMI of Probation (1993), *Annual Report of the Inspector of Probation, 1992/1993*, Home Office, London.

Home Office (1970), *The Report of the Inter-Departmental Committee on Non-Custodial and Semi-Custodial Penalties*, (Wootton Report), HMSO, London.

Home Office (1977), *Prisons and the Prisoner: The Work of the Prison Service in England and Wales*, HMSO, London.

Home Office (1988), *Criminal Statistics in England and Wales 1987*, HMSO, London.

Home Office (1988), *Punishment, Custody and the Community*, HMSO, London.

Home Office (1990), *Crime, Justice and Protecting the Public*, HMSO, London.

Home Office (1991), *Prison Statistics in England and Wales 1990*, HMSO, London.

Home Office (1992a), *Partnership in Dealing with Offenders in the Community: A Decision Document*, HMSO, London.

Home Office (1992b), *National Standards for the Supervision of Offenders in the Community*, London.

Home Office (1993a), *Criminal Statistics in England and Wales 1992*, HMSO, London.

Home Office (1993b), *Digest 2: Information on the Criminal Justice System in England and Wales*, HMSO, London.

Home Office (1994a), *Criminal Statistics in England and Wales 1993*, HMSO, London.

Home Office (1994b), *Prison Statistics in England and Wales 1993*, HMSO, London.

Home Office (1995a), *Strengthening Punishment in the Community*, HMSO, London.

Home Office (1995b), *Statistical Bulletin*, 27 April, London.

Hood, R. (1974), 'Criminology and Penal Change', in Hood, R. (ed.), *Crime and Criminology and Public Policy*, Heinemann, London.

Howard, J. (1977), *The State of the Prisons in England and Wales*, Bicentennial Edition, Professional Books, Abingdon.

Jareborg, N. (1988), *Essays in Criminal Law,* Iustus Forlag, Uppsala.

Jareborg, N. (1995), 'The Swedish Sentencing Reform', in Clarkson, C. and Morgan R. (eds), *The Politics of Sentencing Reform*, Clarendon Press, Oxford.

Joutsen, M. (1995), *The Criminal Justice System of Finland: A General Introduction*, The Ministry of Justice, Helsinki.

Kennedy, A. (1988), *Sacramento Bee*, May 21, Sacramento.

Kalske, J. Nissinen, M. and Tohkanen, M. (eds.), (1990), *Syyttäjän käsikirja*, (The Prosecutor's Manual), Valtion Painatuskeskus, Helsinki.

Krueger, R. A. (1988), *Focus Groups: A Practical Guide for Applied Research,* Sage, Beverley Hills.

Lacey, N. (1995), 'Contingency and Criminalisation' in Loveland, I. (ed.), *The Frontiers of Criminality*, Sweet and Maxwell, London.

Lahti, R. (1989), 'On Finnish and Scandinavian Criminal Policy', in *Cahiers De Defense Sociale*, pp. 64-73.

Lahti, R. (1993), 'Recodifying the Finnish Criminal Code of 1889: Towards a More Efficient, Just and Humane Criminal Law', *Israel Law Review,* vol. 27, (1-2), pp. 100-117.

Lappi-Seppälä, T. (1987), *Rangaistuksen määräämisestä I, Teoria ja yleinen osa,* (Sentencing I: Theory and General Part), Julkaisuja A-sarja, No. 173, Suomalainen Lakimiesyhdistys, Helsinki.

Lappi-Seppälä, T. (1991), Asteikkoratkaisut, päivissä mittaaminen ja rangaistuskäytäntö, (Decisions on Punishment Latitudes, Measuring in Days, and Sentencing Practice), Unpublished Paper.

Lappi-Seppälä, T. (1993), Community Service and the Neo-Classical Framework of Penal Sanctions. In *Rapport fra kontaktseminar om samfunnstjeneste, Reykjavik, Island*, 22-25 October 1992, pp. 12-48. Nordisk Samarbeitsråd for Kriminologi, Oslo.

Lappi-Seppälä, T. (1994a), Vuoden 1994 liikennejuopumusuudistus ja rattijuopumusrangaistusten mittaaminen, (The 1994 Revision of Drunk Driving Legislation and Measurement of Punishment), *Lakimies*, vol. 92 (6), pp. 742-67.

Lappi-Seppälä, T. (1994b), 'Alternative Penal Sanctions' in Ahti Suviranta (ed), *Finnish National Reports to the Fourteenth Congress of the International Academy of Comparative Law*, Finnish Lawyers' Publishing, Helsinki.

Latane, B. Williams, K. and Harkins, S. (1979), 'Many Hands Make Light Work: the Causes and Consequences of Social Loafing', *Journal of Social Psychology*, vol.37, pp. 822-32.

Maguire, M. (1988), *British Journal of Criminology*, vol.28, 1988, pp. 556-8.

Merton, R. K. (1987), 'The Focused Interview and Focus Groups: Continuities and Discontinuities', *Public Opinion Quarterly*, vol.51, pp. 550-566.

Molm, L. (1990), 'Structure, Action, and Outcomes: The Dynamics of Power in Social Exchange', *American Sociological Review*, vol.55, pp. 427-47.

Morgan, D. (1988), *Focus Groups As Qualitative Research*, Sage, Beverley Hills.

Morris, N. and Tonry, M. (1990), *Between Prison and Probation: Intermediate Punishment in a Rational Sentencing System*, Oxford University Press, Oxford.

National Research Institute of Legal Policy (1973), *Criminality in Finland: Annual Report for 1972*, Helsinki.

National Research Institute of Legal Policy (1992), *Criminality in Finland: Annual Report for 1991*, Helsinki.

National Research Institute of Legal Policy (1993), *Criminality in Finland: Annual Report for 1992*, Helsinki.

National Research Institute of Legal Policy (1994), *Criminality in Finland: Annual Report for 1993*, Helsinki.

Nellis, M. and Bottoms, A.E. (1993), 'The View from the Bench and Reflections on the Reduction of Custody', in Bottoms, A.E., *Community Penalties for Young Offenders, Final Report for the Department of Health from Phase II of the Intermediate Treatment Evaluation Project, Part A: the Processual Study*, Cambridge Institute of Criminology, Cambridge.

Nousiainen, T. (1976), Rangaistuksen tuomitsemisesta. (On Sentencing), Finnish Lawyers' Publishing Company, Helsinki.

Nuttall, C. and Pease, K. (1994), 'Changes in the use of Imprisonment in England and Wales 1950-1991', *Criminal Law Review*, p. 321.

Nuutila, A. (1995), Rikosoikeuden ABC-kirja, (The ABC Book of Criminal Law), Turun yliopiston oikeustieteellisen tiedekunnan julkaisuja, Rikosjaprosessioikeuden sarja A:21, University of Turku, Finland.

Oldfield, M. (1993), 'Assessing the Impact of Community Service: lost opportunities and the politics of punishment', in Whitfield, D. and Scott, D. (eds.), *Paying Back: 20 Years of Community Service*, Waterside Press, Winchester.

Patten, J. (1991), *The Times*, February 5.

Paulus, I. (1974), *The Search for Pure Foods: A Sociology of Legislation in Britain*, Martin Robertson: London.

Pease, K. (1994), 'Cross-National Imprisonment Rates: Limitations of Method and Possible Conclusions', *British Journal of Criminology*, vol.34, p. 116.

Peters, A.G. (1986), Main Currents in 'Criminal Law Theory', in van Dijk, J. *et a*l (eds.), *Criminal Law in Action*, Kluwer Academic Publishers, Dordrecht.

Petersilia, J. (1992), 'California's Prison Policy: Causes, Costs, and Consequences', *The Prison Journal,* vol. 1 & 2, pp. 8-36.

Plummer, K. (1979), 'Misunderstanding Labelling Perspectives', in Downes, D. and Rock, P. (eds.), *Deviant Interpretations*, Martin Robertson, Oxford.

Prison Commission (1927), *Annual Report of the Prison Commission 1925/1926*, Home Office, London.

Probation and Aftercare Association (1995), *Annual Report on Activities 1994*, Helsinki.

Robinson, P. and Darley, J. (1995), *Justice, Liability and Blame*, Westview Press, Boulder, Colorado.

Rutherford, A. (1988), 'The English Penal Crisis: Paradox and Possibilities', *Current Legal Problems*, pp. 93-113.

Sackman, H. (1974), *Delphi Assessment: Expert Opinions, Forecasting and Group Procedure*, Rand Corporation, Santa Monica.

Sandoz E. (1990), *A Government of Laws; Political Theory, Religion, and the American Founding*, State University Press, Louisiana.

Silbey, S. (1989), 'A Sociological Interpretation of the Relationship Between Law and Society', in Neuhas, R. *et al* (eds.), *Law and the Ordering of Our Life Together*, Eerdmans, Grand Rapids, Michigan.

Statistics Finland, (1952), *Criminality known to the Police 1951-1952*, Helsinki.

Statistics Finland, (1994), *Yearbook of Justice Statistics*, Helsinki.

Stewart, D. and Shamdasani, P. (1990), *Focus Groups: Theory and Practice*, Sage, Newbury Park, California.

Sveri, K. (1990), 'Criminal Law and Penal Sanctions', in Snare, A. (ed.), *Criminal Violence in Scandinavia: Selected Topics*', Norwegian University Press, Oslo.

Takala, JP. (1993a), *Rangaistus ja siihen soveltuminen: Yhdyskuntapalvelukokeilun alkuvaiheita ja ongelmia*, [Punishment and Suitability for Punishment: Initial phases and problems of Finland's community service experiment], National Research Institute of Legal Policy, Publication No. 120, Helsinki.

Takala, JP. (1993b), 'Finland's Experiment with Community Service: How to Combine Mitigation, Quality Experience and Fairness', in *Rapport fra kontaktseminar om samfunnstjeneste, Reykjavik, Island*, 22-25 October 1992, pp. 32-49, Nordic Research Council for Criminology, Oslo [A shorter version of the paper was published in *The IARCA Journal on Community Corrections* vol. 5 (April), pp. 23-28, 1993].

Takala, JP. (1995), Yhdyskuntapalvelu rangaistusjärjestelmässä, (Community Service in the Penal System), *Uusi Kriminaalihuolto* 12(2), pp. 28-33.

Tonry, M. (1987), *Sentencing Reform Impact*, National Institute of Justice, Office of Communications and Research Utilization, US Department of Justice, Washington, DC.

Tonry, M. (1995), 'Sentencing Reforms Across National Boundaries', in Clarkson, C. and Morgan, R. (eds), *The Politics of Sentencing Reform*, Clarendon Press, Oxford.

Törnudd, P. (1978), *Crime Trends in Finland 1950-1977*, National Research Institute of Legal Policy, Helsinki.

Törnudd, P. (1993), *Fifteen Years of Decreasing Prisoner Rates in Finland*, National Research Institute of Legal Policy, Research Communications No. 8, Helsinki.

Törnudd, P. (1994), 'Sentencing and Punishment in Finland' in *Overcrowded Times*, vol. 6 (No. 6), pp. 1, 11-13, 16.

US Department of Justice, (1993), *National Institute of Justice Program Plan 1993*, Washington DC.

Uusitalo, P. (1968), *Vankila ja työsiirtola rangaistuksena*, (Prison and Labour Colony as a Punishment), Tammi, Helsinki.

van Dijk, J., Haffmans, C., Rüter, F., Schutte, J., and Stolwijk, S. (eds) (1986), *Criminal Law in Action: An Overview of Current Issues in Western Societies*, Kluwer Academic Press, Dordrecht..

van Dijk, J. and Mayhew, P. (1993), 'Criminal Victimisation in the Industrialised World: Key Findings of the 1989 and 1992 International Crime Surveys', in Anna Alvazzi del Frate, Ugljesa Zvekic, and Jan J. M. van Dijk, (eds.) *Understanding Crime: Experiences of Crime and Crime Control*, Publication No. 49, United Nations Inter-Regional Crime and Justice Research Institute, Rome.

Walker, N. and Giller, H. (eds.) (1977), *Penal Policy Making in England*, Cropwood Series No. 9, Institute of Criminology, Cambridge.

Walker, R. (ed.) (1985), *Applied Qualitative Research*, Gower, Aldershot.

Whitfield, D. and Scott, D. (eds.) (1993), *Paying Back: 20 years of Community Service*, Waterside Press, Winchester.

Wise, E. (Series ed.) (1987), *The Penal Code of Finland and Related Laws*, Joutsen, M. (Trans.), The American Series of Foreign Penal Codes, vol. 27, Fred B. Rothman & Co., Littleton, Colorado and Sweet & Maxwell, London.

Woolf, Lord Justice and Judge Tumim, S. (1991), *Report of the Inquiry into Prison Disturbances, April 1990,* cm.1456, Home Office, London.

Zedner, L. (1995), 'Comparative Research in Criminal Justice', in Noaks, L., Maguire, M. and Levi, M. (eds.), *Contemporary Issues in Criminology*, University of Wales Press, Cardiff.

Zimring, F. and Hawkins, G. (1991), *The Scale of Imprisonment*, University of Chicago Press, Chicago.

Index